A SATIRE ANTHOLOGY

"*SATIRE should, like a polished razor keen,
Wound with a touch that's scarcely felt or seen.*"

—*LADY MARY WORTLEY MONTAGU.*

A Satire Anthology

Collected by
Carolyn Wells

Granger Index Reprint Series

BOOKS FOR LIBRARIES PRESS
FREEPORT, NEW YORK

First Published 1905
Reprinted 1970

STANDARD BOOK NUMBER:
8369-6190-0

LIBRARY OF CONGRESS CATALOG CARD NUMBER:
70-128161

MANUFACTURED BY
HALLMARK LITHOGRAPHERS, INC.
IN THE U.S.A.

TO

MINNIE HARPER PILLING

CONTENTS

		PAGE
Chorus of Women	Aristophanes	3
A Would-Be Literary Bore	Horace	4
The Wish for Length of Life	Juvenal	6
The Ass's Legacy	Ruteboeuf	7
A Ballade of Old-Time Ladies (Translated by John Payne)	François Villon	11
A Carman's Account of a Lawsuit	Sir David Lyndsay	12
The Soul's Errand	Sir Walter Raleigh	13
Of a Certain Man	Sir John Harrington	16
A Precise Tailor	Sir John Harrington	16
The Will	John Donne	18
From "King Henry IV"	William Shakespeare	20
From "Love's Labour's Lost"	William Shakespeare	21
From "As You Like It"	William Shakespeare	22
Horace Concocting An Ode	Thomas Dekker	23
On Don Surly	Ben Jonson	24
The Scholar and His Dog	John Marston	25
The Manly Heart	George Wither	26
The Constant Lover	Sir John Suckling	27
The Remonstrance	Sir John Suckling	28
Saintship versus Conscience	Samuel Butler	29
Description of Holland	Samuel Butler	30
The Religion of Hudibras	Samuel Butler	31
Satire on the Scots	John Cleiveland	32
Song	Richard Lovelace	34
The Character of Holland	Andrew Marvell	35
The Duke of Buckingham	John Dryden	37
On Shadwell	John Dryden	38
Satire on Edward Howard	Charles Sackville, Earl of Dorset	39
St. Anthony's Sermon to the Fishes	Abraham á Sancta Clara	39
Introduction to the True-Born Englishman	Daniel Defoe	41

Contents

		PAGE
An Epitaph . . . . *Matthew Prior* . . .		43
The Remedy Worse than the Disease . . . . . . *Matthew Prior* . . .		45
Twelve Articles . . . . . *Jonathan Swift* . . .		46
The Furniture of a Woman's Mind . . . . *Jonathan Swift* . . .		48
From "The Love of Fame" . *Edward Young* . . .		50
Dr. Delany's Villa . . . . *Thomas Sheridan* . .		52
The Quidnunckis . . . . *John Gay*		54
The Sick Man and the Angel *John Gay*		55
Sandys' Ghost . . . . . *Alexander Pope* . . .		57
From "The Epistle to Dr. Arbuthnot" . . . . . . *Alexander Pope* . . .		60
The Three Black Crows . . *John Byrom*		63
An Epitaph . . . . . . *George John Cayley* . .		64
An Epistle to Sir Robert Walpole . . . . *Henry Fielding* . . .		65
The Public Breakfast . . . *Christopher Anstey* . .		67
An Elegy on the Death of a Mad Dog . . . . . . *Oliver Goldsmith* . .		72
On Smollett . . . . . . *Charles Churchill* . .		73
The Uncertain Man . . . . *William Cowper* . . .		74
A Faithful Picture of Ordinary Society . . . . . . *William Cowper* . . .		74
On Johnson . . . . . . *John Wolcott (Peter Pindar)*		75
To Boswell . . . . . . *John Wolcott (Peter Pindar)*		76
The Hen . . . . *Matt. Claudius* . . .		77
Let Us All be Unhappy Together . . . . *Charles Dibdin* . . .		78
The Friar of Orders Gray . . *John O'Keefe* . . .		79
The Country Squire . . . *Tomas Yriarte* . . .		80
The Eggs . . . . *Tomas Yriarte* . . .		82
The Literary Lady . . . . *Richard Brinsley Sheridan*		84

[x]

Contents

		PAGE
Sly Lawyers.	*George Crabbe* . . .	85
Reporters	*George Crabbe* . . .	85
Address to the Unco Guid, or the Rigidly Righteous . .	*Robert Burns*. . . .	86
Holy Willie's Prayer . . .	*Robert Burns*. . . .	88
Kitty of Coleraine	*Edward Lysaght*. . .	91
The Friend of Humanity and the Knife-Grinder . . .	*George Canning* . . .	92
Nora's Vow.	*Sir Walter Scott* . .	94
Job	*Samuel T. Coleridge*. .	95
Cologne	*Samuel T. Coleridge*. .	96
Giles's Hope.	*Samuel T. Coleridge*. .	96
The Battle of Blenheim. . .	*Robert Southey* . . .	97
The Well of St. Keyne . . .	*Robert Southey* . . .	99
The Poet of Fashion . . .	*James Smith*. . . .	101
Christmas Out of Town . .	*James Smith*. . . .	103
Eternal London.	*Thomas Moore*	105
The Modern Puffing System .	*Thomas Moore*	106
Lying	*Thomas Moore*	108
The King of Yvetot (Version of W. M. Thackeray) . . .	*Pierre Jean de Béranger*.	109
Sympathy	*Reginald Heber*. . . .	111
A Modest Wit	*Selleck Osborn* . . .	112
The Philosopher's Scales . .	*Jane Taylor*. . . .	114
From "The Feast of the Poets"	*James Henry Leigh Hunt*.	116
Rich and Poor; or, Saint and Sinner.	*Thomas L. Peacock* . .	117
Mr. Barney Maguire's Account of the Coronation. . . .	*Richard Harris Barham*	119
From "The Devil's Drive" .	*Lord Byron*	123
From "English Bards and Scotch Reviewers" . . .	*Lord Byron*	125
To Woman	*Lord Byron*	126
A Country House Party. . .	*Lord Byron*	127

Contents

		PAGE
Greediness Punished	Friedrich Rückert	130
Woman	Fitz-Greene Halleck	132
The Rich and the Poor Man (From the Russian of Kremnitzer)	Sir John Bowring	132
Ozymandias	Percy Bysshe Shelley	134
Cui Bono	Thomas Carlyle	135
Father-Land and Mother Tongue	Samuel Lover	135
Father Molloy	Samuel Lover	136
Gaffer Gray (From "Hugh Trevor")	Thomas Holcroft	139
Cock'le v. Cackle	Thomas Hood	140
Our Village	Thomas Hood	145
The Devil at Home (From "The Devil's Progress")	Thomas Kibble Hervey	149
How to Make a Novel	Lord Charles Neaves	150
Two Characters	Henry Taylor	151
The Sailor's Consolation	William Pitt	152
Verses on seeing the Speaker asleep in his Chair during One of the Debates of the First Reformed Parliament	Winthrop M. Praed	154
Pelters of Pyramids	Richard Hengist Horne	155
The Annuity	George Outram	156
Malbrouck	Translated by Father Prout	161
A Man's Requirements	Elizabeth Barrett Browning	163
Critics	Elizabeth Barrett Browning	164
The Miser	Edward Fitzgerald	166
Cacoëthes Scribendi	Oliver Wendell Holmes	166
A Familiar Letter to Several Correspondents	Oliver Wendell Holmes	167
Contentment	Oliver Wendell Holmes	171

Contents

		PAGE
How to Make a Man of Consequence	Mark Lemon	173
The Widow Malone	Charles Lever	173
The Pauper's Drive	T. Noel	175
On Lytton	Alfred Tennyson	177
Sorrows of Werther	William Makepeace Thackeray	178
Mr. Molony's Account of the Ball Given to the Nepaulese Ambassador by the Peninsular and Oriental Company	William Makepeace Thackeray	179
Damages, Two Hundred Pounds	William Makepeace Thackeray	182
The Lost Leader	Robert Browning	186
The Pope and the Net	Robert Browning	188
Soliloquy of the Spanish Cloister	Robert Browning	190
Cynical Ode to an Ultra-Cynical Public	Charles Mackay	192
The Great Critics	Charles Mackay	193
The Laureate	William E. Aytoun	194
Woman's Will	John Godfrey Saxe	196
The Mourner á la Mode	John Godfrey Saxe	197
There is no God	Arthur Hugh Clough	199
The Latest Decalogue	Arthur Hugh Clough	200
From "A Fable for Critics"	James Russell Lowell	201
The Pious Editor's Creed	James Russell Lowell	206
Revelry in India	Bartholomew Dowling	210
A Fragment	Grace Greenwood	212
Nothing to Wear	William Allen Butler	213
A Review (The Inn Album, By Robert Browning)	Bayard Taylor	221
The Positivists	Mortimer Collins	224
Sky-Making	Mortimer Collins	226
My Lord Tomnoddy	Robert Barnabas Brough	227
Hiding the Skeleton	George Meredith	229

Contents

		PAGE
Midges	Robert Bulwer Lytton .	230
The Schoolmaster Abroad with his Son	Charles Stuart Calverley.	233
Of Propriety	Charles Stuart Calverley.	235
Peace. A Study	Charles Stuart Calverley.	236
All Saints	Edmund Yates . . .	237
Fame's Penny Trumpet . .	Lewis Carroll . . .	238
The Diamond Wedding . .	Edmund Clarence Stedman	240
True to Poll	Frank C. Burnand . .	247
Sleep On	W. S. Gilbert	249
To the Terrestrial Globe, By a Miserable Wretch . . .	W. S. Gilbert	250
The Ape and the Lady . .	W. S. Gilbert	250
Anglicised Utopia	W. S. Gilbert	252
Etiquette.	W. S. Gilbert	254
The Aesthete	W. S. Gilbert	260
Too Late	Fitz-Hugh Ludlow . .	261
Life in Laconics.	Mary Mapes Dodge . .	263
Distiches	John Hay.	264
The Poet and the Critics . .	Austin Dobson . . .	265
The Love Letter.	Austin Dobson . . .	267
Fame	James Herbert Morse .	269
Five Lives	Edward Rowland Sill .	270
He and She	Eugene Fitch Ware . .	272
What Will We Do? . . .	Robert J. Burdette . .	272
The Tool	Richard Watson Gilder .	273
Give Me a Theme	Richard Watson Gilder .	274
The Poem, To the Critic . .	Richard Watson Gilder .	274
Ballade of Literary Fame . .	A. Lang	274
Chorus of Anglomaniacs (From The Buntling Ball) . . .	Edgar Fawcett . . .	275
The Net of Law	James Jeffrey Roche . .	277
A Boston Lullaby	James Jeffrey Roche . .	277
The V-A-S-E	James Jeffrey Roche . .	278
Thursday	Frederick E. Weatherly .	280

Contents

		PAGE
A Bird in the Hand	Frederick E. Weatherly	281
An Advanced Thinker	Brander Matthews	282
A Thought	J. K. Stephen	283
A Sonnet	J. K. Stephen	284
They Said	Edith M. Thomas	284
To R. K.	J. K. Stephen	286
To Miguel de Cervantes Saavedra	R. K. Munkittrick	287
What's in a Name	R. K. Munkittrick	288
Wed	H. C. Bunner	289
Atlantic City	H. C. Bunner	290
The Font in the Forest	Herman Knickerbocker Vielé	294
The Origin of Sin	Samuel Walter Foss	294
A Philosopher	Samuel Walter Foss	295
The Fate of Pious Dan	Samuel Walter Foss	298
The Meeting of the Clabberhuses	Samuel Walter Foss	300
Wedded Bliss	Charlotte Perkins (Stetson) Gilman	303
A Conservative	Charlotte Perkins (Stetson) Gilman	304
Same Old Story	Harry B. Smith	306
Hem and Haw	Bliss Carman	307
The Sceptics	Bliss Carman	308
The Evolution of a "Name"	Charles Battell Loomis	310
"The Hurt that Honour Feels"	Owen Seaman	310
John Jenkins	Anthony C. Deane	313
A Certain Cure	Anthony C. Deane	316
The Beauties of Nature (A Fragment from an Unpublished Epic)	Anthony C. Deane	317
Paradise. A Hindoo Legend	George Birdseye	319
Hoch! der Kaiser	Rodney Blake	320
On a Magazine Sonnet	Russell Hilliard Loines	321
Earth	Oliver Herford	321

Contents

		Page
A Butterfly of Fashion	*Oliver Herford*	322
General Summary	*Rudyard Kipling*	324
The Conundrum of the Workshops	*Rudyard Kipling*	326
Extracts from the Rubaiyat of Omar Cayenne	*Gelett Burgess*	328
Ballade of Expansion	*Hilda Johnson*	331
Friday Afternoon at the Boston Symphony Hall	*Faulkner Armytage*	332
War is Kind	*Stephen Crane*	336
Lines	*Stephen Crane*	337
From "The House of a Hundred Lights"	*Frederic Ridgely Torrence*	340
The British Visitor	*From The Trollopiad*	343
A Match	*Punch*	343
Wanted a Governess	*Anonymous*	346
Lines by an Old Fogy	*Anonymous*	348

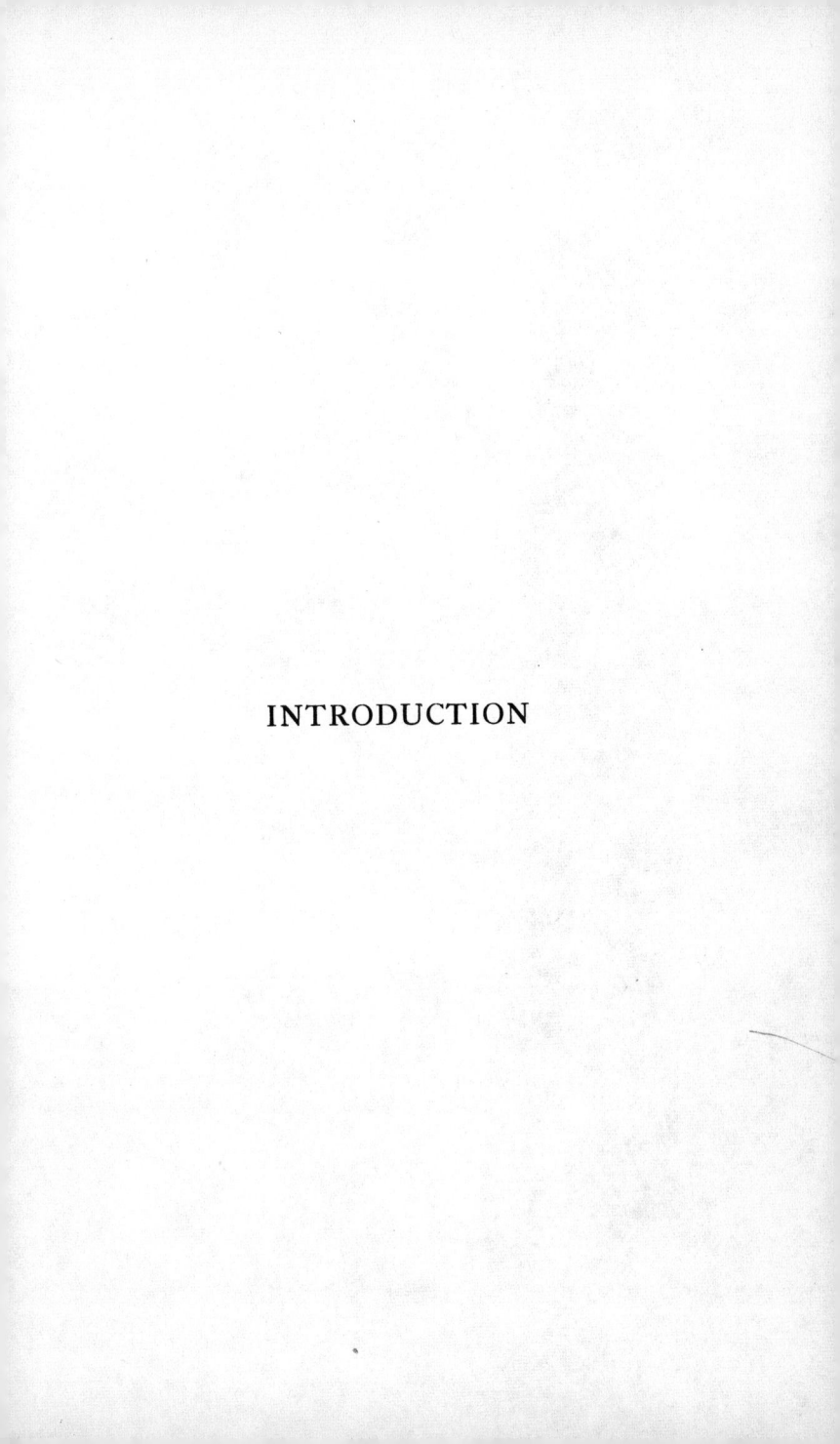

INTRODUCTION

INTRODUCTION

SATIRE, though a form of literature familiar to everyone, is difficult to define. Partaking variously of sarcasm, irony, ridicule, and burlesque, it is exactly synonymous with no one of these.

Satire is primarily dependent on the motive of its writer. Unless meant for satire, it is not the real thing; unconscious satire is a contradiction of terms, or a mere figure of speech.

Secondarily, satire depends on the reader. What seems to us satire to-day, may not seem so to-morrow. Or, what seems satire to a pessimistic mind, may seem merely good-natured chaff to an optimist.

This, of course, refers to the subtler forms of satire. Many classic satires are direct lampoons or broadsides which admit of only one interpretation.

Literature numbers many satirists among its most honoured names; and the best satires show intellect, education, and a keen appreciation of human nature.

Nor is satire necessarily vindictive or spiteful. Often its best examples show a kindly tolerance for

A Satire Anthology

the vice or folly in question, and even hint a tacit acceptance of the conditions condemned. Again, in the hands of a carping and unsympathetic critic, satire is used with vitriolic effects on sins for which the writer has no mercy.

This lashing form of satire was doubtless the earliest type. The Greeks show sardonic examples of it, but the Romans allowed a broader sense of humour to soften the satirical sting.

Following and outstripping Lucilius, Horace is the acknowledged father of satire, and was himself followed, and, in the opinion of some, outstripped by Juvenal.

But the works of the ancient satirists are of interest mainly to scholars, and cannot be included in a collection destined for a popular audience. The present volume, therefore, is largely made up from the products of more recent centuries.

From the times of Horace and Juvenal, down through the mediæval ages to the present day, satires may be divided into the two classes founded by the two great masters: the work of Horace's followers marked by humour and tolerance, that of Juvenal's imitators by bitter invective. On the one side, the years have arrayed such names as Chaucer, Swift, Goldsmith, and Thackeray; on the other, Langland, Dryden, Pope, and Burns.

A scholarly gentleman of our own day classifies

Introduction

satires in three main divisions: those directed at society, those which ridicule political conditions, and those aimed at individual characters.

These variations of the art of satire form a fascinating study, and to one interested in the subject, this small collection of representative satires can be merely a ser es of guide-posts.

It is the compiler's regret that a great mass of material is necessarily omitted for lack of space; other selections are discarded because of their present untimeliness, which deprives them of their intrinsic interest. But an endeavour has been made to represent the greatest and best satiric writers, and also to include at least extracts from the masterpieces of satire.

It is often asked why we have no satire at the present day. Many answers have been given, but one reason is doubtless to be found in the acceleration of the pace of life; fads and foibles follow one another so quickly, that we have time neither to write nor read satiric disquisitions upon them.

Another reason lies in the fact that we have achieved a broader and more tolerant human outlook.

Again, the true satirist must be possessed of earnestness and sincerity. And it is a question whether the mental atmosphere of the twentieth century tends to stimulate and foster those qualities.

A Satire Anthology

These explanations, however, seem to apply to American writers more especially than to English.

The leisurely thinking Briton, with his more personal viewpoint, has produced, and is even now producing, satires marked by strength, honesty, and literary value.

But America is not entirely unrepresented. The work of James Russell Lowell cannot suffer by comparison with that of any contemporary English author; and, though now forgotten because dependent on local and timely interest, many political satires written by Americans during the early part of the nineteenth century show clever and ingenious work founded on a comprehensive knowledge of the truth.

Yet, though the immediate present is not producing masterpieces of satire, the lack is partially made up by the large quantity of really meritorious work that is being done in a satirical vein. In this country and in England are young and middle-aged writers who show evidences of satiric power, which, though it does not make for fame and glory, is yet not without its value.

A SATIRE ANTHOLOGY

A Satire Anthology

CHORUS OF WOMEN

(From the "Thesmophoriazusæ.")

THEY'RE always abusing the women,
   As a terrible plague to men;
   They say we're the root of all evil,
And repeat it again and again—
Of war, and quarrels, and bloodshed,
   All mischief, be what it may.
And pray, then, why do you marry us,
   If we're all the plagues you say?
And why do you take such care of us,
   And keep us so safe at home,
And are never easy a moment
   If ever we chance to roam?
When you ought to be thanking Heaven
   That your plague is out of the way,
You all keep fussing and fretting—
   "Where is my Plague to-day?"
If a Plague peeps out of the window,
   Up go the eyes of men;
If she hides, then they all keep staring
   Until she looks out again.

Aristophanes.

A Satire Anthology

A WOULD-BE LITERARY BORE

IT chanced that I, the other day,
　Was sauntering up the Sacred Way,
　And musing, as my habit is,
Some trivial random fantasies,
When there comes rushing up a wight
Whom only by his name I knew.
"Ha! my dear fellow, how d'ye do?"
Grasping my hand, he shouted. "Why,
As times go, pretty well," said I;
"And you, I trust, can say the same."
But after me as still he came,
"Sir, is there anything," I cried,
"You want of me?" "Oh," he replied,
"I'm just the man you ought to know:
A scholar, author!" "Is it so?
For this I'll like you all the more!"
Then, writhing to escape the bore,
I'll quicken now my pace, now stop,
And in my servant's ear let drop
Some words; and all the while I feel
Bathed in cold sweat from head to heel.
"Oh, for a touch," I moaned in pain,
"Bolanus, of the madcap vein,
To put this incubus to rout!"
As he went chattering on about
Whatever he describes or meets—
The city's growth, its splendour, size.
"You're dying to be off," he cries
(For all the while I'd been stock dumb);
"I've seen it this half-hour. But come,

A Satire Anthology

Let's clearly understand each other;
It's no use making all this pother.
My mind's made up to stick by you;
So where you go, there I go too."
"Don't put yourself," I answered, "pray,
So very far out of your way.
I'm on the road to see a friend
Whom you don't know, that's near his end,
Away beyond the Tiber far,
Close by where Cæsar's gardens are."
"I've nothing in the world to do,
And what's a paltry mile or two?
I like it: so I'll follow you!"
Down dropped my ears on hearing this,
Just like a vicious jackass's,
That's loaded heavier than he likes,
But off anew my torment strikes:
"If well I know myself, you'll end
With making of me more a friend
Than Viscus, ay, or Varius; for,
Of verses, who can run off more,
Or run them off at such a pace?
Who dance with such distinguished grace?
And as for singing, zounds!" says he,
"Hermogenes might envy me!"
Here was an opening to break in:
"Have you a mother, father, kin,
To whom your life is precious?" "None;
I've closed the eyes of everyone."
Oh, happy they, I inly groan;
Now I am left, and I alone.
Quick, quick despatch me where I stand;

A Satire Anthology

Now is the direful doom at hand,
Which erst the Sabine beldam old,
Shaking her magic urn, foretold
In days when I was yet a boy:
"Him shall no poison fell destroy,
Nor hostile sword in shock of war,
Nor gout, nor colic, nor catarrh.
In fulness of time his thread
Shall by a prate-apace be shred;
So let him, when he's twenty-one,
If he be wise, all babblers shun."
          Quintus Horatius Flaccus Horace.

THE WISH FOR LENGTH OF LIFE

PRODUCE the urn that Hannibal contains,
   And weigh the mighty dust that yet remains.
   And this is all? Yet this was once the bold,
The aspiring chief, whom Attic could not hold.
Afric, outstretched from where the Atlantic roars
To Nilus; from the Line to Libya's shores.
Spain conquered, o'er the Pyrenees he bounds.
Nature opposed her everlasting mounds,
Her Alps and snows. O'er these with torrent force
He pours, and rends through rocks his dreadful course.
Yet thundering on, "Think nothing done," he cries,
"Till o'er Rome's prostrate walls I lead my powers,
And plant my standard on her hated towers!"
Big words? But view his figure, view his face!

Ah, for some master hand the lines to trace,
As through the Etrurian swamps, by floods increased,
The one-eyed chief urged his Getulian beast!
But what ensued? Illusive glory, say:
Subdued on Zama's memorable day,
He flies in exile to a petty state,
With headlong haste, and at a despot's gate
Sits, mighty suppliant—of his life in doubt,
Till the Bithynian's morning nap be out.
Nor swords, nor spears, nor stones from engines hurled,
Shall quell the man whose frowns alarmed the world.
The vengeance due to Cannæ's fatal field,
And floods of human gore, a ring shall yield!
Go, madman, go! at toil and danger mock,
Pierce the deep snow, and scale the eternal rock,
To please the rhetoricians, and become
A declamation for the boys of Rome.

Juvenal.

THE ASS'S LEGACY

A PRIEST there was, in times of old,
    Fond of his church, but fonder of his gold,
    Who spent his days, and all his thought,
In getting what he preached was naught.
His chests were full of robes and stuff;
Corn filled his garners to the roof,
Stored up against the fair-times gay
From St. Rémy to Easter day.

A Satire Anthology

An ass he had within his stable,
A beast most sound and valuable;
For twenty years he lent his strength
For the priest, his master, till at length,
Worn out with work and age, he died.
The priest, who loved him, wept and cried;
And, for his service long and hard,
Buried him in his own churchyard.

Now turn we to another thing:
'Tis of a bishop that I sing.
No greedy miser he, I ween;
Prelate so generous ne'er was seen.
Full well he loved in company
Of all good Christians still to be;
When he was well, his pleasure still;
His medicine best when he was ill.

Always his hall was full, and there
His guests had ever best of fare.
Whate'er the bishop lacked or lost,
Was bought at once, despite the cost.
And so, in spite of vent and score,
The bishop's debts grew more and more.
For true it is—this ne'er forget—
Who spends too much gets into debt.
One day his friends all with him sat,
The bishop talking this and that,
Till the discourse on rich clerks ran,
Of greedy priests, and how their plan
Was all good bishops still to grieve,
And of their dues their lords deceive.

A Satire Anthology

And then the priest of whom I've told
Was mentioned—how he loved his gold.
And, because men do often use
More freedom than the truth would choose,
They gave him wealth, and wealth so much,
As those like him could scarcely touch.
"And then, besides, a thing he's done
By which great profit might be won,
Could it be only spoken here."
Quoth the bishop, "Tell it without fear."
"He's worse, my lord, than Bedouin,
Because his own dead ass, Baldwin,
He buried in the sacred ground."
"If this is truth, as shall be found,"
The bishop cried, "a forfeit high
Will on his worldly riches lie.
Summon this wicked priest to me;
I will myself in this case be
The judge.   If Robert's word be true,
Mine are the fine, and forfeit too."

"Disloyal!   God's enemy and mine,
Prepare to pay a heavy fine.
Thy ass thou buriest in the place
Sacred by church.   Now, by God's grace,
I never heard of crime more great.
What!   Christian men with asses wait!
Now, if this thing be proven, know
Surely to prison thou wilt go."
"Sir," said the priest, "thy patience grant;
A short delay is all I want.

Not that I fear to answer now,
But give me what the laws allow."
And so the bishop leaves the priest,
Who does not feel as if at feast;
But still, because one friend remains,
He trembles not at prison pains.
His purse it is which never fails
For tax or forfeit, fine or vails.

The term arrived, the priest appeared,
And met the bishop, nothing feared;
For 'neath his girdle safe there hung
A leathern purse, well stocked and strung
With twenty pieces fresh and bright,
Good money all, none clipped or light.
"Priest," said the bishop, "if thou have
Answer to give to charge so grave,
'Tis now the time."
"Sir, grant me leave
My answer secretly to give.
Let me confess to you alone,
And, if needs be, my sins atone."
The bishop bent his head to hear;
The priest he whispered in his ear:
"Sir, spare a tedious tale to tell.
My poor ass served me long and well,
For twenty years my faithful slave;
Each year his work a saving gave
Of twenty sous, so that, in all,
To twenty livres the sum will fall;
And, for the safety of his soul,
To you, my lord, he left the whole."

"'Twas rightly done," the bishop said,
And gravely shook his godly head;
"And that his soul to heaven may go,
My absolution I bestow."

Now have you heard a truthful lay,
How with rich priests the bishops play;
And Rutebœuf the moral draws
That, spite of kings' and bishops' laws,
No evil times has he to dread
Who still has silver at his need.

Rutebœuf.

A BALLADE OF OLD-TIME LADIES

(Translated by John Payne.)

TELL me, where, in what land of shade,
    Hides fair Flora of Rome? and where
Are Thaïs and Archipiade,
    Cousins-german in beauty rare?
    And Echo, more than mortal fair,
That when one calls by river flow,
    Or marish, answers out of the air?
But what has become of last year's snow?

Where did the learn'd Héloïsa vade,
    For whose sake Abelard did not spare
(Such dole for love on him was laid)
    Manhood to lose and a cowl to wear?

And where is the queen who will'd whilere
That Buridan, tied in a sack, should go
    Floating down Seine from the turret-stair?
But what has become of last year's snow?

Blanche, too, the lily-white queen, that made
    Sweet music as if she a siren were?
Broad-foot Bertha? and Joan, the maid,
    The good Lorrainer the English bare
    Captive to Rouen, and burn'd her there?
Beatrix, Eremburge, Alys—lo!
    Where are they, virgins debonair?
But what has become of last year's snow?

Envoi

Prince, you may question how they fare,
    This week, or liefer this year, I trow:
Still shall this burden the answer bear—
    But what has become of last year's snow?
                  François Villon.

A CARMAN'S ACCOUNT OF A LAWSUIT

MARRY, I lent my gossip my mare, to fetch hame coals,
    And he her drounit into the quarry holes;
And I ran to the consistory, for to pleinyie,
And there I happenit amang ane greedie meinyie.
They gave me first ane thing they call *citandum*,
Within aucht days I gat but *libellandum*;

Within ane month I gat *ad opponendum;*
In half ane year I gat *inter-loquendum;*
And syne I gat—how call ye it?—*ad replicandum;*
Bot I could never ane word yet understand him:
And then they gart me cast out many placks,
And gart me pay for four-and-twenty acts.
Bot or they came half gate to *concludendum,*
The fiend ane plack was left for to defend him.
Thus they postponed me twa year with their train,
Syne, *hodie ad octo,* bade me come again;
And then their rooks they rowpit wonder fast
For sentence, silver, they cryit at the last.
Of *pronunciandum* they made me wonder fain,
Bot I gat never my gude gray mare again.
       Sir David Lyndsay.

THE SOUL'S ERRAND

GO, Soul, the body's guest,
 Upon a thankless errand;
Fear not to touch the best;
 The truth shall be thy warrant.
  Go, since I needs must die,
  And give them all the lie.

Go tell the Court it glows
 And shines like rotten wood;
Go tell the Church it shows
 What's good, but does no good.
  If Court and Church reply,
  Give Court and Church the lie.

Tell Potentates they live
  Acting, but oh! their actions;
Not loved, unless they give,
  Not strong but by their factions.
    If Potentates reply,
    Give Potentates the lie.

Tell men of high condition,
  That rule affairs of state,
Their purpose is ambition;
  Their practice only hate;
    And if they do reply,
    Then give them all the lie.

Tell those that brave it most,
  They beg for more by spending,
Who in their greatest cost
  Seek nothing but commending;
    And if they make reply,
    Spare not to give the lie.

Tell Zeal it lacks devotion;
  Tell Love it is but lust;
Tell Time it is but motion;
  Tell Flesh it is but dust;
    And wish them not reply,
    For thou must give the lie.

Tell Age it daily wasteth;
  Tell Honour how it alters;
Tell Beauty how it blasteth;
  Tell Favour that she falters;
    And as they do reply,
    Give every one the lie.

Tell Wit how much it wrangles
  In fickle points of niceness;
Tell Wisdom she entangles
  Herself in overwiseness;
    And if they do reply,
    Then give them both the lie.

Tell Physic of her boldness;
  Tell Skill it is pretension;
Tell Charity of coldness;
  Tell Law it is contention;
    And if they yield reply,
    Then give them all the lie.

Tell Fortune of her blindness;
  Tell Nature of decay;
Tell Friendship of unkindness;
  Tell Justice of delay;
    And if they do reply,
    Then give them still the lie.

Tell Arts they have no soundness,
  But vary by esteeming;
Tell Schools they lack profoundness,
  And stand too much on seeming.
    If Arts and Schools reply,
    Give Arts and Schools the lie.

Tell Faith it's fled the city;
  Tell how the country erreth;
Tell, Manhood shakes off pity;
  Tell, Virtue least preferreth;
    And if they do reply,
    Spare not to give the lie.

So, when thou hast, as I
   Commanded thee, done blabbing,
Although to give the lie
   Deserves no less than stabbing,
     Yet stab at thee who will,
     No stab the Soul can kill!
         Sir Walter Raleigh.

OF A CERTAIN MAN

THERE was (not certain when) a certain preacher
   That never learned, and yet became a teacher,
Who, having read in Latin thus a text
Of *erat quidam homo*, much perplexed,
He seemed the same with study great to scan,
In English thus, *There was a certain man.*
"But now," quoth he, "good people, note you this,
He said there was: he doth not say there is;
For in these days of ours it is most plain
Of promise, oath, word, deed, no man's certain;
Yet by my text you see it comes to pass
That surely once a certain man there was;
But yet, I think, in all your Bible no man
Can find this text, *There was a certain woman.*"
         Sir John Harrington.

A PRECISE TAILOR

A TAILOR, thought a man of upright dealing—
   True, but for lying, honest, but for stealing—
   Did fall one day extremely sick by chance,
And on the sudden was in wondrous trance;

The fiends of hell mustering in fearful manner,
Of sundry colour'd silks display'd a banner
Which he had stolen, and wish'd, as they did tell,
That he might find it all one day in hell.
The man, affrighted with this apparition,
Upon recovery grew a great precisian:
He bought a Bible of the best translation,
And in his life he show'd great reformation;
He walkéd mannerly, he talkéd meekly,
He heard three lectures and two sermons weekly;
He vow'd to shun all company unruly,
And in his speech he used no oath but truly;
And zealously to keep the Sabbath's rest,
His meat for that day on the eve was drest;
And lest the custom which he had to steal
Might cause him sometimes to forget his zeal,
He gives his journeyman a special charge,
That if the stuff, allowance being large,
He found his fingers were to filch inclined,
Bid him to have the banner in his mind.
This done (I scant can tell the rest for laughter),
A captain of a ship came, three days after,
And brought three yards of velvet and three-quarters,
To make Venetians down below the garters.
He, that precisely knew what was enough,
Soon slipt aside three-quarters of the stuff.
His man, espying it, said in derision,
"Master, remember how you saw the vision!"
"Peace, knave!" quoth he, "I did not see one rag
Of such a colour'd silk in all the flag."

Sir John Harrington.

THE WILL

BEFORE I sigh my last gasp, let me breathe,
  Great Love, some legacies: Here I bequeathe
Mine eyes to Argus, if mine eyes can see;
If they be blind, then, Love, I give them thee;
My tongue to fame; to embassadors mine ears;
    To women or the sea, my tears.
  Thou, Love, hast taught me heretofore,
By making me serve her who had twenty more,
That I should give to none but such as had too much
    before.

My constancy I to the planets give;
My truth to them who at the court do live;
My ingenuity and openness
To Jesuits; to buffoons my pensiveness;
My silence to any who abroad have been;
    My money to a Capuchin.
  Thou, Love, taught'st me, by appointing me
To love there where no love received can be,
Only to give to such as have an incapacity.

My faith I give to Roman Catholics;
All my good works unto the schismatics
Of Amsterdam; my best civility
And courtship to a university;
My modesty I give to soldiers bare;
    My patience let gamesters share.
  Thou, Love, taught'st me, by making me
Love her that holds my love disparity,
Only to give to those that count my gifts indignity.

I give my reputation to those
Which were my friends; mine industry to foes;
To schoolmen I bequeathe my doubtfulness;
My sickness to physicians, or excess;
To Nature all that I in rhyme have writ;
    And to my company my wit.
  Thou, Love, by making me adore
Her who begot this love in me before,
Taught'st me to make as though I gave, when I do
    but restore.

To him for whom the passing bell next tolls
I give my physic-books; my written rolls
Of moral counsel I to Bedlam give;
My brazen medals unto them which live
In want of bread; to them which pass among
    All foreigners, mine English tongue.
  Thou, Love, by making me love one
Who thinks her friendship a fit portion
For younger lovers, dost my gifts thus disproportion.

Therefore I'll give no more, but I'll undo
The world by dying, because love dies too.
Then all your beauties will no more be worth
Than gold in mines where none doth draw it forth;
And all your graces no more use shall have
    Than a sundial in a grave.
  Thou, Love, taught'st me, by making me
Love her who doth neglect both thee and me,
To invent and practise this one way to annihilate
    all three.

John Donne.

A Satire Anthology

SHAKESPEAREAN SATIRE

FROM "KING HENRY IV"

MY liege, I did deny no prisoners;
   But I remember, when the fight was done,
   When I was dry with rage and extreme toil,
Breathless and faint, leaning upon my sword,
Came there a certain lord, neat, trimly dress'd,
Fresh as a bridegroom; and his chin, new reap'd,
Show'd like a stubble-land at harvest-home.
He was perfuméd like a milliner,
And 'twixt his finger and his thumb he held
A pouncet-box, which ever and anon
He gave his nose and took 't away again;
Who, therewith angry, when it next came there,
Took it in snuff: and still he smil'd and talk'd,
And as the soldiers bore dead bodies by,
He call'd them untaught knaves, unmannerly,
To bring a slovenly, unhandsome corse
Betwixt the wind and his nobility.
With many holiday and lady terms
He question'd me; among the rest, demanded
My prisoners in your Majesty's behalf.
I then, all smarting with my wounds being cold,
To be so pester'd with a popinjay,
Out of my grief and my impatience,
Answer'd neglectingly I know not what,
He should, or he should not; for he made me mad
To see him shine so brisk, and smell so sweet,
And talk so like a waiting-gentlewoman

Of guns and drums and wounds—God save
   the mark!—
And telling me the sovereign'st thing on earth
Was parmaceti for an inward bruise;
And that it was great pity, so it was,
This villainous saltpetre should be digg'd
Out of the bowels of the harmless earth,
Which many a good tall fellow had destroy'd
So cowardly; and but for these vile guns,
He would himself have been a soldier.
This bald, unjointed chat of his, my lord,
I answer'd indirectly, as I said;
And I beseech you, let not this report
Come current for an accusation
Betwixt my love and your high Majesty.
                              Shakespeare.

FROM "LOVE'S LABOUR'S LOST"

THIS fellow pecks up wit, as pigeons pease,
   And utters it again when God doth please.
   He is wit's pedler, and retails his wares
At wakes and wassails, meetings, markets, fairs;
And we that sell by gross, the Lord doth know,
Have not the grace to grace it with such show.
This gallant pins the wenches on his sleeve;
Had he been Adam, he had tempted Eve.
He can carve, too, and lisp; why, this is he
That kiss'd his hand away in courtesy;
This is the ape of form, monsieur the nice,
That, when he plays at table, chides the dice
In honourable terms; nay, he can sing
A mean most meanly; and in ushering,

A Satire Anthology

Mend him who can: the ladies call him sweet;
The stairs, as he treads on them, kiss his feet.
This is the flower that smiles on every one,
To show his teeth as white as whale's bone;
And consciences that will not die in debt
Pay him the due of honey-tongued Boyet.

. . . . . .

See where it comes!—Behaviour, what wert thou
Till this man show'd thee? and what art thou now?
Shakespeare.

FROM "*AS YOU LIKE IT*"

ALL the world's a stage,
 And all the men and women merely players:
 They have their exits, and their entrances;
And one man in his time plays many parts,
His acts being seven ages. At first the infant,
Mewling and puking in the nurse's arms:
Then the whining schoolboy, with his satchel,
And shining morning face, creeping like snail
Unwillingly to school: And then the lover,
Sighing like furnace, with a woful ballad
Made to his mistress' eyebrow: Then a soldier,
Full of strange oaths, and bearded like the pard,
Jealous in honour, sudden and quick in quarrel,
Seeking the bubble reputation
Even in the cannon's mouth: And then the justice,
In fair round belly with good capon lin'd,
With eyes severe, and beard of formal cut,

Full of wise saws and modern instances;
And so he plays his part: The sixth age shifts
Into the lean and slipper'd pantaloon,
With spectacles on nose, and pouch on side;
His youthful hose well sav'd, a world too wide
For his shrunk shank; and his big manly voice,
Turning again toward childish treble, pipes
And whistles in his sound: Last scene of all,
That ends this strange eventful history,
Is second childishness and mere oblivion,
Sans teeth, sans eyes, sans taste, sans everything.
Shakespeare.

HORACE CONCOCTING AN ODE

TO thee, whose forehead swells with roses,
    Whose most haunted bower
    Gives life and scent to every flower,
Whose most adoréd name encloses
    Things abstruse, deep, and divine;
    Whose yellow tresses shine
Bright as Eoan fire:
    Oh, me thy priest inspire!
For I to thee and thine immortal name,
In—in—in golden tunes,
For I to thee and thine immortal name—
In—sacred raptures flowing, flowing, swimming,
    swimming:
In sacred raptures swimming,
Immortal name, game, dame, tame, lame, lame,
    lame,

(Foh) hath, shame, proclaim, oh—
In sacred raptures flowing, will proclaim. (No!)
    Oh, me thy priest inspire!
For I to thee and thine immortal name,
In flowing numbers filled with spright and flame,
    (Good! good!)
In flowing numbers filled with spright and flame.
Thomas Dekker.

ON DON SURLY

DON SURLY, to aspire the glorious name
  Of a great man, and to be thought the same,
  Makes serious use of all great trade he knows.
He speaks to men with a rhinocerote's nose,
Which he thinks great; and so reads verses too;
And that is done as he saw great men do.
He has tympanies of business in his face,
And can forget men's names with a great grace.
He will both argue and discourse in oaths,
Both which are great, and laugh at ill-made clothes;
That's greater yet, to cry his own up neat.
He doth, at meals, alone his pheasant eat,
Which is main greatness; and at his still board
He drinks to no man: that's, too, like a lord.
He keeps another's wife, which is a spice
Of solemn greatness; and he dares, at dice,
Blaspheme God greatly; or some poor hind beat,
That breathes in his dog's way: and this is great.
Nay, more, for greatness' sake he will be one
May hear my epigrams, but like of none.

Surly, use other arts; these only can
Style thee a most great fool, but no great man.
Ben Jonson.

THE SCHOLAR AND HIS DOG

I WAS a scholar: seven useful springs
   Did I deflower in quotations
   Of cross'd opinions 'bout the soul of man;
The more I learnt, the more I learnt to doubt.
Delight my spaniel slept, whilst I baus'd leaves,
Toss'd o'er the dunces, pored on the old print
Of titled words: and still my spaniel slept.
Whilst I wasted lamp-oil, baited my flesh,
Shrunk up my veins: and still my spaniel slept.
And still I held converse with Zabarell,
Aquinas, Scotus, and the musty saw
Of antick Donate: still my spaniel slept.
Still on went I; first, *an sit anima;*
Then, an it were mortal. Oh, hold, hold! at that
They're at brain buffets, fell by the ears amain
Pell-mell together; still my spaniel slept.
Then, whether 't were corporeal, local, fixt,
Ex traduce, but whether 't had free will
Or no, hot philosphers
Stood banding factions, all so strongly propt,
I stagger'd, knew not which was firmer part,
But thought, quoted, read, observ'd, and pryed,
Stufft noting-books: and still my spaniel slept.
At length he wak'd, and yawned; and by yon sky,
For aught I know he knew as much as I.
                         John Marston.

THE MANLY HEART

SHALL I, wasting in despair,
   Die because a woman's fair?
   Or my cheeks make pale with care
'Cause another's rosy are?
Be she fairer than the day,
Or the flowery meads in May,
   If she be not so to me,
   What care I how fair she be?

Shall my foolish heart be pined
'Cause I see a woman kind;
Or a well-disposéd nature
Joinéd with a lovely feature?
Be she meeker, kinder, than
Turtle-dove or pelican,
   If she be not so to me,
   What care I how kind she be?

Shall a woman's virtues move
Me to perish for her love?
Or her merit's value known
Make me quite forget my own?
Be she with that goodness blest
Which may gain her name of Best,
   If she seem not such to me,
   What care I how good she be?

'Cause her fortune seems too high,
Shall I play the fool and die?
Those that bear a noble mind
Where they want of riches find,
Think what with them they would do
Who without them dare to woo;
  And unless that mind I see,
  What care I though great she be?

Great or good, or kind or fair,
I will ne'er the more despair;
If she loves me, this believe,
I will die ere she shall grieve;
If she slight me when I woo,
I can scorn and let her go;
  For if she be not for me,
  What care I for whom she be?
George Wither.

THE CONSTANT LOVER

OUT upon it! I have loved
   Three whole days together,
  And am like to love three more,
   If it prove fair weather.

Time shall moult away his wings
  Ere he shall discover
In the whole wide world again
  Such a constant lover.

But the spite on 't is, no praise
　　Is due at all to me:
Love with me had made no stays,
　　Had it any been but she.

Had it any been but she,
　　And that very face,
There had been at least ere this
　　A dozen dozen in her place.
　　　　　　　　Sir John Suckling.

THE REMONSTRANCE

WHY so pale and wan, fond lover?
　　Prithee, why so pale?
　Will, when looking well can't move her,
Looking ill prevail?
Prithee, why so pale?

Why so dull and mute, young sinner?
　　Prithee, why so mute?
Will, when speaking well can't win her,
　　Saying nothing do't?
　　Prithee, why so mute?

Quit, quit, for shame! this will not move,
　　This cannot take her;
If of herself she will not love,
　　Nothing can make her:
　　The devil take her!
　　　　　　　　Sir John Suckling.

SAINTSHIP VERSUS CONSCIENCE

"WHY didst thou choose that cursed sin,
    Hypocrisy, to set up in?"
"Because it is the thriving'st calling,
The only saints' bell that rings all in;
In which all churches are concern'd,
And is the easiest to be learn'd."

. . . . . .

Quoth he, "I am resolv'd to be
Thy scholar in this mystery;
And therefore first desire to know
Some principles on which you go.
What makes a knave a child of God,
And one of us?" "A livelihood."
"What renders beating out of brains,
And murder, godliness?" "Great gains."
"What's tender conscience?" "'Tis a botch
That will not bear the gentlest touch;
But, breaking out, despatches more
Than th' epidemical'st plague-sore."
"What makes y' encroach upon our trade,
And damn all others?" "To be paid."
"What's orthodox and true believing,
Against a conscience?" "A good living."
"What makes rebelling against kings
A good old cause?" "Administ'rings."
"What makes all doctrines plain and clear?"
"About two hundred pounds a year."
"And that which was prov'd true before,
Prov'd false again?" "Two hundred more."

"What makes the breaking of all oaths
A holy duty?" "Food and clothes."
"What, laws and freedom, persecution?"
"Being out of power and contribution."
"What makes a church a den of thieves?"
"A dean and chapter, and white sleeves."
"And what would serve, if these were gone,
To make it orthodox?" "Our own."
"What makes morality a crime,
The most notorious of the time;
Morality, which both the saints
And wicked, too, cry out against?"
"'Cause grace and virtue are within
Prohibited degrees of kin;
And therefore no true saint allows
They shall be suffered to espouse."
Samuel Butler.

DESCRIPTION OF HOLLAND

A COUNTRY that draws fifty foot of water,
In which men live as in the hold of Nature,
And when the sea does in upon them break,
And drowns a province, does but spring a leak;
That always ply the pump, and never think
They can be safe but at the rate they stink;
They live as if they had been run aground,
And, when they die, are cast away and drowned;
That dwell in ships, like swarms of rats, and prey
Upon the goods all nations' fleets convey;
And when their merchants are blown up and crackt,
Whole towns are cast away in storms, and wreckt;

That feed, like cannibals, on other fishes,
And serve their cousin-germans up in dishes:
A land that rides at anchor, and is moored,
In which they do not live, but go aboard.
Samuel Butler.

THE RELIGION OF HUDIBRAS

FOR his religion it was fit
    To match his learning and his wit:
    Twas Presbyterian true blue;
For he was of that stubborn crew
Of errant saints, whom all men grant
To be the true Church militant;
Such as do build their faith upon
The holy text of pike and gun;
Decide all controversies by
Infallible artillery,
And prove their doctrine orthodox,
By apostolic blows and knocks;
Call fire, and sword, and desolation,
A godly, thorough reformation.
Which always must be carried on,
And still be doing, never done;
As if religion were intended
For nothing else but to be mended;
A sect whose chief devotion lies
In odd perverse antipathies;
In falling out with that or this,
And finding somewhat still amiss;
More peevish, cross, and splenetic,
Than dog distract or monkey sick;

That with more care keep holy-day
The wrong, than others the right way;
Compound for sins they are inclin'd to,
By damning those they have no mind to;
Still so perverse and opposite,
As if they worshipped God for spite;
The self-same thing they will abhor
One way, and long another for;
Free-will they one way disavow,
Another, nothing else allow;
All piety consists therein
In them, in other men all sin;
Rather than fail, they will defy
That which they love most tenderly;
Quarrel with minc'd pies, and disparage
Their best and dearest friend, plum porridge;
Fat pig and goose itself oppose,
And blaspheme custard through the nose.
Samuel Butler.

SATIRE ON THE SCOTS

A LAND where one may pray with cursed intent,
Oh, may they never suffer banishment!
Had Cain been Scot, God would have chang'd his doom—
Not forc'd him wander, but confin'd him home.
Like Jews they spread and as infection fly,
As if the devil had ubiquity;

Hence 'tis they live as rovers, and defy
This or that place, rags of geography;
They're citizens o' th' world, they're all in all;
Scotland's a nation epidemical.
And yet they ramble not to learn the mode
How to be drest, or how to lisp abroad. . . .
No, the Scots errant fight, and fight to eat;
Their ostrich-stomachs make their swords their meat;
Nature with Scots as tooth-drawers hath dealt,
Who use to string their teeth upon their belt. . . .
Lord! what a godly thing is want of shirts!
How a Scotch stomach and no meat converts!
They wanted food and raiment; so they took
Religion for their seamstress and their cook.
Unmask them well, their honours and estate,
As well as conscience, are sophisticate.
Shrive but their title and their moneys poize,
A laird and twenty pence pronounc'd with noise,
When constru'd but for a plain yeoman go,
And a good sober twopence, and well so.
Hence, then, you proud impostors! get you gone,
You Picts in gentry and devotion,
You scandal to the stock of verse—a race
Able to bring the gibbet in disgrace!
Hyperbolus by suffering did traduce
The ostracism, and sham'd it out of use.
The Indian that heaven did forswear,
Because he heard some Spaniards were there,
Had he but known what Scots in hell had been,
He would, Erasmus-like, have hung between.
My muse hath done. A voyder for the nonce,

I wrong the devil should I pick their bones;
That dish is his; for when the Scots decease,
Hell, like their nation, feeds on barnacles.
A Scot when from the gallow-tree got loose,
Drops into Styx, and turns a Soland goose.
John Cleiveland.

SONG

WHY should you swear I am forsworn,
    Since thine I vowed to be?
  Lady, it is already morn,
    And 'twas last night I swore to thee
That fond impossibility.

Have I not loved thee much and long,
    A tedious twelve hours' space?
I must all other beauties wrong,
    And rob thee of a new embrace,
    Could I still dote upon thy face.

Not but all joy in thy brown hair
    By others may be found;
But I must search the black and fair,
    Like skilful mineralists that sound
    For treasure in unploughed-up ground.

Then, if when I have loved my round,
    Thou prov'st the pleasant she;
With spoils of meaner beauties crowned,
    I laden will return to thee,
    Even sated with variety.
Richard Lovelace.

THE CHARACTER OF HOLLAND

HOLLAND, that scarce deserves the name of land,
    As but the off-scouring of the British sand,
And so much earth as was contributed
By English pilots when they heaved the lead;
Or what by th' ocean's slow alluvion fell,
Of shipwrecked cockle and the mussel-shell;
This indigested vomit of the sea
Fell to the Dutch by just propriety.
Glad then, as miners who have found the ore,
They, with mad labour, fished the land to shore;
And dived as desperately for each piece
Of earth as if 't had been of ambergreese;
Collecting anxiously small loads of clay,
Less than what building-swallows bear away;
Or than those pills which sordid beetles roll,
Transfusing into them their dunghill soul.
How did they rivet, with gigantic piles,
Thorough the centre their new-catched miles;
And to the stake a struggling country bound,
Where barking waves still bait the forcéd ground;
Building their watery Babel far more high
To reach the sea, than those to scale the sky.
Yet still his claim the injured ocean laid,
And oft at leap-frog o'er their steeples played;
As if on purpose it on land had come
To shew them what's their *mare liberum*.
A daily deluge over them does boil;
The earth and water play at level-coil.

A Satire Anthology

The fish ofttimes the burgher dispossessed,
And sat, not as a meat, but as a guest;
And oft the Tritons and the sea-nymphs saw
Whole shoals of Dutch served up for cabillau;
Or, as they over the new lever ranged,
For pickled herring, pickled heeren changed.
Nature, it seemed, ashamed of her mistake,
Would throw their land away at duck and drake,
Therefore necessity, that first make kings,
Something like government among them brings;
For, as with pigmies, who best kills the crane,
Among the hungry he that treasures grain,
Among the blind the one-eyed blinkard reigns,
So rules among the drowned he that drains.
Not who first see the rising sun commands,
But who could first discern the rising lands.
Who best could know to pump an earth so leak,
Him they their Lord and Country's Father speak.
To make a bank was a great plot of state;
Invent a shovel, and be a magistrate.
Hence some small dike-grave unperceived invades
The power, and grows, as 'twere, a king of spades;
But, for less envy, some joined states endures,
Who look like a commission of the sewers:
For these Half-anders, half wet, and half dry,
Nor bear strict service, nor pure liberty.
'Tis probable religion, after this,
Came next in order, which they could not miss.
How could the Dutch but be converted, when
The apostles were so many fishermen?
Besides, the waters of themselves did rise,
And, as their land, so them did rebaptize.
Andrew Marvell.

THE DUKE OF BUCKINGHAM

SOME of their chiefs were princes of the land:
In the first rank of these did Zimri stand,
A man so various that he seemed to be
Not one, but all mankind's epitome:
Stiff in opinions, always in the wrong,
Was everything by starts, and nothing long;
But, in the course of one revolving moon,
Was chymist, fiddler, statesman, and buffoon;
Then all for women, painting, rhyming, drinking,
Besides ten thousand freaks that died in thinking.
Blest madman, who could every hour employ
With something new to wish or to enjoy!
Railing and praising were his usual themes,
And both, to shew his judgment, in extremes;
So over-violent, or over-civil,
That every man with him was god or devil.
In squandering wealth was his peculiar art;
Nothing went unrewarded but desert:
Beggared by fools, whom still he found too late,
He had his jest, and they had his estate;
He laughed himself from court, then sought relief
By forming parties, but could ne'er be chief;
For, spite of him, the weight of business fell
On Absalom and wise Achitophel.
Thus, wicked but in will, of means bereft,
He left not faction, but of that was left.

John Dryden.

ON SHADWELL

ALL human things are subject to decay,
    And, when Fate summons, monarchs must
       obey.
This Flecknoe found, who, like Augustus, young
Was called to empire, and had governed long.
In prose and verse was owned, without dispute,
Through all the realms of Nonsense absolute.
This aged prince, now flourishing in peace,
And blest with issue of a large increase,
Worn out with business, did at length debate
To settle the succession of the state;
And pondering which of all his sons was fit
To reign, and wage immortal war with Wit,
Cried: "'Tis resolved; for Nature pleads that he
Should only rule who most resembles me.
Shadwell alone my perfect image bears,
Mature in dulness from his tender years;
Shadwell alone of all my sons is he
Who stands confirmed in full stupidity.
The rest to some faint meaning make pretence,
But Shadwell never deviates into sense.
Some beams of wit on other souls may fall,
Strike through, and make a lucid interval,
But Shadwell's genuine night admits no ray;
His rising fogs prevail upon the day.
Besides, his goodly fabric fills the eye,
And seems designed for thoughtless majesty—
Thoughtless as monarch oaks that shade the plain,
And, spread in solemn state, supinely reign.

Heywood and Shirley were but types of thee,
Thou last great prophet of tautology!
Even I, a dunce of more renown than they,
Was sent before but to prepare thy way."
       John Dryden.

SATIRE ON EDWARD HOWARD

THEY lie, dear Ned, who say thy brain is barren,
 When deep conceits, like maggots, breed in carrion.
Thy stumbling foundered jade can trot as high
As any other Pegasus can fly.
So the dull eel moves nimbler in the mud
Than all the swift-finned racers of the flood.
As skilful divers to the bottom fall
Sooner than those who cannot swim at all,
So in this way of writing, without thinking,
Thou hast a strange alacrity in sinking.
    Charles Sackville, Earl of Dorset.

ST. ANTHONY'S SERMON TO THE FISHES

SAINT ANTHONY at church
 Was left in the lurch,
 So he went to the ditches
And preached to the fishes.
 They wriggled their tails,
 In the sun glanced their scales.

The carps, with their spawn,
Are all thither drawn;
Have opened their jaws,
Eager for each clause.
   No sermon beside
     Had the carps so edified.

Sharp-snouted pikes,
Who keep fighting like tikes,
Now swam up harmonious
To hear Saint Antonius.
   No sermon beside
     Had the pikes so edified.

And that very odd fish,
Who loves fast-days, the cod-fish—
The stock-fish, I mean—
At the sermon was seen.
   No sermon beside
     Had the cods so edified.

Good eels and sturgeon,
Which aldermen gorge on,
Went out of their way
To hear preaching that day.
   No sermon beside
     Had the eels so edified.

Crabs and turtles also,
Who always move low,
Made haste from the bottom
As if the devil had got 'em.
   No sermon beside
     The crabs so edified.

Fish great and fish small,
Lords, lackeys, and all,
Each looked at the preacher
Like a reasonable creature.
  At God's word,
  They Anthony heard.

The sermon now ended,
Each turned and descended;
The pikes went on stealing,
The eels went on eeling.
  Much delighted were they,
  But preferred the old way.

The crabs are backsliders,
The stock-fish thick-siders,
The carps are sharp-set—
All the sermon forget.
  Much delighted were they,
  But preferred the old way.
            Abraham á Sancta-Clara.

INTRODUCTION TO THE TRUE-BORN ENGLISHMAN

SPEAK, satire; for there's none can tell like thee
  Whether 'tis folly, pride, or knavery
  That makes this discontented land appear
Less happy now in times of peace than war?
Why civil feuds disturb the nation more
Than all our bloody wars have done before?
Fools out of favour grudge at knaves in place,
And men are always honest in disgrace;

A Satire Anthology

The court preferments make men knaves in course,
But they which would be in them would be worse.
'Tis not at foreigners that we repine,
Would foreigners their perquisites resign;
The grand contention's plainly to be seen,
To get some men put out, and some put in.
For this our senators make long harangues,
And florid members whet their polished tongues.
Statesmen are always sick of one disease,
And a good pension gives them present ease;
That's the specific makes them all content
With any king and any government.
Good patriots at court abuses rail,
And all the nation's grievances bewail;
But when the sovereign's balsam's once applied,
The zealot never fails to change his side;
And when he must the golden key resign,
The railing spirit comes about again.
Who shall this bubbled nation disabuse,
While they their own felicities refuse,
Who the wars have made such mighty pother,
And now are falling out with one another:
With needless fears the jealous nation fill,
And always have been saved against their will:
Who fifty millions sterling have disbursed,
To be with peace and too much plenty cursed:
Who their old monarch eagerly undo,
And yet uneasily obey the new?
Search, satire, search; a deep incision make;
The poison's strong, the antidote's too weak.
'Tis pointed truth must manage this dispute,
And downright English, Englishmen confute.

Whet thy just anger at the nation's pride,
And with keen phrase repel the vicious tide;
To Englishmen their own beginnings show,
And ask them why they slight their neighbours so.
Go back to elder times and ages past,
And nations into long oblivion cast;
To old Britannia's youthful days retire,
And there for true-born Englishmen inquire.
Britannia freely will disown the name,
And hardly knows herself from whence they came;
Wonders that they of all men should pretend
To birth and blood, and for a name contend.
Go back to causes where our follies dwell,
And fetch the dark original from hell.
Speak, satire, for there's none like thee can tell.
                                Daniel Defoe.

AN EPITAPH

INTERRED beneath this marble stone
  Lie sauntering Jack and idle Joan.
    While rolling threescore years and one
Did round this globe their courses run.
If human things went ill or well,
If changing empires rose or fell,
The morning past, the evening came,
And found this couple just the same.
They walked and ate, good folks. What then?
Why, then they walked and ate again;
They soundly slept the night away;
They did just nothing all the day,

Nor sister either had, nor brother;
They seemed just tallied for each other.
Their moral and economy
Most perfectly they made agree;
Each virtue kept its proper bound,
Nor trespassed on the other's ground.
Nor fame nor censure they regarded;
They neither punished nor rewarded.
He cared not what the footman did;
Her maids she neither praised nor chid;
So every servant took his course,
And, bad at first, they all grew worse;
Slothful disorder filled his stable,
And sluttish plenty decked her table.
Their beer was strong, their wine was port;
Their meal was large, their grace was short.
They gave the poor the remnant meat,
Just when it grew not fit to eat.
They paid the church and parish rate,
And took, but read not, the receipt;
For which they claimed their Sunday's due
Of slumbering in an upper pew.
No man's defects sought they to know,
So never made themselves a foe.
No man's good deeds did they commend,
So never raised themselves a friend.
Nor cherished they relations poor,
That might decrease their present store;
Nor barn nor house did they repair,
That might oblige their future heir.
They neither added nor confounded;
They neither wanted nor abounded.

Nor tear nor smile did they employ
At news of grief or public joy.
When bells were rung and bonfires made,
If asked, they ne'er denied their aid;
Their jug was to the ringers carried,
Whoever either died or married.
Their billet at the fire was found,
Whoever was deposed or crowned.
Nor good, nor bad, nor fools, nor wise;
They would not learn, nor could advise;
Without love, hatred, joy, or fear,
They led—a kind of—as it were;
Nor wished, nor cared, nor laughed, nor cried.
And so they lived, and so they died.
Matthew Prior.

THE REMEDY WORSE THAN THE DISEASE

I SENT for Ratcliffe; was so ill,
   That other doctors gave me over:
He felt my pulse, prescribed his pill,
   And I was likely to recover.

But when the wit began to wheeze,
   And wine had warm'd the politician,
Cured yesterday of my disease,
   I died last night of my physician.
Matthew Prior.

TWELVE ARTICLES

I
LEST it may more quarrels breed,
I will never hear you read.

II
By disputing, I will never,
To convince you, once endeavour.

III
When a paradox you stick to,
I will never contradict you.

IV
When I talk, and you are heedless,
I will show no anger needless.

V
When your speeches are absurd,
I will ne'er object a word.

VI
When you, furious, argue wrong,
I will grieve, and hold my tongue.

VII
Not a jest or humorous story
Will I ever tell before ye.

To be chidden for explaining,
When you quite mistake the meaning.

VIII
Never more will I suppose,
You can taste my verse or prose.

IX
You no more at me shall fret,
While I teach and you forget.

X
You shall never hear me thunder,
When you blunder on, and blunder.

XI
Show your poverty of spirit,
And in dress place all your merit;
Give yourself ten thousand airs:
That with me shall break no squares.

XII
Never will I give advice,
Till you please to ask me thrice:
Which if you in scorn reject,
'Twill be just as I expect.
Thus we both shall have our ends,
And continue special friends.

Jonathan Swift.

THE FURNITURE OF A WOMAN'S MIND

A SET of phrases learned by rote;
A passion for a scarlet coat;
When at a play, to laugh or cry,
Yet cannot tell the reason why;
Never to hold her tongue a minute,
While all she prates has nothing in it;
Whole hours can with a coxcomb sit,
And take his nonsense all for wit.
Her learning mounts to read a song,
But half the words pronouncing wrong;
Has every repartee in store
She spoke ten thousand times before;
Can ready compliments supply
On all occasions, cut and dry;
Such hatred to a parson's gown,
The sight would put her in a swoon;
For conversation well endued,
She calls it witty to be rude;
And, placing raillery in railing,
Will tell aloud your greatest failing;
Nor make a scruple to expose
Your bandy leg or crooked nose;
Can at her morning tea run o'er
The scandal of the day before;
Improving hourly in her skill,
To cheat and wrangle at quadrille.
In choosing lace, a critic nice,
Knows to a groat the lowest price;

A Satire Anthology

Can in her female clubs dispute
What linen best the silk will suit,
What colours each complexion match,
And where with art to place a patch.
If chance a mouse creeps in her sight,
Can finely counterfeit a fright;
So sweetly screams, if it comes near her,
She ravishes all hearts to hear her.
Can dexterously her husband tease,
By taking fits whene'er she please;
By frequent practice learns the trick
At proper seasons to be sick;
Thinks nothing gives one airs so pretty,
At once creating love and pity.
If Molly happens to be careless,
And but neglects to warm her hair-lace,
She gets a cold as sure as death,
And vows she scarce can fetch her breath;
Admires how modest woman can
Be so robustious, like a man.
In party, furious to her power,
A bitter Whig, or Tory sour,
Her arguments directly tend
Against the side she would defend;
Will prove herself a Tory plain,
From principles the Whigs maintain,
And, to defend the Whiggish cause,
Her topics from the Tories draws.
Jonathan Swift.

FROM "THE LOVE OF FAME"

BEGIN. Who first the catalogue shall grace?
To quality belongs the highest place.
My lord comes forward; forward let him come!
Ye vulgar! at your peril, give him room:
He stands for fame on his forefathers' feet,
By heraldry proved valiant or discreet.
With what a decent pride he throws his eyes
Above the man by three descents less wise!
If virtues at his noble hands you crave,
You bid him raise his fathers from the grave.
Men should press forward in fame's glorious chase;
Nobles look backward, and so lose the race.
Let high birth triumph! What can be more great?
Nothing—but merit in a low estate.
To virtue's humblest son let none prefer
Vice, though descended from the Conqueror.
Shall men, like figures, pass for high or base,
Slight or important, only by their place?
Titles are marks of honest men, and wise;
The fool or knave, that wears a title, lies.

· · · · ·

On buying books Lorenzo long was bent,
But found, at length, that it reduced his rent;
His farms were flown; when, lo! a sale comes on,
A choice collection—what is to be done?
He sells his last, for he the whole will buy;
Sells even his house—nay, wants whereon to lie

So high the generous ardor of the man
For Romans, Greeks, and Orientals ran.
When terms were drawn, and brought him by the clerk,
Lorenzo signed the bargain—with his mark.
Unlearned men of books assume the care,
As eunuchs are the guardians of the fair.

. . . . . .

The booby father craves a booby son,
And by Heaven's blessing thinks himself undone.

. . . . . .

These subtle wights (so blind are mortal men,
Though satire couch them with her keenest pen)
Forever will hang out a solemn face,
To put off nonsense with a better grace:
As perlers with some hero's head make bold—
Illustrious mark!—where pins are to be sold.
What's the bent brow, or neck in thought reclined?
The body's wisdom to conceal the mind.
A man of sense can artifice disdain,
As men of wealth may venture to go plain;
And be this truth eternal ne'er forgot,
Solemnity's a cover for a sot.
I find the fool, when I behold the screen;
For 'tis the wise man's interest to be seen.

. . . . . .

And what so foolish as the chance of fame?
How vain the prize! how impotent our aim!
For what are men who grasp at praise sublime,
But bubbles on the rapid stream of time,

That rise and fall, that swell, and are no more,
Born, and forgot, ten thousand in an hour?

. . . . . .

Thus all will judge, and with one single aim,
To gain themselves, not give the writer fame.
The very best ambitiously advise,
Half to serve you, and half to pass for wise.
Critics on verse, as squibs on triumphs wait,
Proclaim the glory, and augment the state;
Hot, envious, noisy, proud, the scribbling fry
Burn, hiss, and bounce, waste paper, stink, and die.
Edward Young.

DR. DELANY'S VILLA

WOULD you that Delville I describe?
 Believe me, sir, I will not gibe;
 For who could be satirical
Upon a thing so very small?
You scarce upon the borders enter,
Before you're at the very centre.
A single crow can make it night,
When o'er your farm she takes her flight:
Yet, in this narrow compass, we
Observe a vast variety;
Both walks, walls, meadows, and parterres,
Windows, and doors, and rooms, and stairs,
And hills, and dales, and woods, and fields,
And hay, and grass, and corn, it yields;
All to your haggard brought so cheap in,
Without the mowing or the reaping:

A razor, tho' to say't I'm loth,
Would shave you and your meadows both.
Tho' small's the farm, yet here's a house
Full large to entertain a mouse;
But where a rat is dreaded more
Than savage Caledonian boar;
For, if it's enter'd by a rat,
There is no room to bring a cat.
A little rivulet seems to steal
Down thro' a thing you call a vale,
Like tears adown a wrinkled cheek,
Like rain along a blade of leek:
And this you call your sweet meander,
Which might be suck'd up by a gander,
Could he but force his nether bill
To scoop the channel of the rill.
For sure you'd make a mighty clutter,
Were it as big as city gutter.
Next come I to your kitchen garden,
Where one poor mouse would fare but hard in;
And round this garden is a walk,
No longer than a tailor's chalk;
Thus I compare what space is in it,
A snail creeps round it in a minute.
One lettuce makes a shift to squeeze
Up thro' a tuft you call your trees:
And, once a year, a single rose
Peeps from the bud, but never blows;
In vain then you expect its bloom!
It cannot blow for want of room.

In short, in all your boasted seat,
There's nothing but yourself that's GREAT.
Thomas Sheridan.

THE QUIDNUNCKIS

"HOW vain are mortal man's endeavours?
   (Said, at Dame Elleot's, Master Travers)
   Good Orleans dead! in truth 'tis hard:
Oh, may all statesmen die prepar'd!
I do foresee (and for foreseeing
He equals any man in being)
The army ne'er can be disbanded.
I with the king was safely landed.
Ah, friends, great changes threat the land!
All France and England at a stand!
There's Meroweis—mark! strange work!
And there's the Czar, and there's the Turk—
The Pope—" An Indian merchant by,
Cut short the speech with this reply:
"All at a stand? You see great changes?
Ah, sir, you never saw the Ganges.
There dwells the nation of Quidnunckis
(So Monomotapa calls monkeys);
On either bank, from bough to bough,
They meet and chat (as we may now);
Whispers go round, they grin, they shrug,
They bow, they snarl, they scratch, they hug;
And, just as chance or whim provoke them,
They either bite their friends, or stroke them.
There have I seen some active prig,
To show his parts, bestride a twig.

Lord, how the chatt'ring tribe admire!
Not that he's wiser, but he's higher.
All long to try the vent'rous thing
(For power is but to have one's swing);
From side to side he springs, he spurns,
And bangs his foes and friends by turns.
Thus as in giddy freaks he bounces,
Crack goes the twig, and in he flounces!
Down the swift stream the wretch is borne,
Never, ah, never to return!
Zounds! what a fall had our dear brother!
Morbleu! cries one, and damme, t'other.
The nation gives a general screech;
None cocks his tail, none claws his breech;
Each trembles for the public weal,
And for awhile forgets to steal.
Awhile all eyes intent and steady
Pursue him whirling down the eddy:
But, out of mind when out of view,
Some other mounts the twig anew;
And business on each monkey shore
Runs the same track it ran before."

John Gay.

THE SICK MAN AND THE ANGEL.

IS there no hope? the Sick Man said.
　The silent doctor shook his head,
　　And took his leave with signs of sorrow,
Despairing of his fee to-morrow.
When thus the Man with gasping breath:
"I feel the chilling wound of death;

A Satire Anthology

Since I must bid the world adieu,
Let me my former life review.
I grant, my bargains well were made,
But all men overreach in trade;
'Tis self-defence in each profession;
Sure, self-defence is no transgression.
The little portion in my hands,
By good security on lands,
Is well increased. If unawares,
My justice to myself and heirs
Hath let my debtor rot in jail,
For want of good sufficient bail;
If I by writ, or bond, or deed,
Reduce a family to need,
My will hath made the world amends;
My hope on charity depends.
When I am numbered with the dead,
And all my pious gifts are read,
By heaven and earth 'twill then be known,
My charities were amply shown."
An angel came. "Ah, friend," he cried,
"No more in flattering hope confide.
Can thy good deeds in former times
Outweigh the balance of thy crimes?
What widow or what orphan prays
To crown thy life with length of days?
A pious action's in thy power;
Embrace with joy the happy hour.
Now, while you draw the vital air,
Prove your intention is sincere:
This instant give a hundred pounds;
Your neighbours want, and you abound."

"But why such haste?" the Sick Man whines:
"Who knows as yet what Heaven designs?
Perhaps I may recover still;
That sum, and more, are in my will."
"Fool," says the Vision, "now 'tis plain,
Your life, your soul, your heaven was gain;
From every side, with all your might,
You scraped, and scraped beyond your right;
And after death would fain atone,
By giving what is not your own."
"Where there is life there's hope," he cried;
"Then why such haste?"—so groaned, and died.
John Gay.

SANDYS' GHOST

OR A PROPER NEW BALLAD OF THE NEW OVID'S
METAMORPHOSES, AS IT WAS INTENDED TO BE
TRANSLATED BY PERSONS OF QUALITY

YE Lords and Commons, men of wit
    And pleasure about town,
Read this, ere you translate one bit
    Of books of high renown.

Beware of Latin authors all!
    Nor think your verses sterling,
Though with a golden pen you scrawl,
    And scribble in a Berlin;

For not the desk with silver nails,
    Nor bureau of expense,

Nor standish well japanned avails
  To writing of good sense.

Hear how a ghost in dead of night,
  With saucer eyes of fire,
In woful wise did sore affright
  A wit and courtly squire.

Rare Imp of Phœbus, hopeful youth,
  Like puppy tame that uses
To fetch and carry, in his mouth,
  The works of all the Muses.

Ah, why did he write poetry,
  That hereto was so civil,
And sell his soul for vanity,
  To rhyming and the devil?

A desk he had of curious work,
  With glittering studs about;
Within the same did Sandys lurk,
  Though Ovid lay without.

Now, as he scratched to fetch up thought,
  Forth popped the sprite so thin,
And from the key-hole bolted out,
  All upright as a pin,

With whiskers, band, and pantaloon,
  And ruff composed most duly.
The squire he dropped his pen full soon,
  While as the light burnt bluely.

"Ho! Master Sam," quoth Sandys' sprite,
  "Write on, nor let me scare ye;
Forsooth, if rhymes fall in not right,
  To Budgell seek, or Carey.

"I hear the beat of Jacob's drums;
  Poor Ovid finds no quarter.
See first the merry P—— comes
  In haste, without his garter.

"Then lords and lordlings, squires and knights,
  Wits, witlings, prigs, and peers;
Garth at St. James's, and at White's,
  Beat up for volunteers.

"What Fenton will not do, nor Gay,
  Nor Congreve, Rowe, nor Stanyan,
Tom Burnett or Tom D'Urfey may,
  John Dunton, Steele, or anyone.

"If Justice Philips' costive head
  Some frigid rhymes disburses,
They shall like Persian tales be read,
  And glad both babes and nurses.

"Let Warwick's muse with Ashurst join,
  And Ozell's with Lord Hervey's;
Tickell and Addison combine,
  And Pope translate with Jervas.

"Lansdowne himself, that lively lord,
　Who bows to every lady,
Shall join with Frowde in one accord,
　And be like Tate and Brady.

"Ye ladies, too, draw forth your pen;
　I pray where can the hurt lie?
Since you have brains as well as men,
　As witness Lady Wortley.

"Now, Tonson, 'list thy forces all,
　Review them, and tell noses;
For to poor Ovid shall befall
　A strange metamorphosis;

"A metamorphosis more strange
　Than all his books can vapour."
"To what" (quoth squire) "shall Ovid
　　change?"
Quoth Sandys, "To waste paper."
　　　　　　　　Alexander Pope.

FROM "THE EPISTLE TO DR. ARBUTHNOT"

"SHUT, shut the door, good John!" fatigued I said;
　Tie up the knocker; say I'm sick, I'm dead.
The dog-star rages! nay, 'tis past a doubt,
All Bedlam, or Parnassus, is let out;

Fire in each eye, and papers in each hand,
They rave, recite, and madden round the land.
What walls can guard me, or what shades can hide?
They pierce my thickets, through my grot they glide.
By land, by water, they renew the charge;
They stop the chariot, and they board the barge.
No place is sacred, not the church is free;
Ev'n Sunday shines no Sabbath-day to me;
Then from the Mint walks forth the man of rhyme,
Happy to catch me—just at dinner-time.
Is there a parson much bemus'd in beer,
A maudlin poetess, a rhyming peer,
A clerk foredoom'd his father's soul to cross,
Who pens a stanza when he should engross?
Is there, who, lock'd from ink and paper, scrawls
With desperate charcoal round his darken'd walls?
All fly to Twit'nam, and in humble strain
Apply to me, to keep them mad or vain.
Arthur, whose giddy son neglects the laws,
Imputes to me and my damn'd works the cause;
Poor Cornus sees his frantic wife elope,
And curses wit, and poetry, and Pope.
Friend to my life (which did you not prolong,
The world had wanted many an idle song),
What drop or nostrum can this plague remove?
Or which must end me, a fool's wrath or love?
A dire dilemma—either way I'm sped;
If foes, they write; if friends, they read me dead.
Seiz'd and ty'd down to judge, how wretched I,
Who can't be silent, and who will not lie.
To laugh, were want of goodness and of grace;
And to be grave, exceeds all power of face.

I sit with sad civility; I read
With honest anguish, and an aching head,
And drop at last, but in unwilling ears,
This saving counsel, "Keep your piece nine years."
"Nine years!" cries he, who high in Drury Lane,
Lull'd by soft zephyrs through the broken pane,
Rhymes ere he wakes, and prints before term ends,
Oblig'd by hunger, and request of friends:
"The piece, you think, is incorrect? Why take it;
I'm all submission; what you'd have it, make it."
Three things another's modest wishes bound,
My friendship, and a prologue, and ten pound.
Pitholeon sends to me: "You know his grace.
I want a patron: ask him for a place."
Pitholeon libell'd me. "But here's a letter
Informs you, sir, 'twas when he knew no better.
Dare you refuse him? Curll invites to dine;
He'll write a journal, or he'll turn divine."
Bless me! a packet. "'Tis a stranger sues,
A virgin tragedy, an orphan muse."
If I dislike it, "Juries, death, and rage!"
If I approve, "Commend it to the stage."
There (thank my stars!), my whole commission ends;
The players and I are luckily no friends.
Fir'd that the house reject him, "'Sdeath! I'll print it,
And shame the fools. Your interest, sir, with Lintot."
"Lintot, dull rogue! will think your price too much."
"Not, sir, if you revise it, and retouch."

All my demurs but double his attacks;
At last he whispers, "Do, and we go snacks."
Glad of a quarrel, straight I clap the door:
"Sir, let me see your works and you no more!"
                                Alexander Pope.

THE THREE BLACK CROWS

TWO honest tradesmen meeting in the Strand,
   One took the other briskly by the hand;
   "Hark-ye," said he, "'tis an odd story, this,
About the crows!" "I don't know what it is,"
Replied his friend. "No! I'm surprised at that;
Where I came from it is the common chat;
But you shall hear—an odd affair indeed!
And that it happened, they are all agreed.
Not to detain you from a thing so strange,
A gentleman, that lives not far from 'Change,
This week, in short, as all the alley knows,
Taking a puke, has thrown up three black crows."
"Impossible!" "Nay, but it's really true;
I have it from good hands, and so may you."
"From whose, I pray?" So, having named the man,
Straight to inquire his curious comrade ran.
"Sir, did you tell"—relating the affair.
"Yes, sir, I did; and, if it's worth your care,
Ask Mr. Such-a-one, he told it me.
But, by the bye, 'twas two black crows—not three."
Resolved to trace so wondrous an event,
Whip, to the third, the virtuoso went;
"Sir"—and so forth. "Why, yes; the thing is fact,
Though, in regard to number, not exact;

A Satire Anthology

It was not two black crows—'twas only one;
The truth of that you may depend upon;
The gentleman himself told me the case."
"Where may I find him?" "Why, in such a
　　place."
Away goes he, and, having found him out,
"Sir, be so good as to resolve a doubt."
Then to his last informant he referred,
And begged to know if true what he had heard.
"Did you, sir, throw up a black crow?" "Not I."
"Bless me! how people propagate a lie!
Black crows have been thrown up, three, two, and
　　one;
And here, I find, all comes, at last, to none.
Did you say nothing of a crow at all?"
"Crow—crow—perhaps I might, now I recall
The matter over." "And pray, sir, what was't?"
"Why, I was horrid sick, and, at the last,
I did throw up, and told my neighbor so,
Something that was—as black, sir, as a crow."
　　　　　　　　　　　　John Byrom.

AN EPITAPH

A LOVELY young lady I mourn in my rhymes;
　　She was pleasant, good-natured, and civil
　　　　(sometimes);
Her figure was good; she had very fine eyes,
And her talk was a mixture of foolish and wise.
Her adorers were many, and one of them said
"She waltzed rather well—it's a pity she's dead."
　　　　　　　　　　　　George John Cayley.

AN EPISTLE TO SIR ROBERT WALPOLE

WHILE at the helm of State you ride,
  Our nation's envy, and its pride;
While foreign courts with wonder gaze,
And curse those counsels that they praise;
Would you not wonder, sir, to view
Your bard a greater man than you?
Which that he is, you cannot doubt,
When you have read the sequel out.

You know, great sir, that ancient fellows,
Philosophers, and such folks, tell us,
No great analogy between
Greatness and happiness is seen.
If, then, as it might follow straight,
Wretched to be, is to be great,
Forbid it, gods, that you should try
What 'tis to be so great as I!

The family that dines the latest
Is in our street esteem'd the greatest;
But latest hours must surely fall
'Fore him who never dines at all.
Your taste in architect, you know,
Hath been admired by friend and foe;
But can your earthly domes compare
With all my castles—in the air?
We're often taught, it doth behove us
To think those greater who're above us;

Another instance of my glory,
Who live above you, twice two story,
And from my garret can look down
On the whole street of Arlington.

Greatness by poets still is painted
With many followers acquainted;
This, too, doth in my favour speak;
Your levée is but twice a week;
From mine I can exclude but one day—
My door is quiet on a Sunday.

Nor in the manner of attendance
Doth your great bard claim less ascendance;
Familiar, you to admiration
May be approached by all the nation;
While I, like the Mogul in Indo,
Am never seen but at my window.
If with my greatness you're offended,
The fault is easily amended;
For I'll come down, with wondrous ease,
Into whatever *place* you please.
I'm not ambitious; little matters
Will serve us, great but humble creatures.

Suppose a secretary o' this isle,
Just to be doing with a while;
Admiral, general, judge, or bishop—
Or I can foreign treaties dish up.
If the good genius of the nation
Should call me to negotiation,

Tuscan and French are in my head;
Latin I write, and Greek—I read.
If you should ask, What pleases best?
To get the most, and do the least.
What fittest for? You know, I'm sure:
I'm fittest for—a sinecure.

Henry Fielding.

THE PUBLIC BREAKFAST

NOW my lord had the honour of coming down post,
    To pay his respects to so famous a toast,
In hopes he her ladyship's favour might win,
By playing the part of a host at an inn.
I'm sure he's a person of great resolution,
Though delicate nerves and a weak constitution;
For he carried us all to a place 'cross the river,
And vowed that the rooms were too hot for his liver.
He said it would greatly our pleasure promote,
If we all for Spring Gardens set out in a boat.
I never as yet could his reason explain,
Why we all sallied forth in the wind and the rain;
For sure such confusion was never yet known;
Here a cap and a hat, there a cardinal blown;
While his lordship, embroidered and powdered all o'er,
Was bowing, and handing the ladies ashore.
How the Misses did huddle, and scuddle, and run!
One would think to be wet must be very good fun;

A Satire Anthology

For by waggling their tails, they all seemed to take pains
To moisten their pinions like ducks when it rains.
And 'twas pretty to see how, like birds of a feather,
The people of quality flocked all together;
All pressing, addressing, caressing, and fond,
Just the same as these animals are in a pond.
You've read all their names in the news, I suppose,
But, for fear you have not, take the list as it goes:
    There was Lady Greasewrister,
    And Madam Van-Twister,
    Her ladyship's sister;
    Lord Cram, and Lord Vulter,
    Sir Brandish O'Culter,
    With Marshal Carouzer,
    And old Lady Mouzer,
And the great Hanoverian Baron Panzmowzer;
Besides many others, who all in the rain went,
On purpose to honour this great entertainment.
The company made a most brilliant appearance,
And ate bread and butter with great perseverance;
All the chocolate, too, that my lord set before 'em,
The ladies despatched with the utmost decorum.
Soft musical numbers were heard all around,
The horns and the clarions echoing sound.
Sweet were the strains, as odourous gales that blow
O'er fragrant banks, where pinks and roses grow.
The peer was quite ravish, while close to his side
Sat Lady Bunbutter, in beautiful pride.
Oft turning his eyes, he with rapture surveyed
All the powerful charms she so nobly displayed;

As when at the feast of the great Alexander,
Timotheus, the musical son of Thersander,
Breathed heavenly measures.
        The prince was in pain,
        And could not contain,
While Thais was sitting beside him;
        But, before all his peers,
        Was for shaking the spheres,
Such goods the kind gods did provide him.
        Grew bolder and bolder,
        And cocked up his shoulder,
Like the son of great Jupiter Ammon,
        Till at length, quite opprest,
        He sunk on her breast,
And lay there, as dead as a salmon.

Oh, had I a voice that was stronger than steel,
With twice fifty tongues to express what I feel,
And as many good mouths, yet I never could utter
All the speeches my lord made to Lady Bunbutter!
So polite all the time, that he ne'er touched a bit,
While she ate up his rolls and applauded his wit;
For they tell me that men of true taste, when they treat,
Should talk a great deal, but they never should eat;
And if that be the fashion, I never will give
Any grand entertainment as long as I live;
For I'm of opinion, 'tis proper to cheer
The stomach and bowels as well as the ear.
Nor me did the charming concerto of Abel
Regale like the breakfast I saw on the table;

A Satire Anthology

I freely will own I the muffins preferred
To all the genteel conversation I heard.
E'en though I'd the honour of sitting between
My Lady Stuff-damask and Peggy Moreen,
Who both flew to Bath in the nightly machine.
Cries Peggy: "This place is enchantingly pretty;
We never can see such a thing in the city.
You may spend all your lifetime in Cateaton Street,
And never so civil a gentleman meet;
You may talk what you please, you may search London through,
You may go to Carlisle's, and to Almack's, too,
And I'll give you my head if you find such a host,
For coffee, tea, chocolate, butter, and toast.
How he welcomes at once all the world and his wife,
And how civil to folks he ne'er saw in his life!"
"These horns," cries my lady, "so tickle one's ear,
Lord! what would I give that Sir Simon was here!
To the next public breakfast Sir Simon shall go,
For I find here are folks one may venture to know.
Sir Simon would gladly his lordship attend,
And my lord would be pleased with so cheerful a friend."
So, when we had wasted more bread at a breakfast
Than the poor of our parish have ate for this week past,
I saw, all at once, a prodigious great throng
Come bustling, and rustling, and jostling along;
For his lordship was pleased that the company now
To my Lady Bunbutter should courtesy and bow;

A Satire Anthology

And my lady was pleased, too, and seemed vastly proud
At once to receive all the thanks of a crowd.
And when, like Chaldeans, we all had adored
This beautiful image set up by my lord,
Some few insignificant folk went away,
Just to follow the employments and calls of the day;
But those who knew better their time how to spend,
The fiddling and dancing all chose to attend.
Miss Clunch and Sir Toby performed a cotillion,
Just the same as our Susan and Bob the postilion;
All the while her mamma was expressing her joy
That her daughter the morning so well could employ.
Now, why should the Muse, my dear mother, relate
The misfortunes that fall to the lot of the great?
As homeward we came, 'tis with sorrow you'll hear
What a dreadful disaster attended the peer;
For whether some envious god had decreed
That a naiad should long to ennoble the breed,
Or whether his lordship was charmed to behold
His face in the stream, like Narcissus of old,
In handing old Lady B—— and daughter,
This obsequious lord tumbled into the water;
But a nymph of the flood brought him safe to the boat,
And I left all the ladies a-cleaning his coat.

Christopher Anstey.

A Satire Anthology

AN ELEGY ON THE DEATH OF A MAD DOG

GOOD people all, of every sort,
    Give ear unto my song;
And if you find it wondrous short
    It cannot hold you long.

In Islington there was a man
    Of whom the world might say
That still a godly race he ran
    Whene'er he went to pray.

A kind and gentle heart he had,
    To comfort friends and foes;
The naked every day he clad,
    When he put on his clothes.

And in that town a dog was found,
    As many dogs there be,
Both mongrel, puppy, whelp, and hound,
    And curs of low degree.

This dog and man at first were friends,
    But when a pique began,
The dog, to gain his private ends,
    Went mad, and bit the man.

Around from all the neighbouring streets
    The wondering neighbours ran,
And swore the dog had lost his wits
    To bite so good a man.

A Satire Anthology

The wound it seemed both sore and sad
   To every Christian eye;
And while they swore the dog was mad,
   They swore the man would die.

But soon a wonder came to light,
   That show'd the rogues they lied:
The man recover'd of the bite,
   The dog it was that died.
Oliver Goldsmith.

ON SMOLLETT

WHENCE could arise this mighty critic spleen,
   The muse a trifler, and her theme so mean?
   What had I done that angry Heaven should send
The bitterest foe where most I wished a friend?
Oft hath my tongue been wanton at thy name,
And hailed the honours of thy matchless fame.
For me let hoary Fielding bite the ground,
So nobler Pickle stand superbly bound;
From Livy's temples tear the historic crown,
Which with more justice blooms upon thine own.
Compared with thee, be all life-writers dumb,
But he who wrote the life of Tommy Thumb.
Who ever read "The Regicide" but swore
The author wrote as man ne'er wrote before?
Others for plots and under-plots may call;
Here's the right method—have no plot at all!
Charles Churchill.

A Satire Anthology

THE UNCERTAIN MAN

DUBIUS is such a scrupulous good man—
  Yes, you may catch him tripping, if you can.
  He would not with a peremptory tone
Assert the nose upon his face his own;
With hesitation admirably slow,
He humbly hopes—presumes—it may be so.
His evidence, if he were called by law
To swear to some enormity he saw,
For want of prominence and just belief,
Would hang an honest man and save a thief.
Through constant dread of giving truth offence,
He ties up all his hearers in suspense;
Knows what he knows as if he knew it not;
What he remembers, seems to have forgot;
His sole opinion, whatsoe'er befall,
Centring at last in having none at all.
                              William Cowper.

A FAITHFUL PICTURE OF ORDINARY SOCIETY

THE circle formed, we sit in silent state,
  Like figures drawn upon a dial-plate.
  "Yes, ma'am" and "No, ma'am" uttered
softly, show
Every five minutes how the minutes go.
Each individual, suffering a constraint—
Poetry may, but colours cannot, paint—

As if in close committee on the sky,
Reports it hot or cold, or wet or dry,
And finds a changing clime a happy source
Of wise reflection and well-timed discourse.
We next inquire, but softly and by stealth,
Like conservators of the public health,
Of epidemic throats, if such there are
Of coughs and rheums, and phthisic and catarrh.
That theme exhausted, a wide chasm ensues,
Filled up at last with interesting news:
Who danced with whom, and who are like to wed;
And who is hanged, and who is brought to bed,
But fear to call a more important cause,
As if 'twere treason against English laws.
The visit paid, with ecstasy we come,
As from a seven years' transportation, home
And there resume an unembarrassed brow,
Recovering what we lost we know not how,
The faculties that seemed reduced to naught,
Expression, and the privilege of thought.
                                    William Cowper.

ON JOHNSON

I OWN I like not Johnson's turgid style,
    That gives an inch th' importance of a mile;
    Casts of manure a wagon-load around,
To raise a simple daisy from the ground;
Uplifts the club of Hercules—for what?
To crush a butterfly or brain a gnat;
Creates a whirlwind from the earth, to draw
A goose's feather or exalt a straw;

Sets wheels on wheels in motion—such a clatter—
To force up one poor nipperkin of water;
Bids ocean labour with tremendous roar
To heave a cockle-shell upon the shore;
Alike in every theme his pompous art,
Heaven's awful thunder or a rumbling cart!
John Wolcott (*Peter Pindar*).

TO BOSWELL

O BOSWELL, Bozzy, Bruce, whate'er thy name,
    Thou mighty shark for anecdote and fame,
Thou jackal, leading lion Johnson forth
To eat Macpherson midst his native north,
To frighten grave professors with his roar,
And shake the Hebrides from shore to shore,
        All hail!
Triumphant thou through time's vast gulf shalt sail,
The pilot of our literary whale;
Close to the classic Rambler shalt thou cling,
Close as a supple courtier to a king;
Fate shall not shake thee off with all its power,
Stuck like a bat to some old ivied tower.
Nay, though thy Johnson ne'er had blessed thy eyes,
Paoli's deeds had raised thee to the skies:
Yes, his broad wing had raised thee (no bad hack),
A tomtit twittering on an eagle's back.
John Wolcott (*Peter Pindar*).

THE HEN

WAS once a hen of wit not small
   (In fact, 'twas not amazing),
  And apt at laying eggs withal,
Who, when she'd done, would scream and bawl,
   As if the house were blazing.
A turkey-cock, of age mature,
  Felt thereat indignation;
'Twas quite improper, he was sure—
He would no more the thing endure;
   So, after cogitation,
He to the lady straight repaired,
And thus his business he declared:
  "Madam, pray, what's the matter,
That always, when you've laid an egg,
   You make so great a clatter?
I wish you'd do the thing in quiet.
Do be advised by me, and try it."
"Advised by you!" the lady cried,
And tossed her head with proper pride;
"And what do you know, now I pray,
Of the fashion of the present day,
You creature ignorant and low?
However, if you want to know,
This is the reason why I do it:
I lay my egg, and then review it!"
                Matthew Claudius.

A Satire Anthology

LET US ALL BE UNHAPPY TOGETHER

WE bipeds, made up of frail clay,
    Alas! are the children of sorrow;
    And, though brisk and merry to-day,
We may all be unhappy to-morrow.
For sunshine's succeeded by rain;
    Then, fearful of life's stormy weather,
Lest pleasure should only bring pain,
    Let us all be unhappy together.

I grant the best blessing we know
    Is a friend, for true friendship's a treasure;
And yet, lest your friend prove a foe,
    Oh, taste not the dangerous pleasure.
Thus, friendship's a flimsy affair;
    Thus, riches and health are a bubble;
Thus, there's nothing delightful but care,
    Nor anything pleasing but trouble.

If a mortal could point out that life
    Which on earth could be nearest to heaven,
Let him, thanking his stars, choose a wife
    To whom truth and honour are given.
But honour and truth are so rare,
    And horns, when they're cutting, so tingle,
That, with all my respect to the fair,
    I'd advise him to sigh, and live single.

It appears from these premises plain,
    That wisdom is nothing but folly;
That pleasure's a term that means pain,
    And that joy is your true melancholy;

That all those who laugh ought to cry;
   That 'tis fine frisk and fun to be grieving;
And that, since we must all of us die,
   We should taste no enjoyment while living.
Charles Dibdin.

THE FRIAR OF ORDERS GRAY

I AM a friar of orders gray,
   And down in the valleys I take my way;
   I pull not blackberry, haw, or hip;
Good store of venison fills my scrip;
My long bead-roll I merrily chant;
Where'er I walk no money I want;
And why I'm so plump the reason I tell:
Who leads a good life is sure to live well.
     What baron or squire,
     Or knight of the shire,
    Lives half so well as a holy friar?

After supper, of heaven I dream,
But that is a pullet and clouted cream;
Myself by denial I mortify—
With a dainty bit of a warden-pie;
I'm clothed in sackcloth for my sin—
With old sack wine I'm lined within;
A chirping cup is my matin song,
And the vesper's bell is my bowl, ding-dong.
     What baron or squire,
     Or knight of the shire,
    Lives half so well as a holy friar?
John O'Keefe.

THE COUNTRY SQUIRE

A COUNTRY squire, of greater wealth than wit
    (For fools are often bless'd with fortune's smile),
Had built a splendid house, and furnish'd it
    In splendid style.

"One thing is wanted," said a friend; "for, though
    The rooms are fine, the furniture profuse,
You lack a library, dear sir, for show,
    If not for use."

"'Tis true; but, zounds!" replied the squire with glee,
    "The lumber-room in yonder northern wing
(I wonder I ne'er thought of it) will be
    The very thing.

"I'll have it fitted up without delay
    With shelves and presses of the newest mode.
And rarest wood, befitting every way
    A squire's abode.

"And when the whole is ready, I'll despatch
    My coachman—a most knowing fellow—down,
To buy me, by admeasurement, a batch
    Of books in town."

But ere the library was half supplied
  With all its pomp of cabinet and shelf,
The booby squire repented him, and cried
        Unto himself:

"This room is much more roomy than I thought;
  Ten thousand volumes hardly would suffice
To fill it, and would cost, however bought,
        A plaguy price.

"Now, as I only want them for their looks,
  It might, on second thoughts, be just as good,
And cost me next to nothing, if the books
        Were made of wood.

"It shall be so. I'll give the shaven deal
  A coat of paint—a colourable dress,
To look like calf or vellum, and conceal
        Its nakedness.

And gilt and letter'd with the author's name,
  Whatever is most excellent and rare
Shall be, or seem to be ('tis all the same),
        Assembled there."

The work was done; the simulated hoards
  Of wit and wisdom round the chamber stood.
In bindings some; and some, of course, in boards,
        Were all of wood.

From bulky folios down to slender twelves,
  The choicest tomes in many an even row,
Display'd their letter'd backs upon the shelves,
        A goodly show.

A Satire Anthology

With such a stock, which seemingly surpass'd
  The best collection ever form'd in Spain,
What wonder if the owner grew at last
  Supremely vain?

What wonder, as he paced from shelf to shelf,
  And conn'd their titles, that the Squire began,
Despite his ignorance, to think himself
  A learned man?

Let every amateur, who merely looks
  To backs and bindings, take the hint, and sell
His costly library; for painted books
  Would serve as well.

Tomas Yriarte.

THE EGGS

BEYOND the sunny Philippines
  An island lies, whose name I do not know;
  But that's of little consequence, if so
You understand that there they had no hens,
Till, by a happy chance, a traveller,
After a while, carried some poultry there.
Fast they increased as anyone could wish,
Until fresh eggs became the common dish.
But all the natives ate them boiled, they say,
Because the stranger taught no other way.
At last th' experiment by one was tried—
Sagacious man!—of having his eggs fried.
And oh, what boundless honours, for his pains,
His fruitful and inventive fancy gains!

Another, now, to have them baked devised—
Most happy thought! and still another, spiced.
Who ever thought eggs were so delicate!
Next, someone gave his friends an omelette:
"Ah!" all exclaimed, "what an ingenious feat!"
But scarce a year went by, an artist shouts,
"I have it now! ye're all a pack of louts!
With nice tomatoes all my eggs are stewed."
And the whole island thought the mode so good,
That they would so have cooked them to this day,
But that a stranger, wandering out that way,
Another dish the gaping natives taught,
And showed them eggs cooked *à la Huguenot*.

Successive cooks thus proved their skill diverse,
But how shall I be able to rehearse
All of the new, delicious condiments
That luxury from time to time invents?
Soft, hard, and dropped; and now with sugar sweet,
And now boiled up with milk, the eggs they eat;
In sherbet, in preserves; at last they tickle
Their palates fanciful with eggs in pickle.
All had their day—the last was still the best.
But a grave senior thus one day addressed
The epicures: "Boast, ninnies, if you will,
These countless prodigies of gastric skill,
But blessings on the man *who brought the hens!*"

Beyond the sunny Philippines
Our crowd of modern authors need not go
New-fangled modes of cooking eggs to show.
                              Tomas Yriarte.

THE LITERARY LADY

WHAT motley cares Corilla's mind perplex,
 Whom maids and metaphors conspire to vex!
In studious dishabille behold her sit,
A letter'd gossip and a household wit:
At once invoking, though for different views,
Her gods, her cook, her milliner, and muse.
Round her strew'd room a frippery chaos lies,
A checker'd wreck of notable and wise,
Bills, books, caps, couplets, combs, a varied mass,
Oppress the toilet and obscure the glass;
Unfinish'd here an epigram is laid,
And there a mantua-maker's bill unpaid.
There new-born plays foretaste the town's applause,
There dormant patterns pine for future gauze.
A moral essay now is all her care,
A satire next, and then a bill of fare.
A scene she now projects, and now a dish;
Here Act the First, and here Remove with Fish.
Now, while this eye in a fine frenzy rolls,
That soberly casts up a bill for coals;
Black pins and daggers in one leaf she sticks,
And tears, and threads, and bowls, and thimbles mix.

Richard Brinsley Sheridan.

SLY LAWYERS

LO, that small office! there th' incautious guest
   Goes blindfold in, and that maintains the rest;
   There in his web th' observant spider lies,
And peers about for fat, intruding flies;
Doubtful at first, he hears the distant hum,
And feels them flutt'ring as they nearer come;
They buzz and blink, and doubtfully they tread
On the strong birdlime of the utmost thread;
But when they're once entangled by the gin,
With what an eager clasp he draws them in!
Nor shall they 'scape till after long delay,
And all that sweetens life is drawn away.
                                    George Crabbe.

REPORTERS

FIRST, from each brother's hoard a part they draw,
   A mutual theft that never feared a law;
Whate'er they gain, to each man's portion fall,
And read it once, you read it through them all.
For this their runners ramble day and night,
To drag each lurking deep to open light;
For daily bread the dirty trade they ply,
Coin their fresh tales, and live upon the lie.
Like bees for honey, forth for news they spring—
Industrious creatures! ever on the wing;
Home to their several cells they bear the store,
Culled of all kinds, then roam abroad for more.
                                    George Crabbe.

ADDRESS TO THE UNCO GUID, OR THE RIGIDLY RIGHTEOUS

OH, ye wha are sae guid yoursel',
    Sae pious an' sae holy,
    Ye've nought to do but mark an' tell
Your neibour's fauts an' folly!
Whase life is like a weel-gaun mill,
    Supplied wi' store o' water,
The heapéd happer's ebbing still,
    An' still the clap plays clatter.

Hear me, ye venerable core,
    As counsel for poor mortals,
That frequent pass douce Wisdom's door,
    For glaiket Folly's portals:
I, for their thoughtless, careless sakes,
    Would here propone defences,
Their donsie tricks, their black mistakes,
    Their failings an' mischances.

Ye see your state wi' theirs compar'd,
    An' shudder at the niffer,
But cast a moment's fair regard,
    What mak's the mighty differ?
Discount what scant occasion gave,
    That purity ye pride in,
An' (what's aft mair than a' the lave)
    Your better art o' hiding.

Think, when your castigated pulse
    Gi'es now an' then a wallop,

What ragings must his veins convulse,
   That still eternal gallop.
Wi' wind an' tide fair i' your tail,
   Right on ye scud your sea-way;
But in the teeth o' baith to sail,
   It makes an unco lee-way.

See social life an' glee sit down,
   All joyous an' unthinking,
Till, quite transmugrified, they're grown
   Debauchery an' drinking:
Oh, would they stay to calculate
   Th' eternal consequences;
Or your more dreaded hell to state,
   Damnation of expenses!

Ye high, exalted, virtuous dames,
   Tied up in godly laces,
Before ye gi'e poor frailty names,
   Suppose a change o' cases;
A dear loved lad, convenience snug,
   A treacherous inclination—
But, let me whisper i' your lug,
   Ye're aiblins nae temptation.

Then gently scan your brother man,
   Still gentler sister woman;
Though they may gang a kennin' wrang,
   To step aside is human.
One point must still be greatly dark,
   The moving why they do it;
An' just as lamely can ye mark
   How far, perhaps, they rue it

Who made the heart, 'tis He alone
    Decidedly can try us;
He knows each chord—its various tone,
    Each spring—its various bias;
Then at the balance let's be mute—
    We never can adjust it;
What's done we partly may compute,
    But know not what's resisted.
                Robert Burns.

HOLY WILLIE'S PRAYER

O THOU, wha in the heavens dost dwell,
    Wha, as it pleases best Thysel,
Sends ane to heaven an' ten to hell,
    A' for Thy glory,
And no for ony guid or ill
    They've done before Thee!

I bless and praise Thy matchless might,
When thousands Thou hast left in night,
That I am here, before Thy sight,
    For gifts an' grace,
A burnin' an' a shinin' light
    To a' this place.

What was I, or my generation,
That I should get sic exaltation!

I, wha deserv'd most just damnation,
    For broken laws
Sax thousand years ere my creation,
    Thro' Adam's cause.

When frae my mither's womb I fell,
Thou might hae plung'd me deep in hell,
To gnash my gooms, to weep and wail
    In burnin' lakes,
Whare damnéd devils roar and yell,
    Chain'd to their stakes.

Yet I am here, a chosen sample,
To show Thy grace is great and ample;
I'm here a pillar o' Thy temple,
    Strong as a rock,
A guide, a buckler, an example
    To a' Thy flock!

But yet, O Lord! confess I must,
At times I'm fash'd wi' fleshly lust;
An' sometimes, too, wi' warldly trust,
    Vile self gets in;
But Thou remembers we are dust,
    Defil'd wi' sin.

May be Thou lets this fleshly thorn
Beset Thy servant e'en and morn,
Lest he owre proud and high should turn
    That he's sae gifted:
If sae, Thy han' maun e'en be borne
    Until Thou lift it.

Lord, bless Thy chosen in this place,
For here Thou hast a chosen race:
But God confound their stubborn face,
    An' blast their name,
Wha bring Thy elders to disgrace
    An' open shame!

Lord, mind Gawn Hamilton's deserts;
He drinks, an' swears, an' plays at carts,
Yet has sae mony takin' arts,
    Wi' great and sma',
Frae God's ain priests the people's hearts
    He steals awa.

An' when we chasten'd him therefor,
Thou kens how he bred sic a splore,
As set the warld in a roar
    O' laughin' at us;
Curse Thou his basket and his store,
    Kail an' potatoes!

Lord, hear my earnest cry and pray'r
Against the Presbyt'ry of Ayr!
Thy strong right hand, Lord, mak it bare
    Upo' their heads!
Lord, visit them, an' dinna spare,
    For their misdeeds!

O Lord, my God! that glib-tongu'd Aiken,
My vera heart and saul are quakin',
To think how we stood sweatin', shakin',
    An' pish'd wi' dread,

A Satire Anthology

> While he wi' hingin' lip an' snakin',
> Held up his head.
>
> Lord, in Thy day o' vengeance try him!
> Lord, visit them wha did employ him,
> And pass not in Thy mercy by them,
> Nor hear their pray'r;
> But for Thy people's sake destroy them.
> An' dinna spare!
>
> But, Lord, remember me and mine,
> Wi' mercies temp'ral and divine,
> That I for grace and gear may shine,
> Excell'd by nane,
> An' a' the glory shall be Thine,
> Amen, Amen!

Robert Burns.

KITTY OF COLERAINE

AS beautiful Kitty one morning was tripping,
With a pitcher of milk from the fair of Coleraine,
When she saw me she stumbled, the pitcher down tumbled,
And all the sweet buttermilk watered the plain.
"Oh, what shall I do now? 'twas looking at you, now!
Sure, sure, such a pitcher I'll ne'er meet again;
'Twas the pride of my dairy! O Barney M'Cleary,
You're sent as a plague to the girls of Coleraine!"

A Satire Anthology

I sat down beside her, and gently did chide her
   That such a misfortune should give her such pain;
A kiss then I gave her, and, ere I did leave her,
   She vowed for such pleasure she'd break it again.
'Twas hay-making season—I can't tell the reason—
   Misfortunes will never come single, 'tis plain;
For very soon after poor Kitty's disaster
   The devil a pitcher was whole in Coleraine.
Edward Lysaght.

THE FRIEND OF HUMANITY AND THE KNIFE-GRINDER

FRIEND OF HUMANITY

"NEEDY Knife-grinder, whither are you going?
   Rough is the road, your wheel is out of order;
Bleak blows the blast; your hat has got a hole in't,
   So have your breeches!

"Weary Knife-grinder, little think the proud ones,
Who in their coaches roll along the turnpike
Road, what hard work 'tis crying all day, 'Knives and
   Scissors to grind O!'

"Tell me, Knife-grinder, how came you to grind knives?
Did some rich man tyrannically use you?

A Satire Anthology

Was it the squire? or parson of the parish?
    Or the attorney?

"Was it the squire, for killing of his game? or
Covetous parson, for his tithes distraining?
Or roguish lawyer, made you lose your little
    All in a lawsuit?

"(Have you not read the 'Rights of Man,' by Tom
    Paine?)
Drops of compassion tremble on my eyelids,
Ready to fall, as soon as you have told your
    Pitiful story."

KNIFE-GRINDER

"Story! God bless you! I have none to tell, sir,
Only last night, a-drinking at the Chequers,
This poor old hat and breeches, as you see, were
    Torn in a scuffle.

"Constables came up, for to take me into
Custody; they took me before the justice;
Justice Oldmixon put me in the parish-
    Stocks for a vagrant.

"I should be glad to drink your Honour's health in
A pot of beer, if you will give me sixpence;
But for my part, I never love to meddle
    With politics, sir."

A Satire Anthology

FRIEND OF HUMANITY

"I give thee sixpence! I will see thee damned first—
Wretch! whom no sense of wrongs can rouse to
  vengeance—
Sordid, unfeeling, reprobate, degraded,
    Spiritless outcast!"

(*Kicks the Knife-grinder, overturns his wheel,
and exit in a transport of Republican enthusiasm
and universal philanthropy.*)

George Canning.

NORA'S VOW

HEAR what Highland Nora said:
    "The Earlie's son I will not wed,
    Should all the race of Nature die,
And none be left but he and I.
For all the gold, for all the gear,
And all the lands both far and near,
That ever valour lost and won,
I would not wed the Earlie's son."

"A maiden's vows," old Callum spoke,
"Are lightly made and lightly broke.
The heather on the mountain's height
Begins to bloom in purple light;
The frost-wind soon shall sweep away
That lustre deep from glen and brae;
Yet Nora, ere its bloom be gone,
May blithely wed the Earlie's son."

A Satire Anthology

"The swan," she said, "the lake's clear breast
May barter for the eagle's nest;
The Awe's fierce stream may backward turn,
Ben Cruaichan fall, and crush Kilchurn;
Our kilted clans, when blood is high,
Before their foes may turn and fly;
But I, were all these marvels done,
Would never wed the Earlie's son."

Still in the water-lily's shade
Her wonted nest the wild swan made,
Ben Cruaichan stands as fast as ever,
Still downward foams the Awe's fierce river;
To shun the clash of foeman's steel,
No Highland brogue has turn'd the heel;
But Nora's heart is lost and won—
She's wedded to the Earlie's son!
Sir Walter Scott.

JOB

SLY Beelzebub took all occasions
 To try Job's constancy and patience.
 He took his honour, took his health;
He took his children, took his wealth,
His servants, horses, oxen, cows—
But cunning Satan did *not* take his spouse.

But Heaven, that brings out good from evil,
And loves to disappoint the devil,

Had predetermined to restore
Twofold all he had before;
His servants, horses, oxen, cows—
Short-sighted devil, *not* to take his spouse!
Samuel T. Coleridge.

COLOGNE

IN Köln, a town of monks and bones,
   And pavements fanged with murderous stones,
   And rags, and hags, and hideous wenches,
I counted two-and-seventy stenches,
All well defined, and separate stinks!
Ye nymphs that reign o'er sewers and sinks,
The river Rhine, it is well known,
Doth wash your city of Cologne;
But tell me, nymphs, what power divine
Shall henceforth wash the river Rhine?
Samuel T. Coleridge.

GILES' HOPE

"WHAT! rise again with all one's bones?"
   Quoth Giles. "I hope you fib.
   I trusted, when I went to heaven,
To go without my rib."
Samuel T. Coleridge.

THE BATTLE OF BLENHEIM

IT was a summer's evening;
   Old Casper's work was done,
And he before his cottage-door
   Was sitting in the sun;
And by him sported on the green
His little grandchild Wilhelmine.

She saw her brother Peterkin
   Roll something large and round,
That he beside the rivulet
   In playing there had found.
He came to ask what he had found,
That was so large, and smooth, and round.

Old Casper took it from the boy,
   Who stood expectant by;
And then the old man shook his head,
   And with a natural sigh,
"'Tis some poor fellow's skull," said he,
"Who fell in the great victory.

"I find them in the garden, for
   There's many here about;
And often, when I go to plough,
   The ploughshare turns them out;
For many thousand men," said he,
"Were slain in the great victory."

"Now tell us what 'twas all about,"
  Young Peterkin he cries;
And little Wilhelmine looks up,
  With wonder-waiting eyes:
"Now tell us all about the war,
And what they kill'd each other for."

"It was the English," Casper cried,
  "That put the French to rout;
But what they kill'd each other for,
  I could not well make out;
But everybody said," quoth he,
"That 'twas a famous victory.

"My father lived at Blenheim then,
  Yon little stream hard by;
They burnt his dwelling to the ground,
  And he was forced to fly;
So with his wife and child he fled,
Nor had he where to rest his head.

"With fire and sword the country round
  Was wasted far and wide,
And many a childing mother then
  And new-born infant died.
But things like that, you know, must be
At every famous victory.

"They say it was a shocking sight,
  After the field was won,

For many a thousand bodies here
  Lay rotting in the sun.
But things like that, you know, must be
After a famous victory.

"Great praise the Duke of Marlbro' won,
  And our good Prince Eugene."
"Why, 'twas a very wicked thing!"
  Said little Wilhelmine.
"Nay, nay, my little girl," quoth he,
"It was a famous victory;

"And everybody praised the duke,
  Who such a fight did win."
"But what good came of it at last?"
  Quoth little Peterkin.
"Why, that I cannot tell," said he;
"But 'twas a famous victory."
Robert Southey.

THE WELL OF ST. KEYNE

A WELL there is in the west country,
  And a clearer one never was seen;
  There is not a wife in the west country
But has heard of the Well of St. Keyne.

An oak and an elm-tree stand beside,
  And behind doth an ash-tree grow,
And a willow from the bank above
  Droops to the water below.

A Satire Anthology

A traveller came to the Well of St. Keyne,
   Joyfully he drew nigh,
For from cock-crow he had been travelling,
   And there was not a cloud in the sky.

He drank of the water so cool and clear,
   For thirsty and hot was he;
And he sat down upon the bank
   Under the willow-tree.

There came a man from the house hard by,
   At the well to fill his pail;
On the well-side he rested it,
   And he bade the stranger hail.

"Now art thou a bachelor, stranger?" quoth he,
   "For an' if thou has a wife,
The happiest draught thou hast drank this day
   That ever thou didst in thy life.

"Or has thy good woman, if one thou hast,
   Ever here in Cornwall been?
For an' if she have, I'll venture my life
   She has drank of the Well of St. Keyne."

"I have left a good woman who never was here,"
   The stranger he made reply;
"But that my draught should be better for that,
   I pray you answer me why?"

"St. Keyne," quoth the Cornishman, "many a time
   Drank of this crystal well,

And before the angels summon'd her,
  She laid on the water a spell.

"If the husband of this gifted well
  Shall drink before his wife,
A happy man henceforth is he,
  For he shall be master for life.

"But if the wife should drink of it first,
  God help the husband then!"
The stranger stooped to the Well of St. Keyne,
  And drank of the water again.

"You drank of the well, I warrant, betimes?"
  He to the Cornishman said;
But the Cornishman smiled as the stranger spake,
  And sheepishly shook his head.

"I hasten'd as soon as the wedding was done,
  And left my wife in the porch;
But i' faith she had been wiser than me,
  For she took a bottle to church."
                              Robert Southey.

THE POET OF FASHION

HIS book is successful, he's steeped in renown,
  His lyric effusions have tickled the town;
  Dukes, dowagers, dandies, are eager to trace
The fountain of verse in the verse-maker's face;
While, proud as Apollo, with peers *tête-à-tête*,
From Monday till Saturday dining off plate,

His heart full of hope, and his head full of gain,
The Poet of Fashion dines out in Park Lane.

Now lean-jointured widows who seldom draw corks,
Whose teaspoons do duty for knives and for forks,
Send forth, vellum-covered, a six-o'clock card,
And get up a dinner to peep at the bard;
Veal, sweetbread, boiled chickens, and tongue crown the cloth,
And soup *à la reine*, little better than broth.
While, past his meridian, but still with some heat,
The Poet of Fashion dines out in Sloane Street.

Enrolled in the tribe who subsist by their wits,
Remember'd by starts, and forgotten by fits,
Now artists and actors, the bardling engage,
To squib in the journals, and write for the stage.
Now soup *à la reine* bends the knee to ox-cheek,
And chickens and tongue bow to bubble and squeak.
While, still in translation employ'd by "the Row,"
The Poet of Fashion dines out in Soho.

Pushed down from Parnassus to Phlegethon's brink,
Toss'd, torn, and trunk-lining, but still with some ink,
Now squat city misses their albums expand,
And woo the worn rhymer for "something off-hand";
No longer with stinted effrontery fraught,
Bucklersbury now seeks what St. James' once sought,

And (oh, what a classical haunt for a bard!)
The Poet of Fashion dines out in Barge-yard.
James Smith.

CHRISTMAS OUT OF TOWN

FOR many a winter in Billiter Lane,
  My wife, Mrs. Brown, was not heard to complain;
At Christmas the family met there to dine
On beef and plum-pudding, and turkey and chine.
Our bark has now taken a contrary heel;
My wife has found out that the sea is genteel.
To Brighton we duly go scampering down,
For nobody now spends his Christmas in town.

Our register-stoves, and our crimson-baized doors,
Our weather-proof walls, and our carpeted floors,
Our casements well fitted to stem the north wind,
Our arm-chair and sofa, are all left behind.
We lodge on the Steyne, in a bow-window'd box,
That beckons up-stairs every Zephyr that knocks;
The sun hides his head, and the elements frown,
But nobody now spends his Christmas in town.

In Billiter Lane, at this mirth-moving time,
The lamp-lighter brought us his annual rhyme;
The tricks of Grimaldi were sure to be seen;
We carved a twelfth-cake, and we drew king and queen.
These pastimes gave oil to Time's round-about wheel,
Before we began to be growing genteel;

'Twas all very well for a cockney or clown,
But nobody now spends his Christmas in town.

At Brighton I'm stuck up in Donaldson's shop,
Or walk upon bricks till I'm ready to drop;
Throw stones at an anchor, look out for a skiff,
Or view the Chain-pier from the top of the cliff:
Till winds from all quarters oblige me to halt,
With an eye full of sand and a mouth full of salt,
Yet still I am suffering with folks of renown,
For nobody now spends his Christmas in town.

In gallop the winds at the full of the moon,
And puff up the carpet like Sadler's balloon;
My drawing-room rug is besprinkled with soot,
And there is not a lock in the house that will shut.
At Mahomet's steam-bath I lean on my cane,
And murmur in secret, "Oh, Billiter Lane!"
But would not express what I think for a crown,
For nobody now spends his Christmas in town.

The Duke and the Earl are no cronies of mine;
His Majesty never invites me to dine;
The Marquis won't speak when we meet on the pier,
Which makes me suspect that I'm *nobody* here.
If that be the case, why, then welcome again
Twelfth-cake and snap-dragon in Billiter Lane.
Next winter I'll prove to my dear Mrs. Brown
That *Nobody* now spends his Christmas in town.

James Smith.

ETERNAL LONDON

AND is there, then, no earthly place
    Where we can rest in dream Elysian,
    Without some cursed round English face
Popping up near to break the vision?

'Mid northern lakes, 'mid southern vines,
  Unholy cits we're doomed to meet;
Nor highest Alps, nor Apennines,
  Are sacred from Threadneedle Street.

If up the Simplon's path we wind,
Fancying we leave this world behind,
Such pleasant sounds salute one's ear
As, "Baddish news from 'Change, my dear:
The Funds (phew! curse this ugly hill!)
Are lowering fast (what! higher still?)
And (zooks! we're mounting up to heaven!)
Will soon be down to sixty-seven."
Go where we may, rest where we will,
Eternal London haunts us still.
The trash of Almack's or Fleet-Ditch—
And scarce a pin's-head difference which—
Mixes, though even to Greece we run,
With every rill from Helicon.
And if this rage for travelling lasts,
If cockneys of all sets and castes,
Old maidens, aldermen, and squires,
Will leave their puddings and coal fires,

To gape at things in foreign lands
No soul among them understands;
If Blues desert their coteries,
To show off 'mong the Wahabees;
If neither sex nor age controls,
　Nor fear of Mamelukes forbids
Young ladies, with pink parasols,
　To glide among the Pyramids:
Why, then, farewell all hope to find
A spot that's free from London-kind!
Who knows, if to the West we roam,
But we may find some Blue "at home"
　Among the Blacks of Carolina,
Or, flying to the eastward, see,
Some Mrs. Hopkins taking tea
　And toast upon the Wall of China?
　　　　　　　　Thomas Moore.

THE MODERN PUFFING SYSTEM

UNLIKE those feeble gales of praise
　Which critics blew in former days,
　Our modern puffs are of a kind
That truly, really "raise the wind";
And since they've fairly set in blowing,
We find them the best *trade-winds* going.
What storm is on the deep—and more
Is the great power of Puff on shore,
Which jumps to glory's future tenses
Before the present even commences,
And makes "immortal" and "divine" of us,
Before the world has read one line of us.

[106]

In old times, when the god of song
Drew his own two-horse team along,
Carrying inside a bard or two
Booked for posterity "all through,"
Their luggage a few close-packed rhymes
(Like yours, my friend, for after-times),
So slow the pull to Fame's abode
That folks oft slumbered on the road;
And Homer's self sometimes, they say,
Took to his nightcap on the way.
But now, how different is the story
With our new galloping sons of glory,
Who, scorning all such slack and slow time,
Dash to posterity in no time!
Raise but one general blast of puff
To start your author—that's enough:
In vain the critics sit to watch him,
Try at the starting-post to catch him;
He's off—the puffers carry it hollow—
The critics, if they please, may follow;
Ere they've laid down their first positions,
He's fairly blown through six editions!
In vain doth Edinburgh dispense
Her blue and yellow pestilence
(That plague so awful in my time
To young and touchy sons of rhyme);
The *Quarterly*, at three months' date,
To catch the Unread One comes too late;
And nonsense, littered in a hurry,
Becomes "immortal" spite of Murray.
                              Thomas Moore.

LYING

I do confess, in many a sigh,
  My lips have breath'd you many a lie,
  And who, with such delights in view,
Would lose them for a lie or two?
Nay—look not thus, with brow reproving:
Lies are, my dear, the soul of loving!
If half we tell the girls were true,
If half we swear to think and do,
Were aught but lying's bright illusion,
The world would be in strange confusion!
If ladies' eyes were, every one,
As lovers swear, a radiant sun,
Astronomy should leave the skies,
To learn her lore in ladies' eyes!
Oh no!—believe me, lovely girl,
When nature turns your teeth to pearl,
Your neck to snow, your eyes to fire,
Your yellow locks to golden wire,
Then, only then, can heaven decree,
That you should live for only me,
Or I for you, as night and morn,
We've swearing kiss'd, and kissing sworn.

And now, my gentle hints to clear,
For once, I'll tell you truth, my dear!
Whenever you may chance to meet
A loving youth, whose love is sweet,
Long as you're false and he believes you,
Long as you trust and he deceives you,
So long the blissful bond endures;

And while he lies, his heart is yours.
But, oh! you've wholly lost the youth
The instant that he tells you truth!

Thomas Moore.

THE KING OF YVETOT*

THERE was a king of Yvetot,
   Of whom renown hath little said,
   Who let all thoughts of glory go,
And dawdled half his days abed;
And every night, as night came round,
By Jenny with a nightcap crowned,
   Slept very sound:
 Sing ho, ho, ho! and he, he, he!
 That's the kind of king for me.

And every day it came to pass
   That four lusty meals made he;
And step by step, upon an ass,
   Rode abroad, his realms to see;
And wherever he did stir,
What think you was his escort, sir?
   Why, an old cur.
 Sing ho, ho, ho! and he, he, he!
 That's the kind of king for me.

If e'er he went into excess,
   'Twas from a somewhat lively thirst;
But he who would his subjects bless,
   Odd's fish! must wet his whistle first;

* Version of W. M. Thackeray.

A Satire Anthology

And so, from every cask they got,
Our king did to himself allot
   At least a pot.
  Sing ho, ho, ho! and he, he, he!
  That's the kind of king for me.

To all the ladies of the land
  A courteous king, and kind, was he;
The reason why, you'll understand—
  They named him Pater Patriæ.
Each year he called his fighting men,
And marched a league from home, and then,
   Marched back again.
  Sing ho, ho, ho! and he, he, he!
  That's the kind of king for me.

Neither by force nor false pretence,
  He sought to make his kingdom great,
And made (O princes, learn from hence)
  "Live and let live" his rule of state.
'Twas only when he came to die,
That his people who stood by
   Were known to cry.
  Sing ho, ho, ho! and he, he, he!
  That's the kind of king for me.

The portrait of this best of kings
  Is extant still, upon a sign
That on a village tavern swings,
  Famed in the country for good wine.

The people in their Sunday trim,
Filling their glasses to the brim,
    Look up to him,
  Singing, "Ha, ha, ha!" and "He, he, he!
That's the sort of king for me."
Pierre Jean De Béranger.

SYMPATHY

A KNIGHT and a lady once met in a grove,
    While each was in quest of a fugitive love.
A river ran mournfully murmuring by,
And they wept in its waters for sympathy.

"Oh, never was knight such a sorrow that bore!"
"Oh, never was maid so deserted before!"
"From life and its woes let us instantly fly,
And jump in together for company!"

They search'd for an eddy that suited the deed,
But here was a bramble, and there was a weed.
"How tiresome it is!" said the fair, with a sigh;
So they sat down to rest them in company.

They gazed at each other, the maid and the knight;
How fair was her form, and how goodly his height!
"One mournful embrace," sobb'd the youth, "ere we die!"
So kissing and crying kept company.

A Satire Anthology

"Oh, had I but loved such an angel as you!"
"Oh, had but my swain been a quarter as true!"
"To miss such perfection, how blinded was I!"
Sure now they were excellent company.

At length spoke the lass, 'twixt a smile and a tear,
"The weather is cold for a watery bier;
When summer returns we may easily die,
Till then let us sorrow in company."
Reginald Heber.

A MODEST WIT

A SUPERCILIOUS nabob of the East—
    Haughty, being great—purse-proud, being rich—
A governor, or general, at the least,
    I have forgotten which—
Had in his family a humble youth,
    Who went from England in his patron's suite,
An unassuming boy, in truth
    A lad of decent parts, and good repute.
This youth had sense and spirit;
    But yet with all his sense,
    Excessive diffidence
Obscured his merit.

One day, at table, flushed with pride and wine,
    His honour, proudly free, severely merry,
Conceived it would be vastly fine
    To crack a joke upon his secretary.

"Young man," he said, "by what art, craft, or trade
  Did your good father gain a livelihood?"
"He was a saddler, sir," Modestus said,
  "And in his time was reckoned good."

"A saddler, eh? and taught you Greek,
  Instead of teaching you to sew!
Pray, why did not your father make
  A saddler, sir, of you?"

Each parasite, then, as in duty bound,
The joke applauded, and the laugh went round.
  At length Modestus, bowing low,
Said (craving pardon, if too free he made),
  "Sir, by your leave, I fain would know
Your father's trade!"

"My father's trade! by Heaven, that's too bad!
My father's trade? Why, blockhead, are you mad?
My father, sir, did never stoop so low—
He was a gentleman, I'd have you know."

"Excuse the liberty I take,"
  Modestus said, with archness on his brow,
"Pray, why did not your father make
  A gentleman of you?"
                                            Selleck Osborn.

THE PHILOSOPHER'S SCALES

A MONK, when his rites sacerdotal were o'er,
　　In the depth of his cell with its stone-covered floor,
Resigning to thought his chimerical brain,
Once formed the contrivance we now shall explain;
But whether by magic's or alchemy's powers
We know not; indeed, 'tis no business of ours.

Perhaps it was only by patience and care,
At last, that he brought his invention to bear.
In youth 'twas projected, but years stole away,
And ere 'twas complete he was wrinkled and gray;
But success is secure, unless energy fails,
And at length he produced The Philosopher's Scales.

"What were they?" you ask. You shall presently see.
These scales were not made to weigh sugar and tea.
Oh, no; for such properties wondrous had they,
That qualities, feelings, and thoughts they could weigh,
Together with articles small or immense,
From mountains or planets to atoms of sense.

Naught was there so bulky but there it would lay,
And naught so ethereal but there it would stay,
And naught so reluctant but in it must go:
All which some examples more clearly will show.

The first thing he weighed was the head of Voltaire,
Which retained all the wit that had ever been there.
As a weight, he threw in a torn scrap of a leaf
Containing the prayer of the penitent thief;
When the skull rose aloft with so sudden a spell,
That it bounced like a ball on the roof of the cell.

One time he put in Alexander the Great,
With the garment that Dorcas had made, for a weight;
And though clad in armour from sandals to crown,
The hero rose up, and the garment went down.
A long row of almshouses, amply endowed
By a well-esteemed Pharisee, busy and proud,
Next loaded one scale; while the other was pressed
By those mites the poor widow dropped into the chest:
Up flew the endowment, not weighing an ounce,
And down, down the farthing-worth came with a bounce.

By further experiments (no matter how)
He found that ten chariots weighed less than one plough;
A sword with gilt trapping rose up in the scale,
Though balanced by only a tenpenny nail;
A shield and a helmet, a buckler and spear,
Weighed less than a widow's uncrystallized tear.

A lord and a lady went up at full sail,
When a bee chanced to light on the opposite scale;

Ten doctors, ten lawyers, two courtiers, one earl,
Ten counsellors' wigs, full of powder and curl,
All heaped in one balance and swinging from thence,
Weighed less than a few grains of candor and sense;
A first-water diamond, with brilliants begirt,
Than one good potato just washed from the dirt;
Yet not mountains of silver and gold could suffice
One pearl to outweigh—'twas THE PEARL OF GREAT PRICE.

Last of all, the whole world was bowled in at the grate,
With the soul of a beggar to serve for a weight,
When the former sprang up with so strong a rebuff
That it made a vast rent and escaped at the roof!
When balanced in air, it ascended on high,
And sailed up aloft, a balloon in the sky;
While the scale with the soul in't so mightily fell,
That it jerked the philosopher out of his cell.
Jane Taylor.

FROM "THE FEAST OF THE POETS"

NEXT came Walter Scott, with a fine, weighty face,
   For as soon as his visage was seen in the place,
The diners and barmaids all crowded to know him,
And thank him with smiles for that sweet, pretty poem!

However, he scarcely had got through the door,
When he looked adoration, and bowed to the floor,
For his host was a god—what a very great thing!
And what was still greater in his eyes—a king!
Apollo smiled shrewdly, and bade him sit down,
With, "Well, Mr. Scott, you have managed the town;
Now, pray, copy less—have a little temerity;
Try if you can't also manage posterity.
All you add now only lessens your credit;
And how could you think, too, of taking to edit?
A great deal's endured where there's measure and rhyme,
But prose such as yours is a pure waste of time—
A singer of ballads unstrung by a cough,
Who fairly talks on, till his hearers walk off.
Be original, man; study more, scribble less,
Nor mistake present favor for lasting success;
And remember, if laurels are what you would find,
The crown of all triumph is freedom of mind."
James Henry Leigh Hunt.

RICH AND POOR; OR, SAINT AND SINNER

THE poor man's sins are glaring;
   In the face of ghostly warning,
   He is caught in the fact
 Of an overt act—
Buying greens on Sunday morning.

The rich man's sins are hidden
In the pomp of wealth and station;
    And escape the sight
    Of the children of light,
Who are wise in their generation.

The rich man has a kitchen,
And cooks to dress his dinner;
    The poor, who would roast,
    To the baker's must post,
And thus becomes a sinner.

The rich man has a cellar,
And a ready butler by him;
    The poor must steer
    For his pint of beer,
Where the saint can't choose but spy him.

The rich man's painted windows
Hide the concerts of the quality;
    The poor can but share
    A crack'd fiddle in the air,
Which offends all sound morality.

The rich man is invisible
In the crowd of his gay society;
    But the poor man's delight
    Is a sore in the sight,
And a stench in the nose of piety.
                      Thomas L. Peacock.

MR. BARNEY MAGUIRE'S ACCOUNT OF THE CORONATION

OCH! the Coronation! what celebration
  For emulation can with it compare?
When to Westminster the Royal Spinster
And the Duke of Leinster, all in order did repair!
'Twas there you'd see the new Polishemen
  Make a scrimmage at half after four;
And the Lords and Ladies, and the Miss O'Gradys,
  All standing round before the Abbey door.

Their pillows scorning, that selfsame morning
  Themselves adorning, all by the candle-light,
With roses and lilies, and daffy-down-dillies,
  And gould and jewels, and rich di'monds bright.
And then approaches five hundred coaches,
  With Gineral Dullbeak.—Och! 'twas mighty fine
To see how aisy bould Corporal Casey,
  With his sword drawn, prancing, made them kape the line.

Then the guns' alarums, and the King of Arums,
  All in his Garters and his Clarence shoes,
Opening the massy doors to the bould Ambassydors,
  The Prince of Potboys, and great haythen Jews;
'Twould have made you crazy to see Esterhazy
  All jools from his jasey to his di'mond boots;
With Alderman Harmer, and that swate charmer,
  The famale heiress, Miss Anjä-ly Coutts.

And Wellington, walking with his swoord drawn, talking
  To Hill and Hardinge, haroes of great fame;
And Sir De Lacy, and the Duke Dalmasey
  (They call'd him Sowlt afore he changed his name),
Themselves presading, Lord Melbourne lading
  The Queen, the darling, to her royal chair,
And that fine ould fellow, the Duke of Pell-Mello,
  The Queen of Portingal's Chargy-de-fair.

Then the noble Prussians, likewise the Russians,
  In fine laced jackets with their goulden cuffs,
And the Bavarians, and the proud Hungarians,
  And Everythingarians all in furs and muffs.
Then Misther Spaker, with Misther Pays the Quaker,
  All in the gallery you might persave;
But Lord Brougham was missing, and gone a-fishing,
  Ounly crass Lord Essex would not give him lave.

There was Baron Alten himself exalting,
  And Prince Von Schwartzenburg, and many more;
Och! I'd be bother'd, and entirely smother'd,
  To tell the half of 'em was to the fore;
With the swate Peeresses, in their crowns and dresses,
  And Aldermanesses, and the Boord of Works;
But Mehemet Ali said, quite gintalely,
  "I'd be proud to see the likes among the Turks!"

A Satire Anthology

Then the Queen—Heaven bless her!—och! they did dress her
  In her purple garments and her goulden crown,
Like Venus, or Hebe, or the Queen of Sheby,
  With eight young ladies houlding up her gown.
Sure 'twas grand to see her, also for to he-ar
  The big drums bating and the trumpets blow;
And Sir George Smart, oh! he played a consarto,
  With his four-and-twenty fiddlers all on a row!

Then the Lord Archbishop held a goulden dish up
  For to resave her bounty and great wealth,
Saying, "Plase your Glory, great Queen Vic-tory!
  Ye'll give the Clargy lave to dhrink your health!"
Then his Riverence, retrating, discoorsed the mating:
  "Boys, here's your Queen! deny it if you can!
And if any bould traitor, or infarior craythur,
  Sneezes at that, I'd like to see the man!"

Then the Nobles kneeling, to the Pow'rs appealing—
  "Heaven send your Majesty a glorious reign!"
And Sir Claudius Hunter, he did confront her,
  All in his scarlet gown and goulden chain.
The great Lord May'r, too, sat in his chair, too,
  But mighty sarious, looking fit to cry,
For the Earl of Surrey, all in his hurry,
  Throwing the thirteens, hit him in his eye.

Then there was preaching, and good store of speeching,
  With dukes and marquises on bended knee;

A Satire Anthology

And they did splash her with raal Macasshur,
   And the Queen said, "Ah! then thank ye all for me!"
Then the trumpets braying, and the organ playing,
   And the swate trombones, with their silver tones;
But Lord Rolle was rolling—'twas mighty consoling
   To think his lordship did not break his bones!

Then the crames and custard, and the beef and mustard,
   All on the tombstones like a poulterer's shop;
With lobsters and white-bait, and other swatemeats,
   And wine and nagus, and Imparial Pop!
There was cakes and apples in all the Chapels,
   With fine polonies, and rich, mellow pears.
Och! the Count Von Strogonoff, sure he got prog enough,
   The sly ould divil, undernathe the stairs.

Then the cannons thunder'd, and the people wonder'd,
   Crying, "God save Victoria, our Royal Queen!"
Och! if myself should live to be a hundred,
   Sure it's the proudest day that I'll have seen!
And now, I've ended, what I pretended,
   This narration splendid in swate poe-thry,
Ye dear bewitcher, just hand the pitcher;
   Faith, it's mesilf that's getting mighty dhry.
                    Richard Harris Barham.

FROM "THE DEVIL'S DRIVE."

THE devil returned to hell by two,
    And he stayed at home till five;
    When he dined on some homicides done in
      ragoût,
And a rebel or so in an Irish stew,
And sausages made of a self-slain Jew—
And bethought himself what next to do,
  "And," quoth he, "I'll take a drive.
I walked in the morning, I'll ride to-night;
In darkness my children take most delight,
    And I'll see how my favorites thrive.

"And what shall I ride in?" quoth Lucifer then;
    "If I followed my taste, indeed,
I should mount in a wagon of wounded men,
    And smile to see them bleed.
But these will be furnished again and again,
    And at present my purpose is speed,
To see my manor as much as I may,
And watch that no souls shall be poached away.

"I have a state coach at Carlton House,
  A chariot in Seymour Place,
But they're lent to two friends, who make me amends
  By driving my favorite pace;
And they handle their reins with such a grace,
I have something for both at the end of the race.

A Satire Anthology

"So now for the earth to take my chance."
  Then up to the earth sprung he,
And making a jump from Moscow to France,
  He stepped across the sea,
And rested his hoof on a turnpike road,
No very great way from a bishop's abode.

But first, as he flew, I forgot to say,
That he hovered a moment upon his way
  To look upon Leipsic plain;
And so sweet to his eye was its sulphury glare,
And so soft to his ear was the cry of despair,
  That he perched on a mountain of slain;
And he gazed with delight from its growing height,
Nor often on earth had he seen such a sight,
  Nor his work done half as well:
For the field ran so red with the blood of the dead,
  That it blushed like the waves of hell!
Then loudly and wildly and long laughed he:
"Methinks they have here little need of *me!*"

  .   .   .   .   .   .

But the softest note that soothed his ear
  Was the sound of a widow sighing;
And the sweetest sight was the icy tear,
Which horror froze in the blue eye clear
  Of a maid by her lover lying,
As round her fell her long fair hair;
And she looked to heaven with that frenzied air,
Which seemed to ask if a God were there!
And, stretched by the wall of a ruined hut,
With its hollow cheeks, and eyes half shut,

A child of famine dying:
And the carnage begun, when resistance is done,
  And the fall of the vainly flying!

Lord Byron.

FROM "ENGLISH BARDS AND SCOTCH REVIEWERS"

A MAN must serve his time to ev'ry trade
  Save censure; critics all are ready-made.
  Take hackney'd jokes from Miller, got by rote,
With just enough of learning to misquote;
A mind well skill'd to find or forge a fault,
A turn for punning, call it Attic salt;
To Jeffrey go, be silent and discreet;
His pay is just ten sterling pounds per sheet.
Fear not to lie—'twill seem a sharper hit;
Shrink not from blasphemy—'twill pass for wit;
Care not for feeling; pass your proper jest,
And stand a critic, hated yet caress'd.

And shall we own such judgment? No! as soon
Seek roses in December, ice in June,
Hope constancy in wind, or corn in chaff,
Believe a woman or an epitaph,
Or any other thing that's false, before
You trust in critics, who themselves are sore;
Or yield one single thought to be misled
By Jeffrey's heart or Lambe's Bœotian head.
To these young tyrants, by themselves misplaced,
Combined usurpers on the throne of taste;

To these, when authors bend in humble awe,
And hail their voice as truth, their word as law—
While these are censors, 'twould be sin to spare;
While such are critics, why should I forbear?
But yet, so near all modern worthies run,
'Tis doubtful whom to seek or whom to shun;
Nor know we when to spare or where to strike,
Our bards and censors are so much alike.
Then should you ask me why I venture o'er
The path which Pope and Gifford trod before;
If not yet sicken'd, you can still proceed;
Go on; my rhyme will tell you as you read.
"But hold!" exclaims a friend—"here's some neglect:
This, that, and t'other line seems incorrect."
What then? the self-same blunder Pope has got,
And careless Dryden— "Ay, but Pye has not."
Indeed! 'tis granted, faith! but what care I?
Better to err with Pope than shine with Pye.
Lord Byron.

TO WOMAN

WOMAN, experience might have told me
That all must love thee who behold thee;
Surely experience might have taught,
Thy firmest promises are naught;
But, placed in all thy charms before me,
All I forget, but to adore thee.
O Memory! thou choicest blessing,
When join'd with hope, when still possessing;
But how much cursed by every lover,
When hope is fled, and passion's over!

A Satire Anthology

Woman, that fair and fond deceiver,
How prompt are striplings to believe her!
How throbs the pulse when first we view
The eye that rolls in glossy blue,
Or sparkles black, or mildly throws
A beam from under hazel brows!
How quick we credit every oath,
And hear her plight the willing troth!
Fondly we hope 'twill last for aye,
When, lo! she changes in a day.
This record will forever stand,
"Woman, thy vows are trac'd in sand."
                              Lord Byron.

A COUNTRY HOUSE PARTY

THE gentlemen got up betimes to shoot
    Or hunt: the young, because they liked
        the sport—
The first thing boys like after play and fruit;
    The middle-aged to make the day more short;
For *ennui* is a growth of English root,
    Though nameless in our language: we retort
The fact for words, and let the French translate
That awful yawn which sleep cannot abate.

The elderly walk'd through the library,
    And tumbled books, or criticised the pictures,
Or saunter'd through the gardens piteously,
    And made upon the hothouse several strictures;
Or rode a nag which trotted not too high,
    Or on the morning papers read their lectures;

A Satire Anthology

Or on the watch their longing eyes would fix,
Longing, at sixty, for the hour of six.

But none were *gêné:* the great hour of union
   Was rung by dinner's knell; till then all were
Masters of their own time—or in communion,
   Or solitary, as they chose to bear
The hours, which how to pass is but to few known.
   Each rose up at his own, and had to spare
What time he chose for dress, and broke his fast
When, where, and how he chose for that repast.

The ladies—some rouged, some a little pale—
   Met the morn as they might. If fine, they rode,
Or walk'd; if foul, they read, or told a tale,
   Sung, or rehearsed the last dance from abroad;
Discuss'd the fashion which might next prevail,
   And settled bonnets by the newest code;
Or cramm'd twelve sheets into one little letter,
To make each correspondent a new debtor.

For some had absent lovers, all had friends.
   The earth has nothing like a she-epistle,
And hardly heaven—because it never ends.
   I love the mystery of a female missal,
Which, like a creed, ne'er says all it intends,
   But, full of cunning as Ulysses' whistle
When he allured poor Dolon. You had better
Take care what you reply to such a letter.

A Satire Anthology

Then there were billiards; cards, too, but no dice—
  Save in the clubs, no man of honour plays;
Boats when 'twas water, skating when 'twas ice,
  And the hard frost destroy'd the scenting days:
And angling, too, that solitary vice,
  Whatever Izaak Walton sings or says:
The quaint, old, cruel coxcomb, in his gullet
Should have a hook, and a small trout to pull it.

With evening came the banquet and the wine;
  The conversazione; the duet,
Attuned by voices more or less divine
  (My heart or head aches with the memory yet).
The four Miss Rawbolds in a glee would shine;
  But the two youngest loved more to be set
Down to the harp—because to music's charms
They added graceful necks, white hands and arms.

Sometime a dance (though rarely on field-days,
  For then the gentlemen were rather tired)
Display'd some sylph-like figures in its maze:
  Then there was small-talk ready when required;
Flirtation, but decorous; the mere praise
  Of charms that should or should not be admired.
The hunters fought their fox-hunt o'er again,
And then retreated soberly—at ten.

The politicians, in a nook apart,
  Discuss'd the world, and settled all the spheres:
The wits watch'd every loophole for their art,
  To introduce a *bon mot*, head and ears.
Small is the rest of those who would be smart.

A moment's good thing may have cost them years
Before they find an hour to introduce it;
And then, even *then*, some bore may make them
    lose it.

But all was gentle and aristocratic
  In this our party; polish'd, smooth, and cold,
As Phidian forms cut out of marble Attic.
  There now are no Squire Westerns, as of old;
And our Sophias are not so emphatic,
  But fair as then, or fairer to behold.
We have no accomplish'd blackguards, like Tom
    Jones,
But gentlemen in stays, as stiff as stones.

They separated at an early hour—
  That is, ere midnight, which is London's noon;
But in the country, ladies seek their bower
  A little earlier than the waning moon.
Peace to the slumbers of each folded flower—
  May the rose call back its true colour soon!
Good hours of fair cheeks are the fairest tinters,
And lower the price of rouge—at least some win-
    ters.   *Lord Byron.*

GREEDINESS PUNISHED

IT was the cloister Grabow, in the land of Use-
    dom;
  For years had God's free goodness to fill its
    larder come:
    They might have been contented!

Along the shore came swimming, to give the monks good cheer
Who dwelt within the cloister, two fishes every year:
    They might have been contented!

Two sturgeons—two great fat ones; and then this law was set,
That one of them should yearly be taken in a net:
    They might have been contented!

The other swam away then until next year came round,
Then with a new companion he punctually was found:
    They might have been contented!

So then again they caught one, and served him in the dish,
And regularly caught they, year in, year out, a fish:
    They might have been contented!

One year, the time appointed two such great fishes brought,
The question was a hard one, which of them should be caught:
    They might have been contented!

They caught them both together, but every greedy wight
Just spoiled his stomach by it; it served the gluttons right:
    They might have been contented!

This was the least of sorrows: hear how the cup ran
   o'er!
Henceforward to the cloister no fish came swimming more:
      They might have been contented!

So long had God supplied them of his free grace
   alone,
That now it is denied them, the fault is all their own:
      They might have been contented!
                Friedrich Rückert.

WOMAN

ALL honour to woman, the sweetheart, the wife,
   The delight of our firesides by night and
     by day,
Who never does anything wrong in her life,
   Except when permitted to have her own way.
                Fitz-Greene Halleck.

THE RICH AND THE POOR MAN

SO goes the world. If wealthy, you may call
   This friend, that brother—friends and broth-
     ers all;
Though you are worthless, witless, never mind it;
You may have been a stable-boy—what then?
'Tis wealth, good sir, makes honourable men.
You seek respect, no doubt, and you will find it.

But if you're poor, Heaven help you! Though your sire
Had royal blood within him, and though you
Possess the intellect of angels, too,
'Tis all in vain; the world will ne'er inquire
On such a score. Why should it take the pains?
'Tis easier to weigh purses, sure, than brains.

I once saw a poor devil, keen and clever,
Witty and wise; he paid a man a visit,
And no one noticed him, and no one ever
Gave him a welcome. "Strange," cried I, "whence it is so!"
    He walked on this side, then on that,
    He tried to introduce a social chat;
Now here, now there, in vain he tried;
Some formally and freezingly replied, and some
Said by their silence, "Better stay at home."

    A rich man burst the door—
    As Crœsus rich, I'm sure;
He could not pride himself upon his wit
Nor wisdom, for he had not got a bit:
He had what's better—he had wealth.
    What a confusion! All stand up erect!
These crowd around to ask him of his health;
    These bow in honest duty and respect;
And these arrange a sofa or a chair,
And these conduct him there.
"Allow me, sir, the honour;" then a bow
Down to the earth. Is't possible to show
Meet gratitude for such kind condescension?

The poor man hung his head,
And to himself he said,
"This is indeed beyond my comprehension."
Then looking round,
One friendly face he found,
And said, "Pray tell me, why is wealth preferred
To wisdom?" "That's a silly question, friend,"
Replied the other; "have you never heard,
A man may lend his store
Of gold or silver ore,
But wisdom none can borrow, none can lend?"
Sir John Bowring.
(From the Russian of Kremnitzer.)

OZYMANDIAS

I MET a traveller from an antique land,
   Who said: "Two vast and trunkless legs of stone
Stand in the desert. Near them, on the sand,
Half sunk, a shattered visage lies, whose frown,
And wrinkled lip, and sneer of cold command,
Tell that its sculptor well those passions read
Which yet survive, stamped on these lifeless things,
The hand that mocked them and the heart that fed.
And on the pedestal these words appear:
'My name is Ozymandias, king of kings:
Look on my works, ye mighty, and despair!'
Nothing besides remains. Round the decay
Of that colossal wreck, boundless and bare
The lone and level sands stretch far away."
Percy Bysshe Shelley.

CUI BONO?

WHAT is hope? A smiling rainbow
    Children follow through the wet.
  'Tis not here—still yonder, yonder;
Never urchin found it yet.

What is life? A thawing iceboard
  On a sea with sunny shore.
Gay we sail; it melts beneath us;
  We are sunk, and seen no more.

What is man? A foolish baby;
  Vainly strives, and fights, and frets;
Demanding all, deserving nothing,
  One small grave is what he gets!
                Thomas Carlyle.

FATHER-LAND AND MOTHER-TONGUE

OUR Father-land! And would'st thou know
    Why we should call it Father-land?
  It is, that Adam here below
Was made of earth by Nature's hand;
And he, our father, made of earth,
  Hath peopled earth on ev'ry hand,
And we, in memory of his birth,
  Do call our country "Father-land."

At first, in Eden's bowers, they say,
   No sound of speech had Adam caught,
But whistled like a bird all day,
   And may be 'twas for want of thought.
But Nature, with resistless laws,
   Made Adam soon surpass the birds;
She gave him lovely Eve, because,
   If he'd a wife, they must have words.

And so, the native land, I hold,
   By male descent is proudly mine;
The language, as the tale hath told,
   Was given in the female line.
And thus, we see, on either hand,
   We name our blessings whence they've sprung;
We call our country Father-*land;*
   We call our language Mother-*tongue.*
                               Samuel Lover.

FATHER MOLLOY

OR, THE CONFESSION

PADDY McCABE was dying one day,
   And Father Molloy he came to confess him;
Paddy pray'd hard he would make no delay,
But forgive him his sins and make haste for to bless him.
"First tell me your sins," says Father Molloy,
"For I'm thinking you've not been a very good boy."
"Oh," says Paddy, "so late in the evenin', I fear,
'Twould throuble you such a long story to hear,

A Satire Anthology

For you've ten long miles o'er the mountains to go,
While the road *I've* to travel's much longer, you know.
So give us your blessin' and get in the saddle;
To tell all my sins my poor brain it would addle;
And the docther gave ordhers to keep me so quiet—
'Twould disturb me to tell all my sins, if I'd thry it,
And your Reverence has tould us, unless we tell *all*,
'Tis worse than not makin' confession at all.
So I'll say in a word I'm no very good boy—
And, therefore, your blessin', sweet Father Molloy."

"Well, I'll read from a book," says Father Molloy,
  "The manifold sins that humanity's heir to;
And when you hear those that your conscience annoy,
  You'll just squeeze my hand, as acknowledging thereto."
Then the father began the dark roll of iniquity,
And Paddy, thereat, felt his conscience grow rickety,
And he gave such a squeeze that the priest gave a roar.
"Oh, murdher," says Paddy, "don't read any more,
For, if you keep readin', by all that is thrue,
Your Reverence's fist will be soon black and blue;
Besides, to be throubled my conscience begins,
That your Reverence should have any hand in my sins,
So you'd betther suppose I committed them all,
For whether they're great ones, or whether they're small,

Or if they're a dozen, or if they're fourscore,
'Tis your Reverence knows how to absolve them,
    astore;
So I'll say in a word, I'm no very good boy—
And, therefore, your blessin', sweet Father Molloy."

"Well," says Father Molloy, "if your sins I forgive,
So you must forgive all your enemies truly;
And promise me also that, if you should live,
    You'll leave off your old tricks, and begin to live newly."
"I forgive ev'rybody," says Pat, with a groan,
    "Except that big vagabone Micky Malone;
And him I will murdher if ever I can—"
    "Tut, tut," says the priest, "you're a very bad man;
For without your forgiveness, and also repentance,
You'll ne'er go to heaven, and that is my sentence."
"Poo!" says Paddy McCabe, "that's a very hard case—
With your Reverence and heaven I'm content to make pace;
But with heaven and your Reverence I wondher—
    Och hone—
You would think of comparin' that blackguard Malone.
But since I'm hard press'd, and that I *must* forgive,
I forgive, if I die—but as sure as I live
That ugly blackguard I will surely desthroy!
So, *now* for your blessin', sweet Father Molloy!"
                        Samuel Lover.

GAFFER GRAY

(From "Hugh Trevor.")

HO! why dost thou shiver and shake,
    Gaffer Gray?
  And why does thy nose look so blue?
"'Tis the weather that's cold,
  'Tis I'm grown very old,
And my doublet is not very new,
    Well-a-day!"

Then line thy worn doublet with ale,
    Gaffer Gray!
And warm thy old heart with a glass.
"Nay, but credit I've none,
  And my money's all gone;
Then say how may that come to pass?
    Well-a-day!"

Hie away to the house on the brow,
    Gaffer Gray,
And knock at the jolly priest's door.
"The priest often preaches
  Against worldly riches,
But ne'er gives a mite to the poor,
    Well-a-day!"

The lawyer lives under the hill,
    Gaffer Gray;
Warmly fenced both in back and in front.

"He will fasten his locks,
  And will threaten the stocks,
Should he ever more find me in want,
  Well-a-day!"

The squire has fat beeves and brown ale,
  Gaffer Gray ;
And the season will welcome you there.
"His beeves and his beer,
  And his merry New Year,
Are all for the flush and the fair,
  Well-a-day!"

My keg is but low, I confess,
  Gaffer Gray ;
What then ? While it lasts, man, we'll live.
"The poor man alone,
  When he hears the poor moan,
Of his morsel a morsel will give,
  Well-a-day!"

Thomas Holcroft.

COCKLE *V.* CACKLE

THOSE who much read advertisement and bills,
  Must have seen puffs of Cockle's pills,
    Call'd Anti-bilious,
Which some physicians sneer at, supercilious,
But which we are assured, if timely taken,
May save your liver and bacon;

Whether or not they really give one ease,
    I, who have never tried,
    Will not decide;
But no two things in union go like these,
Viz., quacks and pills—save ducks and pease.
Now Mrs. W. was getting sallow,
Her lilies not of the white kind, but yellow,
And friends portended was preparing for
    A human *pâté périgord;*
She was, indeed, so very far from well,
Her son, in filial fear, procured a box
Of those said pellets to resist bile's shocks,
And, tho' upon the ear it strangely knocks,
To save her by a Cockle from a shell!
But Mrs. W., just like Macbeth,
Who very vehemently bids us "throw
Bark to the Bow-wows," hated physic so,
It seem'd to share "the bitterness of death":
Rhubarb, magnesia, jalap, and the kind,
Senna, steel, asafœtida, and squills,
Powder or draught; but least her throat inclined
To give a course to boluses or pills.
No, not to save her life, in lung or lobe,
For all her lights' or liver's sake,
Would her convulsive thorax undertake
Only one little uncelestial globe!

'Tis not to wonder at, in such a case,
If she put by the pill-box in a place
For linen rather than for drugs intended;
Yet, for the credit of the pills, let's say,
    After they thus were stow'd away,
    Some of the linen mended.

But Mrs. W. by disease's dint,
Kept getting still more yellow in her tint,
When lo! her second son, like elder brother,
Marking the hue on the parental gills,
Brought a new charge of Anti-turmeric Pills,
To bleach the jaundiced visage of his mother;
Who took them — in her cupboard — like the other.
　"Deeper and deeper still," of course,
　　The fatal colour daily grew in force;
Till daughter W., newly come from Rome,
Acting the selfsame filial, pillial part,
To cure mamma, another dose brought home
Of Cockles—not the Cockles of her heart!
These going where the others went before,
Of course she had a very pretty store.
And then some hue of health her cheek adorning,
　　The medicine so good must be,
　　They brought her dose on dose, which she
Gave to the up-stairs cupboard, "night and morning";
Till, wanting room at last for other stocks,
Out of the window one fine day she pitch'd
The pillage of each box, and quite enrich'd
The feed of Mister Burrell's hens and cocks.
　A little Barber of a bygone day,
　　Over the way,
Whose stock in trade, to keep the least of shops,
Was one great head of Kemble—that is, John—
Staring in plaster, with a Brutus on,
And twenty little Bantam fowls, with crops.

Little Dame W. thought, when through the sash
    She gave the physic wings,
    To find the very things
So good for bile, so bad for chicken rash,
For thoughtless cock and unreflecting pullet!
But while they gathered up the nauseous nubbles,
Each peck'd itself into a peck of troubles,
And brought the hand of Death upon its gullet.
They might as well have addled been, or rattled,
For long before the night—ah, woe betide
The pills!—each suicidal Bantam died,
    Unfatted!

    Think of poor Burrell's shock,
Of Nature's debt to see his hens all payers,
And laid in death as Everlasting Layers,
With Bantam's small ex-Emperor, the Cock,
In ruffled plumage and funereal hackle,
Giving, undone by Cockle, a last cackle!
To see as stiff as stone his unlive stock,
It really was enough to move his block.
Down on the floor he dash'd, with horror big,
Mr. Bell's third wife's mother's coachman's wig;
And with a tragic stare like his own Kemble,
Burst out with natural emphasis enough,
    And voice that grief made tremble,
Into that very speech of sad Macduff:
"What! all my pretty chickens and their dam,
    At one fell swoop!
    Just when I'd bought a coop,
To see the poor lamented creatures cram!"
    After a little of this mood,
    And brooding over the departed brood,

With razor he began to ope each craw,
Already turning black, as black as coals;
When lo! the undigested cause he saw—
  "Pison'd by goles!"

To Mrs. W.'s luck a contradiction,
Her window still stood open to conviction;
And by short course of circumstantial labour,
He fix'd the guilt upon his adverse neighbour.
Lord! how he rail'd at her, declaring how,
He'd bring an action ere next term of Hilary;
Then, in another moment, swore a vow
He'd make her do pill-penance in the pillory!
She, meanwhile distant from the dimmest dream
Of combating with guilt, yard-arm or arm-yard,
Lapp'd in a paradise of tea and cream;
When up ran Betty with a dismal scream:
"Here's Mr. Burrell, ma'am, with all his farmyard!"
Straight in he came, unbowing and unbending,
With all the warmth that iron and a barber
  Can harbour;
To dress the head and front of her offending,
The fuming phial of his wrath uncorking;
In short, he made her pay him altogether,
In hard cash, very hard, for ev'ry feather,
Charging, of course, each Bantam as a Dorking.
Nothing could move him, nothing make him supple,
So the sad dame, unpocketing her loss,
Had nothing left but to sit hands across,
And see her poultry "going down ten couple."

  Now birds by poison slain,
As venom'd dart from Indian's hollow cane,

Are edible; and Mrs. W.'s thrift—
>She had a thrifty vein—
Destined one pair for supper to make shift—
Supper, as usual, at the hour of ten.
But ten o'clock arrived, and quickly pass'd—
Eleven—twelve—and one o'clock at last,
Without a sign of supper even then!
At length, the speed of cookery to quicken,
Betty was called, and with reluctant feet,
>Came up at a white heat:
"Well, never I see chicken like them chicken!
My saucepans, they have been a pretty while in 'em!
Enough to stew them, if it comes to that,
To flesh and bones, and perfect rags; but drat
Those Anti-biling Pills! there is no bile in 'em!"
>>*Thomas Hood.*

OUR VILLAGE

OUR village, that's to say, not Miss Mitford's village, but our village of Bullock's Smithy,
>Is come into by an avenue of trees, three oak pollards, two elders, and a withy;
And in the middle there's a green, of about not exceeding an acre and a half;
It's common to all and fed off by nineteen cows, six ponies, three horses, five asses, two foals, seven pigs and a calf!
Besides a pond in the middle, as is held by a sort of common law lease,
And contains twenty ducks, six drakes, three ganders, two dead dogs, four drowned kittens, and twelve geese.

Of course the green's cropt very close, and does famous for bowling when the little village boys play at cricket;
Only some horse, or pig, or cow, or great jackass, is sure to come and stand right before the wicket.
There's fifty-five private houses, let alone barns and workshops, and pig-sties, and poultry huts, and such-like sheds,
With plenty of public-houses—two Foxes, one Green Man, three Bunch of Grapes, one Crown, and six King's Heads.
The Green Man is reckoned the best, as the only one that for love or money can raise
A postillion, a blue jacket, two deplorable lame white horses, and a ramshackle " neat post-chaise!"
There's one parish church for all the people, whatsoever may be their ranks in life or their degrees,
Except one very damp, small, dark, freezing cold, little Methodist Chapel of Ease;
And close by the churchyard, there's a stone-mason's yard, that when the time is seasonable
Will furnish with afflictions sore and marble urns and cherubims, very low and reasonable.
There's a cage comfortable enough; I've been in it with Old Jack Jeffery and Tom Pike;
For the Green Man next door will send you in ale, gin, or anything else you like.
I can't speak of the stocks, as nothing remains of them but the upright post;

But the pound is kept in repairs for the sake of Cob's horse as is always there almost.
There's a smithy of course, where that queer sort of a chap in his way, Old Joe Bradley,
Perpetually hammers and stammers, for he stutters and shoes horses very badly.
There's a shop of all sorts that sells everything, kept by the widow of Mr. Task;
But when you go there it's ten to one she's out of everything you ask.
You'll know her house by the swarm of boys, like flies, about the old sugary cask:
There are six empty houses and not so well papered inside as out.
For bill-stickers won't beware, but stick notices of sales and election placards all about.
That's the Doctor's with a green door, where the garden pots in the window is seen;
A weakly monthly rose that don't blow, and a dead geranium, and a tea plant with five black leaves, and one green.
As for hollyhocks at the cottage doors, and the honeysuckles and jasmines, you may go and whistle;
But the Tailor's front garden grows two cabbages, a dock, a ha'porth of pennyroyal, two dandelions, and a thistle!
There are three small orchards—Mr. Busby's the schoolmaster's is the chief—
With two pear trees that don't bear; one plum, and an apple that every year is stripped by a thief.

There's another small day-school too, kept by the respectable Mrs. Gaby,
A select establishment for six little boys, and one big, and four little girls and a baby;
There's a rectory with pointed gables and strange odd chimneys that never smokes,
For the Rector don't live on his living like other Christian sort of folks;
There's a barber once a week well filled with rough black-bearded, shock-headed churls,
And a window with two feminine men's heads, and two masculine ladies in false curls;
There's a butcher, and a carpenter's, and a plumber, and a small green grocer's, and a baker,
But he won't bake on a Sunday; and there's a sexton that's a coal merchant besides, and an undertaker;
And a toy-shop, but not a whole one, for a village can't compare with the London shops;
One window sells drums, dolls, kites, carts, bats, Clout's balls, and the other sells malt and hops.
And Mrs. Brown, in domestic economy, not to be a bit behind her betters,
Lets her house to a milliner, a watchmaker, a rat-catcher, a cobbler, lives in it herself, and it's the post-office for letters.
Now I've gone through all the village—ay, from end to end, save and except one more house,
But I haven't come to that—and I hope I never shall—and that's the village Poor House!
Thomas Hood.

THE DEVIL AT HOME

THE Devil sits in his easy chair,
    Sipping his sulphur tea,
    And gazing out, with a pensive air,
O'er the broad bitumen sea;
Lulled into sentimental mood
    By the spirits' far-off wail,
That sweetly, o'er the burning flood,
    Floats on the brimstone gale!
The Devil, who can be sad at times,
    In spite of all his mummery,
And grave—though not so prosy quite
    As drawn by his friend Montgomery—
The Devil to-day has a dreaming air,
And his eye is raised, and his throat is bare;
His musings are of many things,
    That, good or ill, befell,
Since Adam's sons macadamized
    The highways into hell:
And the Devil—whose mirth is *never* loud—
    Laughs with a quiet mirth,
As he thinks how well his serpent-tricks
    Have been mimicked upon earth;
Of Eden, and of England soiled,
    And darkened by the foot
Of those who preach with adder-tongues,
    And those who eat the fruit;
Of creeping things, that drag their slime
    Into God's chosen places,
And knowledge leading into crime
    Before the angels' faces;

Of lands, from Nineveh to Spain,
   That have bowed beneath his sway,
And men who did his work, from Cain
   To Viscount Castlereagh!
              Thomas Kibble Hervey.
              From "The Devil's Progress."

HOW TO MAKE A NOVEL

TRY with me, and mix what will make a novel,
   All hearts to transfix in house or hall or hovel:
Put the caldron on, set the bellows blowing;
We'll produce anon something worth the showing.

Never mind your plot—'tisn't worth the trouble;
Throw into the pot what will boil and bubble.
Character's a jest—what's the use of study?
All will stand the test that's black enough and bloody.

Here's the *Newgate Guide,* here's the *Causes Célèbres;*
Tumble in, besides, pistol, gun, and sabre;
These police reports, those Old Bailey trials,
Horrors of all sorts, to match the Seven Vials.

Down into a well, lady, thrust your lover;
Truth, as some folks tell, there he may discover;
Step-dames, sure though slow, rivals of your daughters.
Bring, as from below, Styx and all its waters.

Crime that breaks all bounds, bigamy and arson,
Poison, blood, and wounds, will carry well the farce on;
Now it's just in shape; yet, with fire and murder,
Treason, too, and rape might help it all the further.

Or, by way of change, in your wild narration,
Choose adventures strange of fraud and personation;
Make the job complete; let your vile assassin
Rob, and forge, and cheat, for his victim passin'.

Tame is virtue's school; paint, as more effective,
Villain, knave, and fool, with always a detective;
Hate for love may sit; gloom will do for gladness;
Banish sense and wit, and dash in lots of madness.

Stir the broth about, keep the furnace glowing;
Soon we'll pour it out, in three bright volumes flowing:
Some may jeer and jibe; we know where the shop is
Ready to subscribe for a thousand copies.
Lord Charles Neaves.

TWO CHARACTERS

THAN Lord de Vaux there's no man sooner sees
    Whatever at a glance is visible;
    What is not, he can never see at all.
Quick-witted is he, versatile, seizing points,
He'll see them all successively, distinctly,
But never solving questions. Vain he is;

It is his pride to see things on all sides;
Which best to do he sets them on their corners.
Present before him arguments by scores,
Bearing diversely on the affair in hand,
Yet never two of them can see together,
Or gather, blend, and balance what he sees
To make up one account; a mind it is
Accessible to reason's subtlest rays,
And many enter there, but none converge;
It is an army with no general,
An arch without a key-stone. Then the other,
Good Martin Blondel-Vatre: he is rich
In nothing else but difficulties and doubts.
You shall be told the evil of your scheme,
But not the scheme that's better. He forgets
That policy, expecting not clear gain,
Deals ever in alternatives. He's wise
In negatives, is skilful at erasures,
Expert in stepping backward, an adept
At auguring eclipses. But admit
His apprehensions, and demand, what then?
And you shall find you've turned the blank leaf
     over.
                              Henry Taylor.

THE SAILOR'S CONSOLATION

ONE night came on a hurricane,
    The sea was mountains rolling,
    When Barney Buntline turned his quid,
And said to Billy Bowling:

"A strong nor'-wester's blowing, Bill—
  Hark! don't ye hear it roar now?
Lord help 'em! how I pities all
  Unhappy folks on shore now!

"Foolhardy chaps who live in town—
  What danger they are all in,
And now are quaking in their beds,
  For fear the roof should fall in.
Poor creatures! how they envies us,
  And wishes, I've a notion,
For our good luck, in such a storm
  To be upon the ocean.

"But as for them who're out all day,
  On business from their houses,
And late at night are coming home,
  To cheer the babes and spouses,
While you and I, Bill, on the deck
  Are comfortably lying,
My eyes! what tiles and chimney-pots
  About their heads are flying!

"And very often have we heard
  How men are killed and undone
By overturns of carriages,
  By thieves and fires in London.
We know what risks all landsmen run,
  From noblemen to tailors;
Then, Bill, let us thank Providence
  That you and I are sailors!"

William Pitt.

VERSES ON SEEING THE SPEAKER ASLEEP IN HIS CHAIR DURING ONE OF THE DEBATES OF THE FIRST REFORMED PARLIAMENT

SLEEP, Mr. Speaker; 'tis surely fair,
   If you mayn't in your bed, that you should in your chair;
Louder and longer still they grow,
Tory and Radical, Aye and No;
Talking by night and talking by day.
Sleep, Mr. Speaker—sleep while you may!

Sleep, Mr. Speaker; slumber lies
Light and brief on a Speaker's eyes;
Fielden or Finn in a minute or two
Some disorderly thing will do;
Riot will chase repose away.
Sleep, Mr. Speaker—sleep while you may!

Sleep, Mr. Speaker. Sweet to men
Is the sleep that cometh but now and then;
Sweet to the weary, sweet to the ill,
Sweet to the children that work in the mill.
You have more need of repose than they.
Sleep, Mr. Speaker—sleep while you may!

Sleep, Mr. Speaker; Harvey will soon
Move to abolish the sun and the moon;
Hume will no doubt be taking the sense
Of the House on a question of sixteen pence;

Statesmen will howl, and patriots bray.
Sleep, Mr. Speaker—sleep while you may!

Sleep, Mr. Speaker, and dream of the time,
When loyalty was not quite a crime;
When Grant was a pupil in Canning's school,
And Palmerston fancied Wood a fool.
Lord, how principles pass away!
Sleep, Mr. Speaker—sleep while you may!
Winthrop M. Praed.

PELTERS OF PYRAMIDS

A SHOAL of idlers, from a merchant craft
Anchor'd off Alexandria, went ashore,
And mounting asses in their headlong glee,
Round Pompey's Pillar rode with hoots and taunts,
As men oft say, "What art thou more than we?"
Next in a boat they floated up the Nile,
Singing and drinking, swearing senseless oaths,
Shouting, and laughing most derisively
At all majestic scenes. A bank they reach'd,
And clambering up, play'd gambols among tombs;
And in portentous ruins (through whose depths,
The nightly twilight of departed gods,
Both sun and moon glanced furtive, as in awe)
They hid, and whoop'd, and spat on sacred things.

At length, beneath the blazing sun they lounged
Near a great Pyramid. Awhile they stood
With stupid stare, until resentment grew,

A Satire Anthology

In the recoil of meanness from the vast;
And gathering stones, they with coarse oaths and gibes
(As they would say, "What art thou more than we?")
Pelted the Pyramid! But soon these men,
Hot and exhausted, sat them down to drink—
Wrangled, smok'd, spat, and laugh'd, and drowsily
Curs'd the bald Pyramid, and fell asleep.

Night came. A little sand went drifting by,
And morn again was in the soft blue heavens.
The broad slopes of the shining Pyramid
Look'd down in their austere simplicity
Upon the glistening silence of the sands,
Whereon no trace of mortal dust was seen.
Richard Hengist Horne.

THE ANNUITY

I GAED to spend a week in Fife;
   An unco week it proved to be,
  For there I met a waesome wife
   Lamentin' her viduity.
Her grief brak out sae fierce and fell,
I thought her heart wad burst the shell;
And—I was sae left to mysel'—
   I sell't her an annuity.

The bargain lookit fair eneugh—
   She just was turned o' saxty-three.
I couldna guessed she'd prove sae teugh,
   By human ingenuity.

But years have come, and years have gane,
And there she's yet, as stieve as stane;
The limmer's growin' young again,
   Since she got her annuity.

She's crined awa' to bane and skin,
   But that, it seems, is naught to me;
She's like to live, although she's in
   The last stage o' tenuity.
She munches wi' her wizen'd gums,
An' stumps about on legs o' thrums,
But comes, as sure as Christmas comes,
   To ca' for her annuity.

I read the tables drawn wi' care
   For an insurance company;
Her chance o' life was stated there
   Wi' perfect perspicuity.
But tables here, or tables there,
She's lived ten years beyond her share,
An' 's like to live a dozen mair,
   To ca' for her annuity.

Last Yule she had a fearfu' host;
   I thought a kink might set me free;
I led her out, 'mang snaw and frost,
   Wi' constant assiduity.
But deil ma' care—the blast gaed by,
   And miss'd the auld anatomy—
It just cost me a tooth, forbye
   Discharging her annuity.

A Satire Anthology

If there's a sough o' cholera,
   Or typhus, wha sae gleg as she?
She buys up baths, an' drugs, an' a',
   In siccan superfluity,
She doesna need—she's fever-proof;
The pest walked o'er her very roof—
She tauld me sae; an' then her loof
   Held out for her annuity.

Ae day she fell, her arm she brak—
   A compound fracture as could be;
Nae leech the cure wad undertake,
   Whate'er was the gratuity.
It's cured! she handles 't like a flail—
It does as weel in bits as hale;
But I'm a broken man mysel',
   Wi' her and her annuity.

Her broozled flesh and broken banes
   Are weel as flesh and banes can be;
She beats the toads that live in stanes
   An' fatten in vacuity!
They die when they're exposed to air—
They canna thole the atmosphere;
But her! expose her onywhere,
   She lives for her annuity.

If mortal means could nick her thread,
   Sma' crime it wad appear to me;
Ca't murder—or ca't homicide,
   I'd justify 't, an' do it tae.

But how to fell a withered wife
That's carved out o' the tree of life,
The timmer limmer dares the knife
   To settle her annuity.

I'd try a shot—but whar's the mark?
  Her vital parts are hid frae me;
Her backbone wanders through her sark
  In an unkenn'd corkscrewity.
She's palsified, an' shakes her head
Sae fast about, ye scarce can see 't;
It's past the power o' steel or lead
   To settle her annuity.

She might be drowned, but go she'll not
  Within a mile o' loch or sea;
Or hanged, if cord could grip a throat
  O' siccan exiguity.
It's fitter far to hang the rope—
It draws out like a telescope;
'Twad tak' a dreadfu' length o' drop
   To settle her annuity.

Will poison do it? It has been tried,
  But be 't in hash or fricassee,
That's just the dish she can't abide,
  Whatever kind o' gout it hae.
It's needless to assail her doubts;
She gangs by instinct, like the brutes,
An' only eats an' drinks what suits
   Hersel' and her annuity.

The Bible says the age o' man
  Threescore and ten, perchance, may be;
She's ninety-four. Let them who can,
  Explain the incongruity.
She should hae lived afore the flood;
She's come o' patriarchal blood;
She's some auld Pagan mummified,
  Alive for her annuity.

She's been embalmed inside and oot;
  She's sauted to the last degree;
There's pickle in her very snoot,
  Sae caper-like an' cruety.
Lot's wife was fresh compared to her;
They've kyanized the useless knir;
She canna decompose—nae mair
  Than her accurs'd annuity.

The water-drop wears out the rock,
  As this eternal jaud wears me;
I could withstand the single shock,
  But not the continuity.
It's pay me here, an' pay me there,
An' pay me, pay me, evermair.
I'll gang demented wi' despair—
  I'm charged for her annuity.

George Outram.

MALBROUCK

MALBROUCK, the prince of commanders,
   Is gone to the war in Flanders;
   His fame is like Alexander's;
     But when will he come home?

Perhaps at Trinity Feast, or
Perhaps he may come at Easter.
Egad! he had better make haste, or
   We fear he may never come.

For Trinity Feast is over,
And has brought no news from Dover;
And Easter is past, moreover,
   And Malbrouck still delays.

Milady in her watch-tower
Spends many a pensive hour,
Not well knowing why or how her
   Dear lord from England stays.

While sitting quite forlorn in
That tower, she spies returning
A page clad in deep mourning,
   With fainting steps and slow.

"O page, prithee, come faster!
What news do you bring of your master?
I fear there is some disaster,
   Your looks are so full of woe."

"The news I bring, fair lady,"
With sorrowful accent said he,
"Is one you are not ready
 So soon, alas! to hear.

"But since to speak I'm hurried,"
Added this page, quite flurried,
"Malbrouck is dead and buried!"
 (And here he shed a tear.)

"He's dead! he's dead as a herring!
For I beheld his 'berring,'
And four officers transferring
 His corpse away from the field.

"One officer carried his sabre,
And he carried it not without labour,
Much envying his next neighbour,
 Who only bore a shield.

"The third was helmet-bearer—
That helmet which on its wearer
Filled all who saw with terror,
 And covered a hero's brains.

"Now, having got so far, I
Find that (by the Lord Harry!)
The fourth is left nothing to carry;
 So there the thing remains."

Translated by Father Prout.

A MAN'S REQUIREMENTS

LOVE me, sweet, with all thou art,
    Feeling, thinking, seeing;
  Love me in the lightest part,
    Love me in full being.

Love me with thine open youth
    In its frank surrender;
With the vowing of thy mouth,
    With its silence tender.

Love me with thine azure eyes,
    Made for earnest granting;
Taking colour from the skies—
    Can Heaven's truth be wanting?

Love me with their lids, that fall
    Snow-like at first meeting;
Love me with thine heart, that all
    Neighbours then see beating.

Love me with thine hand, stretched out
    Freely, open-minded:
Love me with thy loitering foot—
    Hearing one behind it.

Love me with thy voice, that turns
    Sudden faint above me;
Love me with thy blush, that burns
    When I murmur, *Love me!*

Love me with thy thinking soul,
  Break it to love-sighing;
Love me with thy thoughts, that roll
  On through living, dying.

Love me in thy gorgeous airs,
  When the world has crown'd thee;
Love me, kneeling at thy prayers,
  With the angels round thee.

Love me pure, as musers do,
  Up the woodlands shady;
Love me gayly, fast and true,
  As a winsome lady.

Though all hopes that keep us brave,
  Further off or nigher,
Love me for the house and grave,
  And for something higher.

Thus, if thou wilt prove me, dear,
  Woman's love no fable,
I will love *thee*—half a year,
  As a man is able.
            Elizabeth Barrett Browning.

CRITICS

MY critic Hammond flatters prettily,
  And wants another volume like the last.
  My critic Belfair wants another book
Entirely different, which will sell (and live?)—
A striking book, yet not a startling book.

A Satire Anthology

The public blames originalities
(You must not pump spring water unawares
Upon a gracious public, full of nerves),
Good things, not subtle, new, yet orthodox,
As easy reading as the dog-eared page
That's fingered by said public fifty years,
Since first taught spelling by its grandmother,
And yet a revelation in some sort;
That's hard, my critic Belfair! So, what next?
My critic Stokes objects to abstract thoughts;
"Call a man John, a woman, Joan," says he,
"And do not prate so of humanities;"
Whereat I call my critic simply Stokes.
My critic Johnson recommends more mirth,
Because a cheerful genius suits the times,
And all true poets laugh unquenchably,
Like Shakespeare and the gods. That's very hard.
The gods may laugh, and Shakespeare; Dante smiled
With such a needy heart on two pale lips,
We cry, "Weep, rather, Dante." Poems are
Men, if true poems; and who dares exclaim
At any man's door, "Here, 'tis understood
The thunder fell last week and killed a wife,
And scared a sickly husband—what of that?
Get up, be merry, shout, and clap your hands,
Because a cheerful genius suits the times?"
None says so to the man—and why, indeed,
Should any to the poem?
Elizabeth Barrett Browning.

THE MISER

A FELLOW all his life lived hoarding gold,
   And, dying, hoarded left it. And behold,
   One night his son saw peering through the house
A man, with yet the semblance of a mouse,
Watching a crevice in the wall, and cried,
"My father?" "Yes," the Mussulman replied,
"Thy father!" "But why watching thus?" "For fear
Lest any smell my treasure buried here."
"But wherefore, sir, so metamousified?"
"Because, my son, such is the true outside
Of the inner soul by which I lived and died."
      Edward Fitzgerald.

CACOËTHES SCRIBENDI

IF all the trees in all the woods were men,
   And each and every blade of grass a pen;
   If every leaf on every shrub and tree
Turned to a sheet of foolscap; every sea
Were changed to ink, and all earth's living tribes
Had nothing else to do but act as scribes,
And for ten thousand ages, day and night,
The human race should write, and write, and write,
Till all the pens and paper were used up,
And the huge inkstand was an empty cup,
Still would the scribblers clustered round its brink
Call for more pens, more paper, and more ink.
      Oliver Wendell Holmes.

A FAMILIAR LETTER TO SEVERAL CORRESPONDENTS

YES, write if you want to—there's nothing like trying;
   Who knows what a treasure your casket may hold?
I'll show you that rhyming's as easy as lying,
   If you'll listen to me while the art I unfold.

Here's a book full of words: one can choose as he fancies,
   As a painter his tint, as a workman his tool;
Just think! all the poems and plays and romances
   Were drawn out of this, like the fish from a pool!

You can wander at will through its syllabled mazes,
   And take all you want—not a copper they cost;
What is there to hinder your picking out phrases
   For an epic as clever as "Paradise Lost"?

Don't mind if the index of sense is at zero;
   Use words that run smoothly, whatever they mean;
Leander and Lillian and Lillibullero
   Are much the same thing in the rhyming machine.

A Satire Anthology

There are words so delicious their sweetness will
    smother
  That boarding-school flavour of which we're
    afraid;
There is "lush" is a good one, and "swirl" is
    another;
  Put both in one stanza, its fortune is made.

With musical murmurs and rhythmical closes
  You can cheat us of smiles when you've nothing
    to tell;
You hand us a nosegay of milliner's roses,
  And we cry with delight, "Oh, how sweet they
    do smell!"

Perhaps you will answer all needful conditions
  For winning the laurels to which you aspire,
By docking the tails of the two prepositions
  I' the style o' the bards you so greatly admire.

As for subjects of verse, they are only too plenty
  For ringing the changes on metrical chimes;
A maiden, a moonbeam, a lover of twenty,
  Have filled that great basket with bushels of
    rhymes.

Let me show you a picture—'tis far from irrele-
    vant—
  By a famous old hand in the arts of design;
'Tis only a photographed sketch of an elephant;
  The name of the draughtsman was Rembrandt of
    Rhine.

How easy! no troublesome colours to lay on;
  It can't have fatigued him, no, not in the least;
A dash here and there with a haphazard crayon,
  And there stands the wrinkled-skinned, baggy-limbed beast.

Just so with your verse—'tis as easy as sketching;
  You can reel off a song without knitting your brow,
As lightly as Rembrandt a drawing or etching;
  It is nothing at all, if you only know how.

Well, imagine you've printed your volume of verses;
  Your forehead is wreathed with the garland of fame;
Your poem the eloquent school-boy rehearses;
  Her album the school-girl presents for your name.

Each morning the post brings you autograph letters;
  You'll answer them promptly—an hour isn't much
For the honour of sharing a page with your betters,
  With magistrates, members of Congress, and such.

Of course you're delighted to serve the committees
  That come with requests from the country all round;
You would grace the occasion with poems and ditties
  When they've got a new school-house, or poor-house, or pound.

With a hymn for the saints, and a song for the sinners,
    You go and are welcome wherever you please;
You're a privileged guest at all manner of dinners;
    You've a seat on the platform among the grandees.

At length your mere presence becomes a sensation;
    Your cup of enjoyment is filled to its brim
With the pleasure Horatian of digitmonstration,
    As the whisper runs round of "That's he!" or "That's him!"

But, remember, O dealer in phrases sonorous,
    So daintily chosen, so tunefully matched,
Though you soar with the wings of the cherubim o'er us,
    The ovum was human from which you were hatched.

No will of your own, with its puny compulsion,
    Can summon the spirit that quickens the lyre;
It comes, if at all, like the sibyl's convulsion,
    And touches the brain with a finger of fire.

So, perhaps, after all, it's as well to be quiet,
    If you've nothing you think is worth saying in prose,
As to furnish a meal of their cannibal diet
    To the critics, by publishing, as you propose.

But it's all of no use, and I'm sorry I've written;
  I shall see your thin volume some day on my shelf;
For the rhyming tarantula surely has bitten,
  And music must cure you, so pipe it yourself.
Oliver Wendell Holmes.

CONTENTMENT

"MAN WANTS BUT LITTLE HERE BELOW"

LITTLE I ask; my wants are few;
    I only wish a hut of stone
    (A very plain brown stone will do)
  That I may call my own;
And close at hand is such a one,
In yonder street that fronts the sun.

Plain food is quite enough for me;
  Three courses are as good as ten;
If Nature can subsist on three,
  Thank Heaven for three—Amen!
I always thought cold victual nice—
My choice would be vanilla-ice.

I care not much for gold or land;
  Give me a mortgage here and there,
Some good bank-stock, some note of hand,
  Or trifling railroad share.
I only ask that Fortune send
A little more than I shall spend.

Honours are silly toys, I know,
  And titles are but empty names;
I would, perhaps, be Plenipo—
  But only near St. James;
I'm very sure I should not care
To fill our Gubernator's chair.

Jewels are baubles; 'tis a sin
  To care for such unfruitful things;
One good-sized diamond in a pin,
  Some, not so large, in rings,
A ruby, and a pearl or so,
Will do for me; I laugh at show.

My dame should dress in cheap attire
  (Good, heavy silks are never dear);
I own, perhaps, I might desire
  Some shawls of true Cashmere—
Some marrowy crapes of China silk,
Like wrinkled skins on scalded milk.

Wealth's wasteful tricks I will not learn,
  Nor ape the glitt'ring upstart fool;
Shall not carved tables serve my turn,
  But *all* must be of buhl?
Give grasping pomp its double care—
I ask but *one* recumbent chair.

Thus humble let me live and die,
  Nor long for Midas' golden touch;
If Heaven more gen'rous gifts deny,
  I shall not miss them much—

A Satire Anthology

Too grateful for the blessing lent
Of simple tastes and mind content!
     Oliver Wendell Holmes.

HOW TO MAKE A MAN OF CONSEQUENCE

A BROW austere, a circumspective eye.
 A frequent shrug of the *os humeri;*
 A nod significant, a stately gait,
A blustering manner, and a tone of weight,
A smile sarcastic, an expressive stare:
Adopt all these, as time and place will bear;
Then rest assur'd that those of little sense
Will deem you sure a man of consequence.
     Mark Lemon.

THE WIDOW MALONE

DID ye hear of the Widow Malone,
    Ohone!
 Who lived in the town of Athlone,
    Alone?
Oh, she melted the hearts
Of the swains in them parts,
So lovely the Widow Malone,
    Ohone!
So lovely the Widow Malone.

Of lovers she had a full score,
>> Or more;
And fortunes they all had galore,
>> In store;
From the minister down
To the Clerk of the Crown,
All were courting the Widow Malone,
>> Ohone!
All were courting the Widow Malone.

But so modest was Mrs. Malone,
>> 'Twas known
No one ever could see her alone,
>> Ohone!
Let them ogle and sigh,
They could ne'er catch her eye,
So bashful the Widow Malone,
>> Ohone!
So bashful the Widow Malone.

Till one Mister O'Brien from Clare—
>> How quare.
It's little for blushing they care
>> Down there—
Put his arm round her waist,
Gave ten kisses at laste—
"Oh," says he, "you're my Molly Malone,
>> My own!"
"Oh," says he, "you're my Molly Malone!"

A Satire Anthology

And the widow they all thought so shy,
My eye!
Ne'er thought of a simper or sigh—
For why?

"But, Lucius," says she,
"Since you've now made so free,
You may marry your Molly Malone,
Ohone!
You may marry your Molly Malone."

There's a moral contained in my song,
Not wrong;
And, one comfort, it's not very long,
But strong:
If for widows you die,
Learn to *kiss*, not to sigh,
For they're all like sweet Mistress Malone,
Ohone!
Oh! they're very like Mistress Malone!
Charles Lever.

THE PAUPER'S DRIVE

THERE'S a grim one-horse hearse in a jolly round trot;
  To the churchyard a pauper is going, I wot;
The road it is rough, and the hearse has no springs;
And hark to the dirge which the sad driver sings:
  Rattle his bones over the stones!
  He's only a pauper, whom nobody owns.

Oh, where are the mourners? Alas! there are none;
He has left not a gap in the world, now he's gone;
Not a tear in the eye of child, woman, or man;
To the grave with his carcass as fast as you can.
    Rattle his bones over the stones!
    He's only a pauper, whom nobody owns.

What a jolting, and creaking, and splashing, and din!
The whip, how it cracks, and the wheels, how they spin!
How the dirt, right and left, o'er the hedges is hurled!
The pauper at length makes a noise in the world!
    Rattle his bones over the stones!
    He's only a pauper, whom nobody owns.

Poor pauper defunct! he has made some approach
To gentility, now that he's stretched in a coach;
He's taking a drive in his carriage at last,
But it will not be long, if he goes on so fast.
    Rattle his bones over the stones!
    He's only a pauper, whom nobody owns.

You bumpkins, who stare at your brother conveyed,
Behold what respect to a cloddy is paid!
And be joyful to think, when by death you're laid low,
You've a chance to the grave like a gemman to go.
    Rattle his bones over the stones!
    He's only a pauper, whom nobody owns.

But a truce to this strain; for my soul it is sad,
To think that a heart in humanity clad
Should make, like the brutes, such a desolate end,
And depart from the light without leaving a friend.
>   Bear soft his bones over the stones!
>   Though a pauper, he's one whom his Maker yet owns.

Thomas Noel.

ON LYTTON

WE know him, out of Shakespeare's art,
    And those fine curses which he spoke—
The Old Timon with his noble heart,
    That strongly loathing, greatly broke.

So died the Old; here comes the New;
    Regard him—a familiar face;
I thought we knew him. What! it's you,
    The padded man that wears the stays;

Who killed the girls, and thrilled the boys
    With dandy pathos when you wrote:
O Lion, you that made a noise,
    And shook a mane *en papillotes*. . .

What profits now to understand
    The merits of a spotless shirt,
A dapper boot, a little hand,
    If half the little soul is dirt? . . .

A Timon you! Nay, nay, for shame!
  It looks too arrogant a jest—
That fierce old man, to take his name,
  You bandbox! Off, and let him rest!
                      Alfred Tennyson.

SORROWS OF WERTHER

WERTHER had a love for Charlotte
  Such as words could never utter;
  Would you know how first he met her?
She was cutting bread and butter.

Charlotte was a married lady,
  And a moral man was Werther,
And, for all the wealth of Indies,
  Would do nothing for to hurt her.

So he sighed and pined and ogled,
  And his passion boiled and bubbled,
Till he blew his silly brains out,
  And no more was by it troubled.

Charlotte, having seen his body
  Borne before her on a shutter,
Like a well-conducted person,
  Went on cutting bread and butter.
               William Makepeace Thackeray.

MR. MOLONY'S ACCOUNT OF THE BALL

GIVEN TO THE NEPAULESE AMBASSADOR BY THE
PENINSULAR AND ORIENTAL COMPANY

OH, will ye choose to hear the news?
    Bedad, I cannot pass it o'er;
  I'll tell you all about the Ball
To the Naypaulase Ambassador.
Begor! this *fête* all balls does bate
  At which I've worn a pump, and I
Must here relate the splendthor great
  Of th' Oriental Company.

These men of sinse dispoised expinse,
  To *fête* these black Achilleses.
"We'll show the blacks," says they, "Almack's,
  And take the rooms at Willis's."
With flags and shawls, for these Nepauls,
  They hung the rooms of Willis up,
And decked the walls, and stairs, and halls,
  With roses and with lilies up.

And Jullien's band it tuck its stand
  So sweetly in the middle there,
And soft bassoons played heavenly chunes,
  And violins did fiddle there.
And when the Coort was tired of spoort,
  I'd lave you, boys, to think there was
A nate buffet before them set,
  Where lashins of good dhrink there was.

At ten, before the ballroom door
  His moighty Excellincy was,
He smoiled and bowed to all the crowd,
  So gorgeous and imminse he was.
His dusky shuit, sublime and mute
  Into the doorway followed him;
And oh, the noise of the blackguard boys,
  As they hurrood and hollowed him!

The noble Chair stud at the stair,
  And bade the dhrums to thump; and he
Did thus evince to that Black Prince
  The welcome of his Company.
Oh, fair the girls, and rich the curls,
  And bright the oys you saw there, was;
And fixed each oye, ye there could spoi,
  On Gineral Jung Behawther was!

This gineral great then tuck his sate,
  With all the other ginerals
(Bedad his troat, his belt, his coat,
  All bleezed with precious minerals);
And as he there, with princely air,
  Recloinin' on his cushion was,
All round about his royal chair
  The squeezin' and the pushin' was.

O Pat, such girls, such jukes, and earls,
  Such fashion and nobilitee!
Just think of Tim, and fancy him
  Amidst the hoigh gentilitee!

There was Lord de L'Huys, and the Portygeese
  Ministhér and his lady there,
And I reckonized, with much surprise,
  Our messmate, Bob O'Grady, there.

There was Baroness Brunow, that looked like Juno,
  And Baroness Rehausen there,
And Countess Roullier, that looked peculiar
  Well, in her robes of gauze in there.
There was Lord Crowhurst (I knew him first,
  When only Misther Pips he was),
And Mick O'Toole, the great big fool,
  That after supper tipsy was.

There was Lord Fingall, and his ladies all,
  And Lords Killeen and Dufferin,
And Paddy Fife, with his fat wife:
  I wondher how he could stuff her in.
There was Lord Belfast, that by me passed,
  And seemed to ask how should *I* go there?
And the Widow Macrae, and Lord A. Hay,
  And the Marchioness of Sligo there.

Yes, jukes, and earls, and diamonds, and pearls,
  And pretty girls, was sporting there;
And some beside (the rogues!) I spied,
  Behind the windies, coorting there.
Oh, there's one I know, bedad would show
  As beautiful as any there,
And I'd like to hear the pipers blow,
  And shake a fut with Fanny there!
        William Makepeace Thackeray.

DAMAGES, TWO HUNDRED POUNDS.

SPECIAL jurymen of England, who admire your country's laws,
  And proclaim a British jury worthy of the realm's applause,
Gayly compliment each other at the issue of a cause
Which was tried at Guildford 'Sizes, this day week, as ever was.

Unto that august tribunal comes a gentleman in grief
(Special was the British jury, and the judge, the Baron Chief)—
Comes a British man and husband, asking of the law relief,
For his wife was stolen from him; he'd have vengeance on the thief.

Yes, his wife, the blessed treasure with the which his life was crowned,
Wickedly was ravished from him by a hypocrite profound;
And he comes before twelve Britons, men for sense and truth renowned,
To award him for his damage twenty hundred sterling pound.

A Satire Anthology

He by counsel and attorney there at Guildford does appear,
Asking damage of the villain who seduced his lady dear;
But I can't help asking, though the lady's guilt was all too clear,
And though guilty the defendant, wasn't the plaintiff rather queer?

First the lady's mother spoke, and said she'd seen her daughter cry
But a fortnight after marriage—early times for piping eye;
Six months after, things were worse, and the piping eye was black,
And this gallant British husband caned his wife upon the back.

Three months after they were married, husband pushed her to the door,
Told her to be off and leave him, for he wanted her no more.
As she would not go, why, he went: thrice he left his lady dear—
Left her, too, without a penny, for more than a quarter of a year.

Mrs. Frances Duncan knew the parties very well indeed;
She had seen him pull his lady's nose, and make her lip to bleed;

If he chanced to sit at home, not a single word he said;
Once she saw him throw the cover of a dish at his lady's head.

Sarah Green, another witness, clear did to the jury note
How she saw this honest fellow seize his lady by the throat;
How he cursed her and abused her, beating her into a fit,
Till the pitying next-door neighbours crossed the wall and witnessed it.

Next door to this injured Briton Mr. Owers, a butcher, dwelt;
Mrs. Owers's foolish heart toward this erring dame did melt
(Not that she had erred as yet—crime was not developed in her),
But, being left without a penny, Mrs. Owers supplied her dinner—
God be merciful to Mrs. Owers, who was merciful to this sinner!

Caroline Naylor was their servant, said they led a wretched life;
Saw this most distinguished Briton fling a teacup at his wife;
He went out to balls and pleasures, and never once, in ten months' space,
Sat with his wife, or spoke her kindly. This was the defendant's case.

A Satire Anthology

Pollock, C. B., charged the jury; said the woman's guilt was clear:
That was not the point, however, which the jury came to hear;
But the damage to determine which, as it should true appear,
This most tender-hearted husband, who so used his lady dear—

Beat her, kicked her, caned her, cursed her, left her starving, year by year.
Flung her from him, parted from her, wrung her neck, and boxed her ear—
What the reasonable damage this afflicted man could claim
By the loss of the affections of this guilty, graceless dame?

Then the honest British twelve, to each other turning round,
Laid their clever heads together with a wisdom most profound:
And towards his lordship looking, spoke the foreman wise and sound:
"My Lord, we find for this here plaintiff, damages two hundred pound."

So, God bless the special jury! pride and joy of English ground,
And the happy land of England, where true justice does abound!

British jurymen and husbands, let us hail this verdict proper:
If a British wife offends you, Britons, you've a right o whop her.

Though you promised to protect her, though you promised to defend her,
You are welcome to neglect her; to the devil you may send her;
You may strike her, curse, abuse her; so declares our law renowned;
And if after this you lose her, why, you're paid two hundred pound.

William Makepeace Thackeray.

THE LOST LEADER

I

JUST for a handful of silver he left us,
    Just for a riband to stick in his coat—
    Found the one gift of which fortune bereft us,
Lost all the others, she lets us devote;
They, with the gold to give, doled him out silver,
So much was theirs who so little allowed:
How all our copper had gone for his service!
    Rags—were they purple, his heart had been proud!
We that had loved him so, followed him, honoured him,
    Lived in his mild and magnificent eye,
Learned his great language, caught his clear accents,
    Made him our pattern, to live and to die?

Shakespeare was of us, Milton was for us,
    Burns, Shelley, were with us—they watched from
        their graves!
He alone breaks from the van and the freemen,
    He alone sinks to the rear and the slaves!

II

We shall march prospering, not thro' his presence;
    Songs may inspirit us, not from his lyre;
Deeds will be done, while he boasts his quiescence,
    Still bidding crouch whom the rest bade aspire.
Blot out his name, then; record one lost soul more,
    One task more declined, one more footpath untrod;
One more devils' triumph, and sorrow for angels,
    One wrong more to man, one more insult to God!
Life's night begins; let him never come back to us!
    There would be doubt, hesitation, and pain,
Forced praise on our part—the glimmer of twilight,
    Never glad, confident morning again!
Best fight on well, for we taught him—strike gallantly,
    Menace our heart ere we master his own;
Then let him receive the new knowledge, and wait us,
    Pardoned in heaven, the first by the throne!

Robert Browning.

THE POPE AND THE NET

WHAT! he on whom our voices unanimously ran,
Made Pope at our last Conclave? Full low his life began:
His father earned the daily bread as just a fisherman.

So much the more his boy minds book, gives proof of mother-wit,
Becomes first Deacon, and then Priest, then Bishop; see him sit
No less than Cardinal ere long, while no one cries "Unfit!"

But some one smirks, some other smiles, jogs elbow, and nods head;
Each winks at each: "I' faith, a rise! Saint Peter's net, instead
Of swords and keys, is come in vogue!" You think he blushes red?

Not he, of humble, holy heart! "Unworthy me," he sighs;
"From fisher's drudge to Church's prince—it is indeed a rise!
So, here's my way to keep the fact forever in my eyes!"

And straightway in his palace-hall, where commonly is set
Some coat-of-arms, some portraiture ancestral, lo, we met
His mean estate's reminder in his fisher-father's net!

Which step conciliates all and some, stops cavil in a trice:
"The humble, holy heart that holds of new-born pride no spice,
He's just the saint to choose for Pope!" Each adds. "'Tis my advice."

So Pope he was; and when we flocked—its sacred slipper on—
To kiss his foot we lifted eyes, alack, the thing was gone—
That guarantee of lowlihead—eclipsed that star which shone!

Each eyed his fellow; one and all kept silence. I cried "Pish!
I'll make me spokesman for the rest, express the common wish:
Why, Father, is the net removed?" "Son, it hath caught the fish."

Robert Browning.

SOLILOQUY OF THE SPANISH CLOISTER

G R-R-R—there go, my heart's abhorrence!
    Wate your damned flower-pots, do!
If hate killed men, Brother Lawrence,
  God's blood, would not mine kill you!
What! your myrtle-bush wants trimming?
  Oh, that rose has prior claims—
Needs its leaden vase filled brimming?
  Hell dry you up with its flames!

At the meal we sit together:
  Salve tibi! I must hear
Wise talk of the kind of weather,
  Sort of season, time of year;
Not a plenteous cork-crop; scarcely
  Dare we hope oak-galls, I doubt:
What's the Latin name for "parsley"?
  Wha 's the Greek name for swine's snout?

Whew! we'll have our platter burnished,
  Laid with care on our own shelf;
With a fire-new spoon we're furnished,
  And a goblet for ourself,
Rinsed like something sacrificial
  Ere 'tis fit to touch our chaps
Marked with L for our initial!
  (He-he! There his lily snaps!)

Saint, forsooth! While brown Dolores
  Squats outside the convent bank
With Sanchicha, telling stories,
  Steeping tresses in the tank,
Blue-black, lustrous, thick like horsehairs,
  Can't I see his dead eye glow
Bright as 't were a Barbary corsair's?
  (That is, if he'd let it show!)

When he finishes refection,
  Knife and fork he never lays
Crosswise, to my recollection,
  As do I, in Jesu's praise.
I the Trinity illustrate,
  Drinking watered orange pulp—
In three sips the Arian frustrate,
  While he drains his at one gulp.

Oh, those melons! If he's able,
  We're to have a feast, so nice!
One goes to the abbot's table,
  All of us get each a slice.
How go on your flowers? None double?
  Not one fruit-sort can you spy?
Strange! And I, too, at such trouble
  Keep them close-nipped on the sly!

There's a great text in Galatians,
  Once you trip on it, entails
Twenty-nine distinct damnations,
  One sure, if another fails.

If I trip him just a-dying,
  Sure of heaven as sure can be,
Spin him round and send him flying
  Off to hell, a Manichee?

Or, my scrofulous French novel
  On gray paper, with blunt type!
Simply glance at it, you grovel
  Hand and foot in Belial's gripe.
If I double down its pages
  At the woful sixteenth print,
When he gathers his greengages,
  Ope a sieve and slip it in't?

Or, there's Satan! One might venture
  Pledge one's soul to him, yet leave
Such a flaw in the indenture
  As he'd miss till, past retrieve,
Blasted lay that rose-acacia
  We're so proud of! *Hy, Zy, Hine* . . .
'St, there's Vespers! *Plena gratia,*
  Ave, Virgo! Gr-r-r—you swine!
                    Robert Browning.

CYNICAL ODE TO AN ULTRA-CYNICAL PUBLIC

YOU prefer a buffoon to a scholar,
    A harlequin to a teacher,
    A jester to a statesman,
An anonyma flaring on horseback
To a modest and spotless woman—
        Brute of a public!

You think that to sneer shows wisdom;
That a gibe outvalues a reason;
That slang, such as thieves delight in,
Is fit for the lips of the gentle,
And rather a grace than a blemish—
        Thick-headed public!

You think that if merit's exalted,
'Tis excellent sport to decry it,
And trail its good name in the gutter;
And that cynics, white-gloved and cravatted,
Are the cream and quintessence of all things—
        Ass of a public!

You think that success must be merit;
That honour and virtue and courage
Are all very well in their places,
But that money's a thousand times better—
Detestable, stupid, degraded
        Pig of a public!

Charles Mackay.

THE GREAT CRITICS

WHOM shall we praise?
    Let's praise the dead!
  In no men's ways
Their heads they raise,
  Nor strive for bread
With you or me.
So, do you see,
  We'll praise the dead!

A Satire Anthology

Let living men
   Dare but to claim
From tongue or pen
   Their meed of fame,
We'll cry them down,
Spoil their renown,
Deny their sense,
Wit, eloquence,
   Poetic fire,
   All they desire.
   Our say is said,
   Long live the dead!
              Charles Mackay.

THE LAUREATE

WHO would not be
   The Laureate bold,
   With his butt of sherry
To keep him merry,
And nothing to do but to pocket his gold?

'Tis I would be the Laureate bold!
When the days are hot, and the sun is strong,
I'd lounge in the gateway all the day long,
With her Majesty's footmen in crimson and gold.
I'd care not a pin for a waiting-lord;
But I'd lie on my back on the smooth greensward,
With a straw in my mouth, and an open vest,
And the cool wind blowing upon my breast,

And I'd vacantly stare at the clear blue sky,
And watch the clouds that are listless as I,
        Lazily, lazily!
And I'd pick the moss and the daisies white,
And chew their stalks with a nibbling bite;
And I'd let my fancies roam abroad
In search of a hint for a birthday ode,
        Crazily, crazily!

Oh, that would be the life for me,
With plenty to get and nothing to do,
But to deck a pet poodle with ribbons of blue,
And whistle all day to the Queen's cockatoo,
        Trance-somely, trance-somely!
Then the chambermaids, that clean the rooms,
Would come to the windows and rest on their brooms,
With their saucy caps and their crispéd hair,
And they'd toss their heads in the fragrant air,
And say to each other, "Just look down there,
At the nice young man, so tidy and small,
Who is paid for writing on nothing at all,
        Handsomely, handsomely!"

They would pelt me with matches and sweet pastilles,
And crumpled-up balls of the royal bills,
Giggling and laughing, and screaming with fun,
As they'd see me start, with a leap and a run,
From the broad of my back to the points of my toes,
When a pellet of paper hit my nose,
        Teasingly, sneezingly.

Then I'd fling them bunches of garden flowers,
And hyacinths plucked from the castle bowers;
And I'd challenge them all to come down to me,
And I'd kiss them all till they kisséd me,
    Laughingly, laughingly.

Oh, would not that be a merry life,
Apart from care and apart from strife,
With the Laureate's wine and the Laureate's pay,
And no deductions at quarter-day?
Oh, that would be the post for me!
With plenty to get and nothing to do,
But to deck a pet poodle with ribbons of blue,
And whistle a tune to the Queen's cockatoo,
And scribble of verses remarkably few,
And empty at evening a bottle or two,
    Quaffingly, quaffingly!

    'Tis I would be
      The Laureate bold,
    With my butt of sherry
    To keep me merry,
And nothing to do but to pocket my gold!
              William E. Aytoun.

WOMAN'S WILL

MEN, dying, make their wills, but wives
    Escape a work so sad;
  Why should they make what all their lives
The gentle dames have had?
              John Godfrey Saxe.

THE MOURNER À LA MODE

I SAW her last night at a party
    (The elegant party at Mead's),
And looking remarkably hearty
    For a widow so young in her weeds;
Yet I know she was suffering sorrow
    Too deep for the tongue to express—
Or why had she chosen to borrow
    So much from the language of dress?

Her shawl was as sable as night;
    And her gloves were as dark as her shawl;
And her jewels—that flashed in the light—
    Were black as a funeral pall;
Her robe had the hue of the rest,
    (How nicely it fitted her shape!)
And the grief that was heaving her breast
    Boiled over in billows of crape!

What tears of vicarious woe,
    That else might have sullied her face,
Were kindly permitted to flow
    In ripples of ebony lace
While even her fan, in its play,
    Had quite a lugubrious scope,
And seemed to be waving away
    The ghost of the angel of Hope!

Yet rich as the robes of a queen
  Was the sombre apparel she wore;
I'm certain I never had seen
  Such a sumptuous sorrow before;
And I couldn't help thinking the beauty,
  In mourning the loved and the lost,
Was doing her conjugal duty
  Altogether regardless of cost!

One surely would say a devotion
  Performed at so vast an expense
Betrayed an excess of emotion
  That was really something immense;
And yet, as I viewed, at my leisure,
  Those tokens of tender regard,
I thought: It is scarce without measure—
  The sorrow that goes by the yard!

Ah, grief is a curious passion;
  And yours—I am sorely afraid
The very next phase of the fashion
  Will find it beginning to fade;
Though dark are the shadows of grief,
  The morning will follow the night;
Half-tints will betoken relief,
  Till joy shall be symboled in white!

Ah, well! it were idle to quarrel
  With fashion, or aught she may do;
And so I conclude with a moral
  And metaphor—warranted new:

When measles come handsomely out,
  The patient is safest, they say;
And the sorrow is mildest, no doubt,
  That works in a similar way!

John Godfrey Saxe.

THERE IS NO GOD

"THERE is no God," the wicked saith,
  "And truly it's a blessing,
For what he might have done with us
  It's better only guessing."

"There is no God," a youngster thinks,
  "Or really, if there may be,
He surely didn't mean a man
  Always to be a baby."

"There is no God, or if there is,"
  The tradesman thinks, "'twere funny
If he should take it ill in me
  To make a little money."

"Whether there be," the rich man says
  "It matters very little,
For I and mine, thank somebody,
  Are not in want of victual."

Some others, also, to themselves,
  Who scarce so much as doubt it,
Think there is none, when they are well,
  And do not think about it.

But country folks who live beneath
    The shadow of the steeple;
The parson and the parson's wife,
    And mostly married people;

Youths green and happy in first love,
    So thankful for illusion;
And men caught out in what the world
    Calls guilt, in first confusion;

And almost every one when age,
    Disease, or sorrows strike him,
Inclines to think there is a God,
    Or something very like him.
                Arthur Hugh Clough.

THE LATEST DECALOGUE

THOU shalt have one God only; who
    Would be at the expense of two?
    No graven images may be
Worshipped, except the currency.
Swear not at all; for, for thy curse
Thine enemy is none the worse.
At church on Sunday to attend
Will serve to keep the world thy friend.
Honour thy parents; that is, all
From whom advancement may befall.
Thou shalt not kill; but need'st not strive
Officiously to keep alive.
Do not adultery commit;
Advantage rarely comes of it.

Thou shalt not steal; an empty feat,
When it's so lucrative to cheat.
Bear not false witness; let the lie
Have time on its own wings to fly.
Thou shalt not covet, but tradition
Approves all forms of competition.
Arthur Hugh Clough.

FROM "A FABLE FOR CRITICS"

"THERE is Bryant, as quiet, as cool, and as dignified
    As a smooth, silent iceberg, that never is ignified,
Save when by reflection 'tis kindled o' nights,
With a semblance of flame by the chill Northern Lights.
He may rank (Griswold says so) first bard of your nation
(There's no doubt that he stands in supreme ice-olation);
Your topmost Parnassus he may set his heel on,
But no warm applauses come, peal following peal on;
He's too smooth and too polished to hang any zeal on;
Unqualified merits, I'll grant, if you choose, he has 'em,
But he lacks the one merit of kindling enthusiasm;
If he stir you at all, it is just, on my soul,
Like being stirred up with the very North Pole.

. . . . . .

A Satire Anthology

"Mr. Quivis, or somebody quite as discerning,
Some scholar who's hourly expecting his learning,
Calls B. the American Wordsworth; but Wordsworth
May be rated at more than your whole tuneful herd's worth.
No, don't be absurd, he's an excellent Bryant;
But, my friends, you'll endanger the life of your client
By attempting to stretch him up into a giant.

. . . . . .

"There is Whittier, whose swelling and vehement heart
Strains the strait-breasted drab of the Quaker apart,
And reveals the live Man, still supreme and erect
Underneath the bemummying wrappers of sect;
There was ne'er a man born who had more of the swing
Of the true lyric bard, and all that kind of thing;
And his failures arise (though he seem not to know it)
From the very same cause that has made him a poet—
A fervour of mind which knows no separation
'Twixt simple excitement and pure inspiration,
As my pythoness erst sometimes erred from not knowing
If 'twere I, or mere wind, through her tripod was blowing;
Let his mind once get head in its favourite direction,
And the torrent of verse bursts the dams of reflection,

While, borne with the rush of the metre along,
The poet may chance to go right or go wrong,
Content with the whirl and delirium of song;
Then his grammar's not always correct, nor his rhymes,
And he's prone to repeat his own lyrics sometimes,
Not his best, though, for those are struck off at white-heats,
When the heart in his breast like a trip-hammer beats,
And can ne'er be repeated again any more
Than they could have been carefully plotted before:
Like old What's-his-name there at the battle of Hastings
(Who, however, gave more than mere rhythmical bastings),
Our Quaker leads off metaphorical fights
For reform and whatever they call human rights,
Both singing and striking in front of the war,
And hitting his foes with the mallet of Thor:
Anne haec, one exclaims, on beholding his knocks,
Vestis filii tui, O leather-clad Fox?
Can that be my son, in the battle's mid din,
Preaching brotherly love and then driving it in
To the brain of the tough old Goliath of sin,
With the smoothest of pebbles from Castaly's spring
Impressed on his hard moral sense with a sling?

.   .   .   .   .   .

"There is Hawthorne, with genius so shrinking and rare
That you hardly at first see the strength that is there;

A Satire Anthology

A frame so robust, with a nature so sweet,
So earnest, so graceful, so lithe and so fleet,
Is worth a descent from Olympus to meet;
'Tis as if a rough oak that for ages had stood,
With his gnarled bony branches like ribs of the wood,
Should bloom, after cycles of struggle and scathe,
With a single anemone trembly and rathe;
His strength is so tender, his wildness so meek,
That a suitable parallel sets one to seek—
He's a John Bunyan Fouqué, a Puritan Tieck;
When nature was shaping him, clay was not granted
For making so full-sized a man as she wanted,
So, to fill out her model, a little she spared
From some finer-grained stuff for a woman prepared,
And she could not have hit a more excellent plan
For making him fully and perfectly man.
The success of her scheme gave her so much delight,
That she tried it again, shortly after, in Dwight;
Only, while she was kneading and shaping the clay,
She sang to her work in her sweet, childish way,
And found, when she'd put the last touch to his soul,
That the music had somehow got mixed with the whole.

. . . . . .

"There's Holmes, who is matchless among you for wit—
A Leyden-jar always full-charged, from which flit
The electrical tingles of hit after hit;
In long poems 'tis painful sometimes, and invites
A thought of the way the new telegraph writes,

Which pricks down its little sharp sentences spitefully,
As if you got more than you'd title to rightfully,
And you find yourself hoping its wild Father Lightning
Would flame in for a second and give you a fright'ning.
He has perfect sway of what I call a sham metre,
But many admire it, the English pentameter,
And Campbell, I think, wrote most commonly worse,
With less nerve, swing, and fire in the same kind of verse,
Nor e'er achieved aught in't so worthy of praise
As the tribute of Holmes to the grand 'Marseillaise.'
You went crazy, last year, over Bulwer's 'New Timon';
Why, if B., to the day of his dying, should rhyme on,
Heaping verses on verses and tomes upon tomes,
He could ne'er reach the best point and vigour of Holmes.
His are just the fine hands, too, to weave you a lyric
Full of fancy, fun, feeling, or spiced with satyric
In a measure so kindly, you doubt if the toes
That are trodden upon are your own or your foes."

James Russell Lowell.

THE PIOUS EDITOR'S CREED

I DU believe in Freedom's cause,
    Ez fur away ez Paris is;
I love to see her stick her claws
    In them infarnal Pharisees;
It's wal enough agin a king
    To dror resolves an' triggers,
But libbaty's a kind o' thing
    That don't agree with niggers.

I du believe the people want
    A tax on teas an' coffees;
Thet nothin' aint extravygunt,
    Purvidin' I'm in office;
Fer I hev loved my country sence
    My eye-teeth fill'd their sockets,
An' Uncle Sam I reverence,
    Partic'larly his pockets.

I du believe in any plan
    O' levyin' the taxes,
Ez long, ez, like a lumberman,
    I get jest wut I axes:
I go free-trade thru thick an' thin,
    Because it kind o' rouses
The folks to vote—an' keeps us in
    Our quiet custom-houses.

I du believe it's wise an' good
  To send out furrin missions,
Thet is, on sartin understood
  An' orthydox conditions—
I mean nine thousan' dolls. per ann.,
  Nine thousan' more fer outfit,
An' me to recommend a man
  The place 'ould jest about fit.

I du believe in special ways
  O' prayin' an' convartin';
The bread comes back in many days,
  An' butter'd, tu, fer sartin;
I mean in preyin' till one busts
  On wut the party chooses,
An' in convartin' public trusts
  To very privit uses.

I du believe hard coin's the stuff
  Fer 'lectioneers to spout on;
The people's ollers soft enough
  To make hard money out on;
Dear Uncle Sam pervides fer his,
  An' gives a good-sized junk to all,
I don't care how hard money is,
  Ez long ez mine's paid punctooal.

I du believe with all my soul
  In the great Press's freedom,
To p'int the people to the goal,
  An' in the traces lead 'em.

Palsied the arm thet forges yokes
  At my fat contracts squintin',
An' wither'd be the nose thet pokes
  Inter the Gov'ment printin'!

I du believe that I should give
  Wut's his'n unto Cæsar,
For it's by him I move an' live,
  Frum him my bread an' cheese air;
I du believe thet all o' me
  Doth bear his souperscription—
Will, conscience, honour, honesty,
  An' things o' thet description.

I du believe in prayer an' praise
  To him thet hez the grantin'
O' jobs—in everythin' thet pays,
  But most of all in Cantin';
This doth my cup with marcies fill,
  This lays all thought o' sin to rest;
I don't believe in princerple,
  But, oh! I du in interest.

I du believe in bein' this
  Or thet, ez it may happen,
One way or t'other hendiest is
  To ketch the people nappin'.
It aint by princerples nor men
  My preudunt course is steadied;
I scent which pays the best, an' then
  Go into it bald-headed.

I du believe thet holdin' slaves
  Comes nat'ral tu a Presidunt,
Let 'lone the rowdedow it saves
  To hev a well-broke precedunt;
Fer any office, small or gret,
  I couldn't ax with no face,
Without I'd ben, thru dry an' wet,
  Th' unrizzest kind o' doughface.

I du believe wutever trash
  'Ill keep the people in blindness,
Thet we the Mexicuns can thrash
  Right inter brotherly kindness;
Thet bomb-shells, grape, an' powder, 'n' ball
  Air good-will's strongest magnets;
Thet peace, to make it stick at all,
  Must be druv in with bagnets.

In short, I firmly du believe
  In Humbug generally,
Fer it's a thing thet I perceive
  To hev a solid vally;
This heth my faithful shepherd ben,
  In pasture sweet heth led me,
An' this'll keep the people green,
  To feed ez they hev fed me.
              James Russell Lowell.

REVELRY IN INDIA

WE meet 'neath the sounding rafter,
    And the walls around are bare;
As they echo the peals of laughter,
    It seems that the dead are there;
But stand to your glasses steady,
    We drink to our comrades' eyes.
Quaff a cup to the dead already,
    And hurrah for the next that dies!

Not here are the goblets flowing,
    Not here is the vintage sweet;
'T is cold, as our hearts are growing,
    And dark as the doom we meet.
But stand to your glasses steady,
    And soon shall our pulses rise.
A cup to the dead already—
    Hurrah for the next hat dies!

Not a sigh for the lot that darkles,
    Not a tear for the friends that sink;
We'll fall, 'midst the wine-cup's sparkles,
    As mute as the wine we drink.
So stand to your glasses steady,
    'Tis in this that our respite lies.
One cup to the dead already—
    Hurrah for the next that dies!

Time was when we frowned at others;
  We thought we were wiser then;
Ha, ha! let those think of their mothers,
  Who hope to see them again.
No! stand to your glasses steady;
  The thoughtless are here the wise
A cup to the dead already—
  Hurrah for the next that dies!

There's many a hand that's shaking,
  There's many a cheek that's sunk;
But soon, though our hearts are breaking,
  They'll burn with the wine we've drunk.
So stand to your glasses steady,
  'Tis here the revival lies.
A cup to the dead already—
  Hurrah for the next that dies!

There's a mist on the glass congealing,
  'Tis the hurricane's fiery breath;
And thus does the warmth of feeling
  Turn ice in the grasp of death.
Ho! stand to your glasses steady;
  For a moment the vapour flies.
A cup to the dead already—
  Hurrah for the next that dies!

Who dreads to the dust returning?
  Who shrinks from the sable shore,
Where the high and haughty yearning
  Of the soul shall sing no more?

Ho! stand to your glasses steady;
  This world is a world of lies.
A cup to the dead already—
  Hurrah for the next that dies!

Cut off from the land that bore us,
  Betrayed by the land we find,
Where the brightest have gone before us,
  And the dullest remain behind—
Stand, stand to your glasses steady!
  'Tis all we have left to prize.
A cup to the dead already—
  And hurrah for the next that dies!
                    Bartholomew Dowling.

A FRAGMENT

HOW hardly doth the cold and careless world
    Requite the toil divine of genius-souls,
      Their wasting cares and agonizing throes!
I had a friend, a sweet and precious friend,
One passing rich in all the strange and rare,
And fearful gifts of song.
                On one great work,
A poem in twelve cantos, she had toiled
From early girlhood, e'en till she became
An olden maid.
            Worn with intensest thought,
She sunk at last—just at the "finis" sunk!—
And closed her eyes for ever! The soul-gem
Had fretted through its casket!
                          As I stood

Beside her tomb, I made a solemn vow
To take in charge that poor, lone orphan work,
And edit it!
        My publisher I sought,
A learned man and good. He took the work,
Read here and there a line, then laid it down,
And said, "It would not pay." I slowly turned,
And went my way with troubled brow, "but more
In sorrow than in anger."
Grace Greenwood.

NOTHING TO WEAR

MISS Flora McFlimsey, of Madison Square,
    Has made three separate journeys to Paris;
And her father assures me, each time she was there,
    That she and her friend Mrs. Harris
(Not the lady whose name is so famous in history,
But plain Mrs. H., without romance or mystery)
Spent six consecutive weeks without stopping,
In onè continuous round of shopping;
Shopping alone, and shopping together,
At all hours of the day and in all sorts of weather;
For all manner of things that a woman can put
On the crown of her head or the sole of her foot,
Or wrap round her shoulders, or fit round her waist,
Or that can be sewed on, or pinned on, or laced,
Or tied on with a string, or stitched on with a bow,
In front or behind, above or below;

For bonnets, mantillas, capes, collars, and shawls;
Dresses for breakfasts, and dinners, and balls;
Dresses to sit in, and stand in, and walk in,
Dresses to dance in, and flirt in, and talk in;
Dresses in which to do nothing at all;
Dresses for winter, spring, summer, and fall—
All of them different in colour and pattern,
Silk, muslin, and lace, crape, velvet, and satin,
Brocade, and broadcloth, and other material
Quite as expensive and much more ethereal:
In short, for all things that could ever be thought of,
Or milliner, modiste, or tradesman be bought of,
   From ten-thousand-francs robes to twenty-sous frills;
In all quarters of Paris, and to every store,
While McFlimsey in vain stormed, scolded, and swore,
   They footed the streets, and he footed the bills.

The last trip, their goods shipped by the steamer *Argo*,
Formed, McFlimsey declares, the bulk of her cargo,
Not to mention a quantity kept from the rest,
Sufficient to fill the largest-sized chest,
Which did not appear on the ship's manifest,
But for which the ladies themselves manifested
Such particular interest that they invested
Their own proper persons in layers and rows
Of muslins, embroideries, worked underclothes,
Gloves, handkerchiefs, scarfs, and such trifles as those;

Then, wrapped in great shawls, like Circassian beauties,
Gave *good-by* to the ship, and *go-by* to the duties.
Her relations at home all marvelled, no doubt,
Miss Flora had grown so enormously stout
　For an actual belle and a possible bride;
But the miracle ceased when she turned inside out,
　And the truth came to light, and the dry-goods beside,
Which, in spite of collector and custom-house sentry,
Had entered the port without any entry.
And yet, though scarce three months have passed since the day
This merchandise went, on twelve carts, up Broadway,
This same Miss McFlimsey, of Madison Square,
The last time we met, was in utter despair,
Because she had nothing whatever to wear!

NOTHING TO WEAR! Now, as this is a true ditty,
　I do not assert—this you know is between us—
That she's in a state of absolute nudity,
　Like Powers's Greek Slave, or the Medici Venus,
But I do mean to say I have heard her declare,
　When at the same moment she had on a dress
　Which cost five hundred dollars, and not a cent less,
　And jewelry worth ten times more, I should guess,
That she had not a thing in the wide world to wear!
I should mention just here, that out of Miss Flora's
Two hundred and fifty or sixty adorers,

A Satire Anthology

I had just been selected as he who should throw all
The rest in the shade, by the gracious bestowal
On myself, after twenty or thirty rejections,
Of those fossil remains which she called her "affections,"
And that rather decayed but well-known work of art,
Which Miss Flora persisted in styling "her heart."
So we were engaged. Our troth had been plighted
  Not by moonbeam or starbeam, by fountain or grove,
But in a front parlour, most brilliantly lighted,
  Beneath the gas-fixtures we whispered our love—
Without any romance, or raptures, or sighs,
Without any tears in Miss Flora's blue eyes,
Or blushes, or transports, or such silly actions;
It was one of the quietest business transactions,
With a very small sprinkling of sentiment, if any,
And a very large diamond imported by Tiffany.
On her virginal lips while I printed a kiss,
She exclaimed, as a sort of parenthesis,
And by way of putting me quite at my ease,
"You know, I'm to polka as much as I please,
And flirt when I like—now stop—don't you speak—
And you must not come here more than twice in the week,
Or talk to me either at party or ball,
But a'ways be ready to come when I call:
So don't prose to me about duty and stuff—
If we don't break this off, there will be time enough
For that sort of thing; but the bargain must be,
That as long as I choose I am perfectly free:

[216]

For this is a sort of engagement, you see,
Which is binding on you, but not binding on me."

Well, having thus wooed Miss McFlimsey, and
    gained her,
With the silks, crinolines, and hoops that contained
    her,
I had, as I thought, a contingent remainder
At least in the property, and the best right
To appear as its escort by day and by night;
And it being the week of the Stuckups' grand
    ball—
  Their cards had been out for a fortnight or so,
  And set all the Avenue on the tiptoe—
I considered it only my duty to call
  And see if Miss Flora intended to go.
I found her—as ladies are apt to be found
When the time intervening between the first sound
Of the bell and the visitor's entry is shorter
Than usual—I found—I won't say I caught—her
Intent on the pier-glass, undoubtedly meaning
To see if perhaps it didn't need cleaning.
She turned as I entered. "Why, Harry, you sinner,
I thought that you went to the Flashers' to dinner!"
"So I did," I replied; "but the dinner is swallowed,
  And digested, I trust; for 'tis now nine or more:
So being relieved from that duty, I followed
  Inclination, which led me, you see, to your
    door.
And now will your Ladyship so condescend
As just to inform me if you intend
Your beauty and graces and presence to lend

(All of which, when I own, I hope no one will borrow)
To the Stuckups, whose party, you know, is tomorrow?"
The fair Flora looked up with a pitiful air,
And answered quite promptly, "Why, Harry, *mon cher*,
I should like above all things to go with you there;
But really and truly, I've nothing to wear."

"Nothing to wear? Go just as you are:
Wear the dress you have on, and you'll be by far,
I engage, the most bright and particular star
   On the Stuckup horizon." I stopped, for her eye,
Notwithstanding this delicate onset of flattery,
Opened on me at once a most terrible battery
   Of scorn and amazement. She made no reply,
But gave a slight turn to the end of her nose
   (That pure Grecian feature), as much as to say,
"How absurd that any sane man should suppose
That a lady would go to a ball in the clothes,
   No matter how fine, that she wears every day!"
So I ventured again, "Wear your crimson brocade."
(Second turn-up of nose). "That's too dark by a shade."
"Your blue silk." "That's too heavy." "Your pink—" "That's too light."
"Wear tulle over satin." "I can't endure white."
"Your rose-coloured, then, the best of the batch."
"I haven't a thread of point lace to match."

"Your brown moire-antique." "Yes, and look
    like a Quaker."
"The pearl-coloured—" "I would, but that
    plaguy dressmaker
Has had it a week." "Then that exquisite lilac,
In which you would melt the heart of a Shylock."
(Here the nose took again the same elevation):
"I wouldn't wear that for the whole of creation."
"Why not? It's my fancy, there's nothing could strike it
  As more *comme il faut*." "Yes, but, dear me, that lean
Sophronia Stuckup has got one just like it,
  And I won't appear dressed like a chit of sixteen."
"Then that splendid purple, that sweet mazarine,
That superb *point d'aiguille*, that imperial green,
That zephyr-like tarlatan, that rich grenadine—"
  "Not one of all which is fit to be seen,"
Said the lady, becoming excited and flushed.
"Then wear," I exclaimed, in a tone which quite crushed
Opposition, "that gorgeous toilette which you sported
  In Paris last spring, at the grand presentation,
  When you quite turned the head of the head of the nation;
And by all the grand court were so very much courted."
The end of the nose was portentously tipped up,
  And both the bright eyes shot forth indignation,
  As she burst upon me with the fierce exclamation,
"I have worn it three times at the least calculation,

A Satire Anthology

And that and most of my dresses are ripped up!"
Here I *ripped out* something, perhaps rather rash—
  Quite innocent, though; but, to use an expression
More striking than classic, it "settled my hash,"
  And proved very soon the last act of our session.
"Fiddlesticks, is it, sir? I wonder the ceiling
Doesn't fall down and crush you! Oh, you men have no feeling.
You selfish, unnatural, illiberal creatures,
Who set yourselves up as patterns and preachers,
Your silly pretence—why, what a mere guess it is!
Pray, what do you know of a woman's necessities?
I have told you and shown you I've nothing to wear,
And it's perfectly plain you not only don't care,
But you do not believe me" (here the nose went still higher):
"I suppose, if you dared, you would call me a liar.
Our engagement is ended, sir—yes, on the spot;
You're a brute, and a monster, and—I don't know what."
I mildly suggested the words Hottentot,
Pickpocket, and cannibal, Tartar, and thief,
As gentle expletives which might give relief;
But this only proved as a spark to the powder,
And the storm I had raised came faster and louder;
It blew, and it rained, thundered, lightened, and hailed
Interjections, verbs, pronouns, till language quite failed

To express the abusive, and then its arrears
Were brought up all at once by a torrent of tears;
And my last faint, despairing attempt at an obs-
Ervation was lost in a tempest of sobs.

Well, I felt for the lady, and felt for my hat, too,
Improvised on the crown of the latter a tattoo,
In lieu of expressing the feelings which lay
Quite too deep for words, as Wordsworth would say;
Then, without going through the form of a bow,
Found myself in the entry—I hardly knew how—
On doorstep and sidewalk, past lamp-post and square,
At home and up-stairs, in my own easy chair;
Poked my feet into slippers, my fire into blaze,
  And said to myself, as I lit my cigar:
  Supposing a man had the wealth of the Czar
Of the Russias to boot, for the rest of his days,
On the whole, do you think he would have much to spare
If he married a woman with nothing to wear?
William Allen Butler.

A REVIEW

THE INN ALBUM, BY ROBERT BROWNING.

WHAT'S this, a book? 16mo. Osgood's page,
  Fair, clear, Olympian-typed, and save a scant
O' the margin, stiff i' the hurried binding, good!

A Satire Anthology

Intituled how?—"The Inn Album, Robert Brown-
    ing, Author."
Why should he not say, as well,
The Hotel Register?—cis-Atlantic term!
Nay, an he should, the action might purvey
To lower comprehensions: so not he!
Reflect, 'tis Browning! he neglects, prepense,
All forms of form: what *he* gives must we take,
Sweet, bitter, sour, absinthean, adipose,
Conglomerate, jellied, potted, salt, or dried,
As the mood holds him; ours is not to choose!
Well (here huge sighs be heard), commending us
To Heaven's high mercy, let us read.

                              Three hours:
The end is reached; but who begins review,
Forgetful o' beginning, with the end?
Turn back!—why, here's a line supplies us with
Curt comment on the whole, though travesty—
"Hail, calm obliquity, lugubrious plot! . . ."
Yea, since obliquity the straight path is,
And Passion worships as her patron saint
The Holy Vitus, and from Language fall
The rusty chains of rhythm and harmony,
Why not exclaim, "Hail, sham obliquity!"
"Too hard," you murmur, sweet, submissive minds?
But take a bite o' the original pie! Set teeth,
'Ware cherry-stones, and if a herring-spine
Stick crosswise i' the throat, go gulp, shed tears,
But blame us not! So runs the opening:

   .   .   .   .   .   .

A Satire Anthology

This bard's a Browning! there's no doubt of that;
But, ah, ye gods, *the sense!* Are we so sure
If sense be sense unto our common-sense,
Low sense to higher, high to low, no sense
All sense to those, all sense no sense to these?
That's where your poet tells! and you've no right
(Insensate sense with sensuous thought being mixed)
To ask analysis! How can else review,
Save in the dialect of his verse, be writ?
So write we: (would we might foresee the end!)
So has he taught us, i' "The Ring and the
    Book,"
De gustibus, concerning taste, *non est*
There's no—disputing, *disputandum* (Ha!
'Tis not so difficult)—and we submit.

   .   .   .   .   .   .

                       This Album-book—
"Hail, sham obliquity, lugubrious plot!"—
Is well-nigh read; you end the tangle, smash!
Here's Browning's recipe: take heaps o' hate,
Take boundless love, hydraulic-pressed, in bales,
Distilments keen of baseness and of pride,
And innocence and cunning; mix 'em well,
And put a body round 'em! Add the more
O' this, or that, you have another—stay!
The sex don't count; make female of the male,
Male female, all the better; let them meet,
Talk, love, hate, cross, till satisfied; then, kill!
So here: lord, finding situation tough
(Between two fires, hate and a horsewhip-threat),
Writes i' the Album, goes without and waits.

A Satire Anthology

Superb One, having read, takes hand of snob,
Accepts his love till death; then lord comes back.
What did he write? "Refinement every inch,
From brow to boot-end"—'twas a threat to tell
The country curate of his wife's disgrace—
He, the disgracer! Snob gets wild at that,
Screams, jumps, and clutches . . .

All at once we see
One character dead, but how, we don't quite know.
Then she, Superb One, writes in Album, dies
By force of will (no hint of instrument!),
Leaving the snob alone and much surprised.
Cousin is heard without; but ere the door
Opens, the story closes. Only this remains,
The last conundrum, hardly guessable
By the unbrowninged mind. Since what it means,
If aught the meaning, means some other thing,
And that thing something else, but this not that,
Nor that the other; we adopt the lines
As most expressing what we fail express,
Our solemn verdict, handkerchief and all,
Upon the book.

. . . . . .

The meaning, ask you, O ingenuous soul?
Why, were there such for you, what then were left
To puzzle brain with, pump conjecture dry,
And prove you little where the poet's great?
Great must he be, you therefore little. Go!
The curtain falls, the candles are snuffed out:
End, damned obliquity, lugubrious plot!
Bayard Taylor.

THE POSITIVISTS

LIFE and the Universe show spontaneity:
  Down with ridiculous notions of Deity!
    Churches and creeds are all lost in the mists;
  Truth must be sought with the Positivists.

Wise are their teachers beyond all comparison,
Comte, Huxley, Tyndall, Mill, Morley, and Harrison.
  Who will adventure to enter the lists
  With such a squadron of Positivists?

Social arrangements are awful miscarriages;
Cause of all crime is our system of marriages.
  Poets with sonnets, and lovers with trysts,
  Kindle the ire of the Positivists.

Husbands and wives should be all one community,
Exquisite freedom with absolute unity.
  Wedding-rings worse are than manacled wrists—
  Such is the creed of the Positivists.

There was an ape in the days that were earlier;
Centuries passed, and his hair became curlier;
  Centuries more gave a thumb to his wrist—
  Then he was Man, and a Positivist.

If you are pious (mild form of insanity),
Bow down and worship the mass of humanity.
  Other religions are buried in mists;
  We're our own Gods, say the Positivists.
Mortimer Collins.

SKY-MAKING

TO PROFESSOR TYNDALL

JUST take a trifling handful, O philosopher,
  Of magic matter, give it a slight toss over
    The ambient ether, and I don't see why
    You shouldn't make a sky.

O hours Utopian which we may anticipate!
Thick London fog how easy 'tis to dissipate,
  And make the most pea-soupy day as clear
  As Bass's brightest beer!

Poet-professor! now my brain thou kindlest;
I am become a most determined Tyndallist.
  If it is known a fellow can make skies,
  Why not make bright blue eyes?

This to deny, the folly of a dunce it is;
Surely a girl as easy as a sunset is.
  If you can make a halo or eclipse,
  Why not two laughing lips?

The creed of Archimedes, erst of Sicily,
And of D'Israeli . . . *forti nil difficile*,
  Is likewise mine. Pygmalion was a fool
    Who should have gone to school.

Why should an author scribble rhymes or articles?
Bring me a dozen tiny Tyndall particles;
  Therefrom I'll coin a dinner, Nash's wine,
    And a nice girl to dine.
                Mortimer Collins.

MY LORD TOMNODDY

MY Lord Tomnoddy's the son of an earl;
  His hair is straight, but his whiskers curl;
  His lordship's forehead is far from wide,
But there's plenty of room for the brains inside.
He writes his name with indifferent ease;
He's rather uncertain about the "d's";
But what does it matter, if three or one,
To the Earl of Fitzdotterel's eldest son?

My Lord Tomnoddy to college went;
Much time he lost, much money he spent;
Rules, and windows, and heads, he broke;
Authorities wink'd—young men will joke!
He never peep'd inside of a book;
In two years' time a degree he took,
And the newspapers vaunted the honours won
By the Earl of Fitzdotterel's eldest son.

My Lord Tomnoddy came out in the world;
Waists were tighten'd and ringlets curl'd;
Virgins languish'd, and matrons smil'd.
'Tis true, his lordship is rather wild;
In very queer places he spends his life;
There's talk of some children by nobody's wife;
But we mustn't look close into what is done
By the Earl of Fitzdotterel's eldest son.

My Lord Tomnoddy must settle down—
There's a vacant seat in the family town!
('Tis time he should sow his eccentric oats)—
He hasn't the wit to apply for votes:
He cannot e'en learn his election speech;
Three phrases he speaks, a mistake in each,
And then breaks down; but the borough is won
For the Earl of Fitzdotterel's eldest son.

My Lord Tomnoddy prefers the Guards
(The House is a bore), so, it's on the cards!
My lord's a lieutenant at twenty-three;
A captain at twenty-six is he;
He never drew sword, except on drill;
The tricks of parade he has learnt but ill;
A full-blown colonel at thirty-one
Is the Earl of Fitzdotterel's eldest son!

My Lord Tomnoddy is thirty-four;
The earl can last but a few years more;
My Lord in the Peers will take his place;
Her Majesty's councils his words will grace.

Office he'll hold, and patronage sway;
Fortunes and lives he will vote away.
And what are his qualifications?—ONE!
He's the Earl of Fitzdotterel's eldest son.
Robert Barnabas Brough.

HIDING THE SKELETON

AT dinner she is hostess, I am host.
    Went the feast ever cheerfuller? She keeps
  The topic over intellectual deeps
In buoyancy afloat. They see no ghost.
With sparkling surface-eyes we ply the ball:
  It is in truth a most contagious game;
  HIDING THE SKELETON shall be its name.
Such play as this the devils might appal!
But here's the greater wonder, in that we,
  Enamour'd of our acting and our wits,
  Admire each other like true hypocrites.
Warm-lighted glances, Love's ephemeræ,
Shoot gayly o'er the dishes and the wine.
  We waken envy of our happy lot.
  Fast, sweet, and golden shows our marriage knot.
Dear guests, you now have seen Love's corpse-light shine!
George Meredith.

MIDGES

SHE is talking æsthetics, the dear, clever teacher!
    Upon man, and his functions, she speaks with a smile;
Her ideas are divine upon art, upon nature,
    The sublime, the heroic, and Mr. Carlyle.

I no more am found worthy to join in the talk, now,
    So I follow with my surreptitious cigar;
While she leads our poetical friend up the walk, now,
    Who quotes Wordsworth, and praises her "Thoughts on a Star."

Meanwhile, there is dancing in yonder green bower
    A swarm of young midges! They dance high and low;
'Tis a sweet little species that lives but one hour,
    And the eldest was born half an hour ago.

One impulsive young midge I hear ardently pouring
    In the ear of a shy little wanton in gauze,
His eternal devotion, his ceaseless adoring,
    Which shall last till the universe breaks from its laws.

His passion is not, he declares, the mere fever
    Of a rapturous moment: it knows no control;
It will burn in his breast through existence for ever,
    Immutably fixed in the deeps of his soul!

She wavers, she flutters: male midges are fickle;
  Dare she trust him her future? she asks with a sigh.
He implores, and a tear is beginning to trickle.
  She is weak: they embrace, and . . . the lovers pass by.

While they pass me, down here on a rose-leaf has lighted
  A pale midge, his feelers all drooping and torn;
His existence is withered; its future is blighted;
  His hopes are betrayed, and his breast is forlorn.

By the midge his heart trusted his heart is deceived; now
  In the virtue of midges no more he believes;
From love in its falsehood, once wildly believed, now
  He will bury his desolate life in the leaves.

His friends would console him—the noblest and sagest
  Of midges have held that a midge lives again;
In eternity, say they, the strife thou now wagest
  With sorrow, shall cease; but their words were in vain!

Can eternity bring back the seconds now wasted
  In hopeless desire? or restore to his breast
The belief he has lost, with the bliss he once tasted,
  Embracing the midge that his being held best?

His friends would console him: life yet is before him;
  Many hundred long seconds he still has to live;
In the State yet a mighty career spreads before him;
  Let him seek in the great world of action to
      strive!

There's Fame! there's Ambition! and, grander than
    either,
  There is Freedom! the progress and march of the
      race!
But to Freedom his breast beats no longer, and
    neither
  Ambition nor action her loss can replace.

If the time had been spent in acquiring æsthetics
  I have squandered in learning this language of
      midges,
There might, for my friend in her peripatetics,
  Have been now two asses to help o'er the bridges.

As it is, I'll report her the whole conversation.
  It would have been longer, but, somehow or other
(In the midst of that misanthrope's long lamenta-
    tion),
  A midge in my right eye became a young mother.

Since my friend is so clever, I'll ask her to tell me
  Why the least living thing (a mere midge in the
      egg)
Can make a man's tears flow, as now it befell me.
  Oh, you dear, clever woman, explain it, I beg!
                              Robert Bulwer Lytton.

THE SCHOOLMASTER ABROAD WITH HIS SON

O WHAT harper could worthily harp it,
  Mine Edward! this wide-stretching wold
  (Look out wold) with its wonderful carpet
Of emerald, purple, and gold!
Look well at it—also look sharp, it
  Is getting so cold.

The purple is heather (erica);
  The yellow, gorse—call'd sometimes "whin."
Cruel boys on its prickles might spike a
  Green beetle as if on a pin.
You may roll in it, if you would like a
  Few holes in your skin.

You wouldn't? Then think of how kind you
  Should be to the insects who crave
Your compassion—and then, look behind you
  At yon barley-ears! Don't they look brave
As they undulate (undulate, mind you,
  From unda, a wave).

The noise of those sheep-bells, how faint it
  Sounds here (on account of our height)!
And this hillock itself—who could paint it,
  With its changes of shadow and light?
Is it not—(never, Eddy, say "Ain't it")—
  A marvellous sight?

Then yon desolate, eerie morasses,
  The haunts of the snipe and the hern—
(I shall question the two upper classes
  On aquatiles, when we return)—
Why, I see on them absolute masses
  Of filix or fern.

How it interests e'en a beginner
  (Or tyro) like dear little Ned!
Is he listening? As I am a sinner,
  He's asleep—he is wagging his head.
Wake up! I'll go home to my dinner,
  And you to your bed.

The boundless, ineffable prairie;
  The splendour of mountain and lake,
With their hues that seem ever to vary;
  The mighty pine-forests which shake
In the wind, and in which the unwary
  May tread on a snake;

And this wold with its heathery garment
  Are themes undeniably great.
But—although there is not any harm in't—
  It's perhaps little good to dilate
On their charms to a dull little varmint
  Of seven or eight.
Charles Stuart Calverley.

OF PROPRIETY

STUDY first Propriety, for she is indeed the pole-star
    Which shall guide the artless maiden through the mazes of Vanity Fair;
Nay, she is the golden chain which holdeth together Society,
The lamp by whose light young Psyche shall approach unblamed her Eros.
Verily, Truth is as Eve, which was ashamed, being naked;
Wherefore doth Propriety dress her with the fair foliage of artifice;
And when she is drest, behold, she knoweth not herself again!
I walked in the forest, and above me stood the yew—
Stood like a slumbering giant, shrouded in impenetrable shade;
Then I pass'd into the citizen's garden, and marked a tree clipt into shape
(The giant's locks had been shorn by the Delilah-shears of Decorum),
And I said, "Surely Nature is goodly; but how much goodlier is Art!"
I heard the wild notes of the lark floating far over the blue sky,
And my foolish heart went after him, and, lo! I blessed him as he rose.

Foolish! for far better is the trained boudoir bullfinch,
Which pipeth the semblance of a tune, and mechanically draweth up the water;
And the reinless steed of the desert, though his neck be clothed with thunder,
Must yield to him that danceth and "moveth in the circles" at Astley's.
For verily, O my daughter, the world is a masquerade,
And God made thee one thing, that thou mightest make thyself another.
A maiden's heart is as champagne, ever aspiring and struggling upward,
And it needed that its motions be checked by the silvered cork of Propriety;
He that can afford the price, his be the precious treasure;
Let him drink deeply of its sweetness, nor grumble if it tasteth of the cork.

Charles Stuart Calverley.

PEACE: *A Study*

HE stood, a worn-out City clerk—
   Who'd toil'd, and seen no holiday,
   For forty years from dawn to dark—
Alone beside Caermarthen Bay.

He felt the salt spray on his lips;
   Heard children's voices on the sands;

Up the sun's path he saw the ships
  Sail on and on to other lands;

And laugh'd aloud. Each sight and sound
  To him was joy too deep for tears;
He sat him on the beach, and bound
  A blue bandana round his ears;

And thought how, posted near his door,
  His own green door on Camden Hill,
Two bands at least, most likely more,
  Were mingling at their own sweet will

Verdi with Vance. And at the thought
  He laugh'd again, and softly drew
That *Morning Herald* that he'd bought
  Forth from his breast, and read it through.
                              Charles Stuart Calverley.

ALL-SAINTS

IN a church which is furnish'd with mullion and gable,
  With altar and reredos, with gargoyle and groin,
The penitents' dresses are sealskin and sable,
  The odour of sanctity's eau-de-Cologne.

But only could Lucifer, flying from Hades,
  Gaze down on this crowd with its panniers and paints,
He would say, as he look'd at the lords and the ladies,
  "Oh, where is All-Sinners', if this is All-Saints'?"
                                    Edmund Yates.

FAME'S PENNY TRUMPET

Affectionately dedicated to all "original researchers" who pant for "endowment."

BLOW, blow your trumpets till they crack,
    Ye little men of little souls!
  And bid them huddle at your back,
Gold-sucking leeches, shoals on shoals!

Fill all the air with hungry wails—
  "Reward us, ere we think or write!
Without your gold mere knowledge fails
  To sate the swinish appetite!"

And, where great Plato paced serene,
  Or Newton paused with wistful eye,
Rush to the chase with hoofs unclean,
  And Babel-clamour of the sky!

Be yours the pay, be theirs the praise;
  We will not rob them of their due,
Nor vex the ghosts of other days
  By naming them along with you.

They sought and found undying fame;
    They toiled not for reward nor thanks;
Their cheeks are hot with honest shame
    For you, the modern mountebanks,

Who preach of justice, plead with tears
    That love and mercy should abound,
While marking with complacent ears
    The moaning of some tortured hound;

Who prate of wisdom—nay, forbear,
    Lest Wisdom turn on you in wrath,
Trampling, with heel that will not spare,
    The vermin that beset her path!

Go, throng each other's drawing-rooms,
    Ye idols of a petty clique;
Strut your brief hour in borrowed plumes,
    And make your penny trumpets squeak;

Deck your dull talk with pilfered shreds
    Of learning from a nobler time,
And oil each other's little heads
    With mutual flattery's golden slime;

And when the topmost height ye gain,
    And stand in glory's ether clear,
And grasp the prize of all your pain—
    So many hundred pounds a year—

Then let Fame's banner be unfurled!
    Sing pæans for a victory won!
Ye tapers, that would light the world,
    And cast a shadow on the Sun;

Who still shall pour his rays sublime,
    One crystal flood, from east to west,
When ye have burned your little time,
    And feebly flickered into rest!
Lewis Carroll.

THE DIAMOND WEDDING

O LOVE! Love! Love! What times were those,
    Long ere the age of belles and beaux,
    And Brussels lace and silken hose,
When, in the green Arcadian close,
You married Psyche under the rose,
    With only the grass for bedding!
Heart to heart, and hand to hand,
You followed Nature's sweet command,
Roaming lovingly through the land,
    Nor sighed for a Diamond Wedding.

So have we read, in classic Ovid,
How Hero watched for her belovéd,
    Impassioned youth, Leander.
She was the fairest of the fair,
And wrapt him round with her golden hair,
Whenever he landed cold and bare,
With nothing to eat and nothing to wear,
    And wetter than any gander;

For Love was Love, and better than money;
The slyer the theft, the sweeter the honey;
And kissing was clover, all the world over,
  Wherever Cupid might wander.

So thousands of years have come and gone,
And still the moon is shining on,
  Still Hymen's torch is lighted;
And hitherto, in this land of the West,
Most couples in love have thought it best
  To follow the ancient way of the rest,
  And quietly get united.

But now, True Love, you're growing old—
Bought and sold, with silver and gold,
  Like a house, or a horse and carriage!
      Midnight talks,
      Moonlight walks,
The glance of the eye and sweetheart sigh,
The shadowy haunts, with no one by,
  I do not wish to disparage,
      But every kiss
      Has a price for its bliss,
  In the modern code of marriage;
      And the compact sweet
      Is not complete
Till the high contracting parties meet
  Before the altar of Mammon;
And the bride must be led to a silver bower,
Where pearls and rubies fall in a shower
  That would frighten Jupiter Ammon!

I need not tell
How it befell,
(Since Jenkins has told the story
Over and over and over again,
In a style I cannot hope to attain,
  And covered himself with glory!)
How it befell, one summer's day,
The king of the Cubans strolled this way—
King January's his name, they say—
And fell in love with the Princess May,
  The reigning belle of Manhattan;
Nor how he began to smirk and sue,
And dress as lovers who come to woo,
Or as Max Maretzek and Jullien do,
When they sit full-bloomed in the ladies' view,
  And flourish the wondrous baton.

He wasn't one of your Polish nobles,
Whose presence their country somehow troubles,
  And so our cities receive them;
Nor one of your make-believe Spanish grandees,
Who ply our daughters with lies and candies,
  Until the poor girls believe them.
No, he was no such charlatan—
Count de Hoboken Flash-in-the-pan,
  Full of gasconade and bravado—
But a regular, rich Don Rataplan
  Santa Claus de la Muscovado
  Señor Grandissimo Bastinado.
His was the rental of half Havana,
And all Matanzas; and Santa Anna,

Rich as he was, could hardly hold
A candle to light the mines of gold
Our Cuban owned, choke-full of diggers;
And broad plantations, that, in round figures,
Were stocked with at least five thousand niggers!

"Gather ye rosebuds while ye may!"
The señor swore to carry the day,
To capture the beautiful Princess May,
   With his battery of treasure;
Velvet and lace she should not lack;
Tiffany, Haughwout, Ball & Black,
Genin and Stewart his suit should back,
   And come and go at her pleasure;
Jet and lava, silver and gold,
Garnets, emeralds rare to behold,
Diamonds, sapphires, wealth untold,
All were hers, to have and to hold—
   Enough to fill a peck measure!

He didn't bring all his forces on
At once, but, like a crafty old Don,
Who many a heart had fought and won,
   Kept bidding a little higher;
And every time he made his bid,
And what she said, and all they did,
      'Twas written down
      For the good of the town,
By Jeems, of *The Daily Flyer*.

A coach and horses, you'd think, would buy
For the Don an easy victory;
   But slowly our Princess yielded.

A diamond necklace caught her eye,
But a wreath of pearls first made her sigh.
She knew the worth of each maiden glance,
And, like young colts that curvet and prance,
She led the Don a deuce of a dance,
 In spite of the wealth he wielded.
She stood such a fire of silks and laces,
Jewels and gold dressing-cases,
And ruby brooches, and jets and pearls,
That every one of her dainty curls
Brought the price of a hundred common girls;
 Folks thought the lass demented!
But at last a wonderful diamond ring,
An infant Kohinoor, did the thing,
And, sighing with love, or something the same,
  (What's in a name?)
 The Princess May consented.

 Ring! ring the bells, and bring
 The people to see the marrying!
Let the gaunt and hungry and ragged poor
Throng round the great cathedral door,
To wonder what all the hubbub's for,
 And sometimes stupidly wonder
At so much sunshine and brightness which
Fall from the church upon the rich,
 While the poor get all the thunder.

 Ring, ring, merry bells, ring!
  O fortunate few,
  With letters blue,
 Good for a seat and a nearer view!

A Satire Anthology

Fortunate few, whom I dare not name;
Dilettanti! Crême de la crême!
We commoners stood by the street façade,
And caught a glimpse of the cavalcade.
      We saw the bride
         In diamond pride
With jewelled maidens to guard her side—
Six lustrous maidens in tarlatan.
She led the van of the caravan;
  Close behind her, her mother
(Dressed in gorgeous *moire antique*
That told as plainly as words could speak,
  She was more antique than the other)
  Leaned on the arm of Don Rataplan
Santa Claus de la Muscovado
Señor Grandissimo Bastinado.
  Happy mortal! fortunate man!
And Marquis of El Dorado!

In they swept, all riches and grace,
Silks and satins, jewels and lace;
In they swept from the dazzled sun,
And soon in the church the deed was done.
Three prelates stood on the chancel high:
A knot that gold and silver can buy,
Gold and silver may yet untie,
  Unless it is tightly fastened;
What's worth doing at all's worth doing well,
And the sale of a young Manhattan belle
  Is not to be pushed or hastened;
So two Very Reverends graced the scene,
And the tall Archbishop stood between,
  By prayer and fasting chastened.

A Satire Anthology

The Pope himself would have come from Rome,
But Garibaldi kept him at home.
Haply these robed prelates thought
Their words were the power that tied the knot;
But another power that love-knot tied,
And I saw the chain round the neck of the bride—
A glistening, priceless, marvellous chain,
Coiled with diamonds again and again,
　As befits a diamond wedding;
Yet still 'twas a chain, and I thought she knew it,
And half-way longed for the will to undo it,
　By the secret tears she was shedding.

But isn't it odd to think, whenever
We all go through that terrible River,
Whose sluggish tide alone can sever
(The Archbishop says) the Church decree,
By floating one in to Eternity,
And leaving the other alive as ever,
As each wades through that ghastly stream,
The satins that rustle and gems that gleam,
Will grow pale and heavy, and sink away
To the noisome river's bottom-clay!
Then the costly bride and her maidens six
Will shiver upon the bank of the Styx,
Quite as helpless as they were born—
Naked souls, and very forlorn.
The Princess, then, must shift for herself,
And lay her royalty on the shelf;
She, and the beautiful empress yonder,
Whose robes are now the wide world's wonder

And even ourselves, and our dear little wives,
Who calico wear each morn of their lives,
And the sewing-girls, and *les chiffonniers*,
In rags and hunger—a gaunt array—
And all the grooms of the caravan—
Aye, even the great Don Rataplan
Santa Claus de la Muscovado
Señor Grandissimo Bastinado—
That gold-encrusted, fortunate man—
All will land in naked equality;
The lord of a ribboned principality
  Will mourn the loss of his *cordon*.
Nothing to eat and nothing to wear
Will certainly be the fashion there!
Ten to one, and I'll go it alone,
Those most used to a rag and bone,
Though here on earth they labour and groan,
Will stand it best, as they wade abreast
  To the other side of Jordan.
          Edmund Clarence Stedman.

TRUE TO POLL

I'LL sing you a song, not very long,
  But the story somewhat new
  Of William Kidd, who, whatever he did,
To his Poll was always true.
He sailed away in a galliant ship
  From the port of old Bris*tol*,
      And the last words he uttered,
      As his hankercher he fluttered,
Were, "My heart is true to Poll."

His heart was true to Poll,
His heart was true to Poll.
   It's no matter what you do
   If your heart be only true:
And his heart *was* true to Poll.

'Twas a wreck. Will*am*, on shore he swam,
   And looked about for an inn;
When a noble savage lady, of a colour rather shady,
   Came up with a kind of grin:
"Oh, marry *me*, and a king you'll be,
   And in a palace loll;
      Or we'll eat you willy-nilly."
      So he gave his *hand*, did Billy,
But his *heart* was true to Poll.

Away a twelvemonth sped, and a happy life he led
   As the King of the Kikeryboos;
His paint was red and yellar, and he used a big umbrella,
   And he wore a pair of over-*shoes;*
He'd corals and knives, and twenty-six wives,
   Whose beauties I cannot here extol;
      One day they all revolted,
      So he back to Bristol bolted,
For his *heart* was true to Poll.

His heart was true to Poll,
His heart was true to Poll.
   It's no matter what you do,
   If your heart be only true:
And his heart *was* true to Poll.
         Frank C. Burnand.

SLEEP ON

FEAR no unlicensed entry,
    Heed no bombastic talk,
    While guards the British sentry
Pall Mall and Birdcage Walk.
Let European thunders
    Occasion no alarms,
Though diplomatic blunders
    May cause a cry, "To arms!"
Sleep on, ye pale civilians;
    All thunder-clouds defy;
On Europe's countless millions
    The sentry keeps his eye!

Should foreign-born rapscallions
    In London dare to show
Their overgrown battalions,
    Be sure I'll let you know.
Should Russians or Norwegians
    Pollute our favoured clime
With rough barbaric legions,
    I'll mention it in time.
So sleep in peace, civilians,
    The Continent defy;
While on its countless millions
    The sentry keeps his eye!

W. S. Gilbert.

TO THE TERRESTRIAL GLOBE

BY A MISERABLE WRETCH

ROLL on, thou ball, roll on!
    Through pathless realms of space
        Roll on!
What though I'm in a sorry case?
What though I cannot meet my bills?
What though I suffer toothache's ills?
What though I swallow countless pills?
      Never *you* mind!
        Roll on!

Roll on, thou ball, roll on!
Through seas of inky air
        Roll on!
It's true I've got no shirts to wear;
It's true my butcher's bill is due;
It's true my prospects all look blue;
But don't let that unsettle you.
      Never *you* mind!
        Roll on!
          (It rolls on.)
            W. S. Gilbert.

THE APE AND THE LADY

A LADY fair, of lineage high,
    Was loved by an ape, in the days gone by;
    The maid was radiant as the sun;
The ape was a most unsightly one.

    So it would not do—
    His scheme fell through;
For the maid, when his love took formal shape,
    Expressed such terror
    At his monstrous error,
That he stammered an apology and made his 'scape,
The picture of a disconcerted ape.

With a view to rise in the social scale,
He shaved his bristles and he docked his tail;
He grew mustachios, and he took his tub,
And he paid a guinea to a toilet club.
    But it would not do—
    The scheme fell through;
For the maid was Beauty's fairest queen,
    With golden tresses,
    Like a real princess's,
While the ape, despite his razor keen,
Was the apiest ape that ever was seen!

He bought white ties, and he bought dress suits;
He crammed his feet into bright, tight boots;
And to start his life on a brand-new plan,
He christened himself Darwinian man!
    But it would not do—
    The scheme fell through;
For the maiden fair, whom the monkey craved,
    Was a radiant being,
    With a brain far-seeing;
While a man, however well behaved,
At best is only a monkey shaved!

W. S. Gilbert.

ANGLICISED UTOPIA

SOCIETY has quite forsaken all her wicked courses,
   Which empties our police courts, and abolishes divorces.
(Divorce is nearly obsolete in England.)
No tolerance we show to undeserving rank and splendour,
For the higher his position is, the greater the offender.
(That's a maxim that is prevalent in England.)
No peeress at our drawing-room before the Presence passes
Who wouldn't be accepted by the lower-middle classes.
Each shady dame, whatever be her rank, is bowed out neatly;
In short, this happy country has been Anglicised completely!
   It really is surprising
   What a thorough Anglicising
We've brought about—Utopia's quite another land;
   In her enterprising movements,
   She is England, with improvements,
Which we dutifully offer to our mother-land!

Our city we have beautified—we've done it willy-nilly—
And all that isn't Belgrave Square is Strand and Piccadilly.

(They haven't any slummeries in England.)
We have solved the labour question with discrimination polished,
So poverty is obsolete, and hunger is abolished.
  (They are going to abolish it in England.)
The Chamberlain our native stage has purged, beyond a question,
Of "risky situation and indelicate suggestion";
No piece is tolerated if it's costumed indiscreetly—
In short, this happy country has been Anglicised completely!
    It really is surprising
    What a thorough Anglicising
  We've brought about—Utopia's quite another land;
    In her enterprising movements,
    She is England, with improvements,
  Which we dutifully offer to our mother-land!

Our peerage we've remodelled on an intellectual basis,
Which certainly is rough on our hereditary races.
  (They are going to remodel it in England.)
The brewers and the cotton lords no longer seek admission,
And literary merit meets with proper recognition—
  (As literary merit does in England!)
Who knows but we may count among our intellectual chickens
Like them an Earl of Thackeray, and p'r'aps a Duke of Dickens—

Lord Fildes and Viscount Millais (when they come)
    we'll welcome sweetly,
And then this happy country will be Anglicised
    completely!
    It really is surprising
    What a thorough Anglicising
We've brought about—Utopia's quite another
    land;
    In her enterprising movements,
    She is England, with improvements,
Which we dutifully offer to our mother-land!
W. S. Gilbert.

ETIQUETTE

THE *Ballyshannon* foundered off the coast of
    Cariboo,
    And down in fathoms many went the captain
    and the crew;
Down went the owners—greedy men whom hope
    of gain allured:
Oh, dry the starting tear, for they were heavily
    insured.

Besides the captain and the mate, the owners and
    the crew,
The passengers were also drowned excepting only
    two:
Young Peter Gray, who tasted teas for Baker,
    Croop, and Co.,
And Somers, who from Eastern shores imported
    indigo.

These passengers, by reason of their clinging to a mast,
Upon a desert island were eventually cast.
They hunted for their meals, as Alexander Selkirk used,
But they couldn't chat together—they had not been introduced.

For Peter Gray, and Somers, too, though certainly in trade,
Were properly particular about the friends they made;
And somehow thus they settled it, without a word of mouth,
That Gray should take the northern half, while Somers took the south.

On Peter's portion oysters grew—a delicacy rare,
But oysters were a delicacy Peter couldn't bear.
On Somer's side was turtle, on the shingle lying thick,
Which Somers couldn't eat, because it always made him sick.

Gray gnashed his teeth with envy as he saw a mighty store
Of turtle unmolested on his fellow-creature's shore.
The oysters at his feet aside impatiently he shoved,
For turtle and his mother were the only things he loved.

And Somers sighed in sorrow as he settled in the south,
For the thought of Peter's oysters brought the water to his mouth.
He longed to lay him down upon the shelly bed, and stuff:
He had often eaten oysters, but had never had enough.

How they wished an introduction to each other they had had
When on board the *Ballyshannon!* And it drove them nearly mad
To think how very friendly with each other they might get,
If it wasn't for the arbitrary rule of etiquette!

One day, when out a-hunting for the *mus ridiculus*,
Gray overheard his fellow-man soliloquising thus:
"I wonder how the playmates of my youth are getting on,
M'Connell, S. B. Walters, Paddy Byles, and Robinson?"

These simple words made Peter as delighted as could be;
Old chummies at the Charterhouse were Robinson and he.
He walked straight up to Somers, then he turned extremely red,
Hesitated, hummed and hawed a bit, then cleared his throat, and said:

"I beg your pardon—pray forgive me if I seem too bold,
But you have breathed a name I knew familiarly of old.
You spoke aloud of Robinson—I happened to be by.
You know him?" "Yes, extremely well." "Allow me, so do I."

It was enough: they felt they could more pleasantly get on,
For (ah, the magic of the fact!) they each knew Robinson!
And Mr. Somers' turtle was at Peter's service quite,
And Mr. Somers punished Peter's oyster-beds all night.

They soon became like brothers from community of wrongs;
They wrote each other little odes and sang each other songs;
They told each other anecdotes disparaging their wives;
On several occasions, too, they saved each other's lives.

They felt quite melancholy when they parted for the night,
And got up in the morning soon as ever it was light;
Each other's pleasant company they reckoned so upon,
And all because it happened that they both knew Robinson!

They lived for many years on that inhospitable
   shore,
And day by day they learned to love each other
   more and more.
At last, to their astonishment, on getting up one day,
They saw a frigate anchored in the offing of the bay.

To Peter an idea occurred. "Suppose we cross
   the main?
So good an opportunity may not be found again."
And Somers thought a minute, then ejaculated,
   "Done!
I wonder how my business in the City's getting on?"

"But stay," said Mr. Peter; "when in England, as
   you know,
I earned a living tasting teas for Baker, Croop, and
   Co.,
I may be superseded—my employers think me
   dead!"
"Then come with me," said Somers, "and taste
   indigo instead."

But all their plans were scattered in a moment
   when they found
The vessel was a convict ship from Portland outward bound;
When a boat came off to fetch them, though they
   felt it very kind,
To go on board they firmly but respectfully declined.

As both the happy settlers roared with laughter at the joke,
They recognized a gentlemanly fellow pulling stroke:
'Twas Robinson—a convict, in an unbecoming frock!
Condemned to seven years for misappropriating stock!!!

They laughed no more, for Somers thought he had been rather rash
In knowing one whose friend had misappropriated cash;
And Peter thought a foolish tack he must have gone upon
In making the acquaintance of a friend of Robinson.

At first they didn't quarrel very openly, I've heard;
They nodded when they met, and now and then exchanged a word:
The word grew rare, and rarer still the nodding of the head,
And when they meet each other now, they cut each other dead.

To allocate the island they agreed by word of mouth,
And Peter takes the north again, and Somer takes the south;
And Peter has the oysters, which he hates, in layers thick,
And Somers has the turtle—turtle always makes him sick.

W. S. Gilbert.

THE ÆSTHETE

IF you're anxious for to shine in the high æsthetic
   line, as a man of culture rare,
You must get up all the germs of the tran-
   scendental terms, and plant them everywhere;
You must lie upon the daisies, and discourse in
   novel phrases of your complicated state of mind
(The meaning doesn't matter, if it's only idle chatter
   of a transcendental kind).
   And every one will say,
   As you walk your mystic way,
"If this young man expresses himself in terms too
   deep for me,
Why, what a very singularly deep young man this
   deep young man must be!"

Be eloquent in praise of the very dull old days
   which have long since passed away,
And convince 'em, if you can, that the reign of good
   Queen Anne was Culture's palmiest day.
Of course you will pooh-pooh whatever's fresh and
   new, and declare it's crude and mean,
And that Art stopped short in the cultivated court
   of the Empress Josephine.
   And every one will say,
   As you walk your mystic way,
"If that's not good enough for him which is good
   enough for me,
Why, what a very cultivated kind of youth this kind
   of youth must be!"

Then a sentimental passion of a vegetable fashion
    must excite your languid spleen,
An attachment *à la Plato* for a bashful young potato,
    or a not-too-French French bean.
Though the Philistines may jostle, you will rank
    as an apostle in the high æsthetic band,
If you walk down Piccadilly with a poppy or a lily
    in your mediæval hand.
        And every one will say,
        As you walk your flowery way,
"If he's content with a vegetable love, which would
    certainly not suit me,
Why, what a most particularly pure young man this
    pure young man must be!"
                                W. S. Gilbert.

TOO LATE!

"Ah! si la jeunesse savait,—si la vieillesse pouvait!"

THERE sat an old man on a rock,
    And unceasing bewailed him of Fate,
    That concern where we all must take stock,
Though our vote has no hearing or weight;
And the old man sang him an old, old song—
Never sang voice so clear and strong
That it could drown the old man's for long,
    For he sang the song, "Too late! too late!"

When we want, we have for our pains
    The promise that if we but wait
Till the want has burned out of our brains,
    Every means shall be present to state;

[261]

A Satire Anthology

While we send for the napkins, the soup gets cold;
While the bonnet is trimming, the face grows old;
When we've matched our buttons, the pattern is sold,
    And everything comes too late—too late!

"When strawberries seemed like red heavens,
    Terrapin stew a wild dream,
When my brain was at sixes and sevens,
    If my mother had 'folks' and ice-cream,
Then I gazed with a lickerish hunger
At the restaurant-man and fruit-monger—
But oh! how I wished I were younger,
    When the goodies all came in a stream—in a stream!

"I've a splendid blood-horse, and—a liver
    That it jars into torture to trot;
My row-boat's the gem of the river—
    Gout makes every knuckle a knot!
I can buy boundless credits on Paris and Rome,
But no palate for *ménus*, no eyes for a dome—
Those belonged to the youth who must tarry at home,
    When no home but an attic he'd got—he'd got!

"How I longed, in that lonest of garrets,
    Where the tiles baked my brains all July,
For ground to grow two pecks of carrots,
    Two pigs of my own in a sty,
A rosebush, a little thatched cottage,
Two spoons, love, a basin of pottage!

Now in freestone I sit, and my dotage,
  With a woman's chair empty close by—close by!

"Ah, now, though I sit on a rock,
  I have shared one seat with the great;
I have sat—knowing naught of the clock—
  On love's high throne of state;
But the lips that kissed, and the arms that caressed,
To a mouth grown stern with delay were pressed,
And circled a breast that their clasp had blessed,
  Had they only not come too late—too late!"
Fitz-Hugh Ludlow.

LIFE IN LACONICS

Given a roof, and a taste for rations,
And you have the key to the "wealth of nations."

Given a boy, a tree, and a hatchet,
And virtue strives in vain to match it.

Given a pair, a snake, and an apple,
You make the whole world need a chapel.

Given "no cards," broad views, and a hovel,
You have a realistic novel.

Given symptoms and doctors with potion and pill,
And your heirs will ere long be contesting your will.

That good leads to evil there's no denying:
If it were not for *truth* there would be no *lying*.

"I'm nobody!" should have a hearse;
But then, "I'm somebody!" is worse.

"Folks say," *et cetera!* Well, they shouldn't,
And if they knew you well, they wouldn't.

When you coddle your life, all its vigor and grace
Shrink away with the whisper,"We're in the wrong
    place."
                     Mary Mapes Dodge.

DISTICHES

WISELY a woman prefers to a lover a man
    who neglects her.
This one may love her some day; some
day the lover will not.

There are three species of creatures who, when they
    seem coming, are going;
When they seem going, they come: Diplomats,
    women, and crabs.

As the meek beasts in the Garden came flocking
    for Adam to name them,
Men for a title to-day crawl to the feet of a king.

A Satire Anthology

What is a first love worth except to prepare for a second?
What does the second love bring? Only regret for the first.

                      John Hay.

THE POET AND THE CRITICS

IF those who wield the rod forget,
  'Tis truly, *Quis custodiet?*

A certain bard (as bards will do)
Dressed up his poems for review.
His type was plain, his title clear,
His frontispiece by Fourdrinier.
Moreover, he had on the back
A sort of sheepskin zodiac—
A mask, a harp, an owl—in fine,
A neat and "classical" design.
But the *in*-side? Well, good or bad,
The inside was the best he had
Much memory, more imitation,
Some accidents of inspiration,
Some essays in that finer fashion
Where fancy takes the place of passion;
And some (of course) more roughly wrought
To catch the advocates of thought.

In the less-crowded age of Anne,
Our bard had been a favoured man;

Fortune, more chary with the sickle,
Had ranked him next to Garth or Tickell;
He might have even dared to hope
A line's malignity from Pope!
But now, when folks are hard to please,
And poets are as thick as—peas,
The Fates are not so prone to flatter,
Unless, indeed, a friend . . . No matter.

The book, then, had a minor credit.
The critics took, and doubtless read it.
Said A.: "These little songs display
No lyric gift, but still a ray,
A promise. They will do no harm."
'Twas kindly, if not *very* warm.
Said B.: "The author may, in time,
Acquire the rudiments of rhyme;
His efforts now are scarcely verse."
This, certainly, could not be worse.

Sorely discomfited, our bard
Worked for another ten years—hard.
Meanwhile the world, unmoved, went on;
New stars shot up, shone out, were gone;
Before his second volume came,
His critics had forgot his name:
And who, forsooth, is bound to know
Each laureate *in embryo!*
They tried and tested him, no less,
The pure assayers of the Press.
Said A.: "*The author may, in time . . .*"
Or much what B. had said of rhyme.

Then B.: "*These little songs display . . .*"
And so forth, in the sense of A.
Over the bard I throw a veil.

There is no moral to this tale.
Austin Dobson.

THE LOVE-LETTER

"J'ai vu les mœurs de mon temps, et j'ai publié cette lettre."—*La Nouvelle Héloïse.*

IF this should fail, why, then I scarcely know
    What could succeed. Here's brilliancy (and
        banter),
Byron *ad lib.*, a chapter of Rousseau;
   If this should fail, then *tempora mutantur;*
Style's out of date, and love, as a profession,
Acquires no aid from beauty of expression.

"The men who think as I, I fear, are few"
    (Cynics would say 'twere well if they were
        fewer);
"I am not what I seem"—(indeed, 'tis true;
    Though, as a sentiment, it might be newer);
"Mine is a soul whose deeper feelings lie
More deep than words"—(as these exemplify).

"I will not say when first your beauty's sun
    Illumed my life"—(it needs imagination);
"For me to see you and to love were one"—
    (This will account for some precipitation);

"Let it suffice that worship more devoted
Ne'er throbbed," *et cetera*. The rest is quoted.

"If Love can look with all-prophetic eye"—
    (Ah, if he could, how many would be single!)
"If truly spirit unto spirit cry"—
    (The ears of some most terribly must tingle!)
"Then I have dreamed you will not turn your face."
This next, I think, is more than commonplace.

"Why should we speak, if Love, interpreting,
    Forestall the speech with favour found before?
Why should we plead? it were an idle thing,
    If Love himself be Love's ambassador!"
Blot, as I live! Shall we erase it? No;
'Twill show we write *currente calamo*.

"My fate, my fortune, I commit to you"—
    (In point of fact, the latter's not extensive);
"Without you I am poor indeed" (strike through—
    'Tis true, but crude; 'twould make her apprehensive);
"My life is yours—I lay it at your feet"
(Having no choice but Hymen or the Fleet).

"Give me the right to stand within the shrine
    Where never yet my faltering feet intruded;
Give me the right to call you wholly mine"—
    (That is, consols and three-per-cents. included);
"To guard your rest from every care that cankers—
To keep your life"—(and balance at your banker's).

"Compel me not to long for your reply;
    Suspense makes havoc with the mind"—(and muscles);
"Winged Hope takes flight" (which means that I must fly,
    Default of funds, to Paris or to Brussels);
"I cannot wait! My own, my queen—Priscilla!
Write by return." And *now* for a manilla!

"Miss Blank," at "Blank." Jemima, let it go;
    And I, meanwhile, will idle with "Sir Walter."
Stay, let me keep the first rough copy, though—
    'Twill serve again. There's but the name to alter,
And Love, that starves, must knock at every portal,
In forma pauperis. We are but mortal!
                      Austin Dobson.

FAME

ALL over the world we sing of Fame,
    Bright as a bubble, and hollow;
      With a breath men make it and give it a name;
All over the world they sing the same,
    And the beautiful bubble follow.

Its rounded, splendid, gossamer walls
    Hide more than our fairy fancies:
For here, in the vaulted, antique halls,
'Mid oriel splendours, a light foot falls,
    And a fairy figure dances.

And men will do for a glancing eye,
   And foot that tarries never,
More, far more than look and sigh;
For men will fight, and man will die,
   But follow it on for ever.
              James Herbert Morse.

FIVE LIVES

FIVE mites of monads dwelt in a round drop
   That twinkled on a leaf by a pool in the sun.
   To the naked eye they lived invisible;
Specks, for a world of whom the empty shell
Of a mustard-seed had been a hollow sky.

One was a meditative monad, called a sage;
And, shrinking all his mind within, he thought:
"Tradition, handed down for hours and hours,
Tells that our globe, this quivering crystal world,
Is slowly dying. What if, seconds hence
When I am very old, yon shimmering doom
Comes drawing down and down, till all things end?"
Then with a wizen smirk he proudly felt
No other mote of God had ever gained
Such giant grasp of universal truth.

One was a transcendental monad; thin
And long and slim of mind; and thus he mused:
"Oh, vast, unfathomable monad-souls!
Made in the image"—a horse frog croaks from the
   pool,

A Satire Anthology

"Hark! 'twas some god, voicing his glorious thought
In thunder-music.   Yea, we hear their voice,
And we may guess their minds from ours, their work.
Some taste they have like ours, some tendency
To wriggle about, and munch a trace of scum."
He floated up on a pin-point bubble of gas,
That burst, pricked by the air, and he was gone.

One was a barren-minded monad, called
A positivist, and he knew positively:
"There was no world beyond this certain drop.
Prove me another!   Let the dreamers dream
Of their faint gleams, and noises from without,
And higher and lower; life is life enough."
Then swaggering half a hair's-breath hungrily,
He seized upon an atom of bug, and fed.

One was a tattered monad, called a poet,
And with a shrill voice ecstatic thus he sang:
"Oh, little female monad's lips!
Oh, little female monad's eyes!
Ah, the little, little, female, female monad!"
The last was a strong-minded monadess,
Who dashed amid the infusoria,
Danced high and low, and wildly spun and dove,
Till the dizzy others held their breath to see.

But while they led their wondrous little lives,
Æonian moments had gone wheeling by,
The burning drop had shrunk with fearful speed;
A glistening film—'twas gone; the leaf was dry.
The little ghost of an inaudible squeak
Was lost to the frog that goggled from his stone;

Who, at the huge, slow tread of a thoughtful ox
Coming to drink, stirred sideways fatly, plunged,
Launched backward twice, and all the pool was still.

Edward Rowland Sill.

HE AND SHE

WHEN I am dead you'll find it hard,
    Said he,
  To ever find another man
    Like me.

What makes you think, as I suppose
    You do,
I'd ever want another man
    Like you?

Eugene Fitch Ware.

WHAT WILL WE DO?

WHAT will we do when the good days come—
  When the prima donna's lips are dumb,
  And the man who reads us his "little things"
Has lost his voice like the girl who sings;
When stilled is the breath of the cornet-man,
And the shrilling chords of the quartette clan;
When our neighbours' children have lost their drums—
Oh, what will we do when the good time comes?

Oh, what will we do in that good, blithe time,
When the tramp will work—oh, thing sublime!
And the scornful dame who stands on your feet
Will "Thank you, sir," for the proffered seat;
And the man you hire to work by the day,
Will allow you to do his work your way;
And the cook who trieth your appetite
Will steal no more than she thinks is right;
When the boy you hire will call you "Sir,"
Instead of "Say" and "Guverner";
When the funny man is humorsome—
How can we stand the millennium?
Robert J. Burdette.

THE TOOL

THE man of brains, of fair repute and birth,
    Who loves high place above all else of earth—
Who loves it so, he'll go without the power,
If he may hold the semblance but an hour;
Willing to be some sordid creature's tool,
So he but seem a little while to rule—
On him even moral pigmies would look down;
Were prizes given for shame, he'd wear the crown.
Richard Watson Gilder.

GIVE ME A THEME

"GIVE me a theme," the little poet cried,
   "And I will do my part."
"'Tis not a theme you need," the world replied;
   "You need a heart."
               Richard Watson Gilder.

THE POEM, TO THE CRITIC

WEIGH me, if you're fain;
   Measure me, if it is your plan;
Know your little thimble-brain
   Hold me never can.
               Richard Watson Gilder.

BALLADE OF LITERARY FAME

"All these for fourpence."

OH, where are the endless romances
   Our grandmothers used to adore?
The knights with their helms and their lances,
Their shields and the favours they wore?
And the monks with their magical lore?
They have passed to oblivion and *Nox;*
They have fled to the shadowy shore—
They are all in the Fourpenny Box!

And where the poetical fancies
  Our fathers rejoiced in, of yore?
The lyric's melodious expanses,
  The epics in cantos a score.
They have been, and are not. No more
  Shall the shepherds drive silvery flocks,
Nor the ladies their languors deplore—
  They are all in the Fourpenny Box!

And the music! The songs and the dances?
  The tunes that time may not restore?
And the tomes where divinity prances?
  And the pamphlets where heretics roar?
They have ceased to be even a bore,—
  The divine, and the sceptic who mocks;
They are "cropped," they are "foxed" to the core,
  They are all in the Fourpenny Box!

Envoi

Suns beat on them; tempests downpour,
  On the chest without cover or locks,
Where they lie by the Bookseller's door—
  They are all in the Fourpenny Box!
               Andrew Lang.

CHORUS OF ANGLOMANIACS

IT is positively false to call us frantic,
   For the soundness of our mental state is sure,
Yet we look upon this side of the Atlantic
  As a tract of earth unpleasant to endure.

We consider dear old England as the fountain
    Of all institutions reputably sane;
We abominate and loathe a Rocky Mountain;
    We regard a rolling prairie with disdain.

We assiduously imitate the polish
    That we notice round the English nabob hang;
We unfailingly endeavour to abolish
    From our voices any trace of nasal twang.

Every patriotic duty we leave undone,
    With aversion such as Hebrews hold for pork,
Since we venerate the very name of London
    In proportion to our hatred of New York.

No treaty could in any manner soften
    Our contempt for native tailors when we dress;
If we bet, we "lay a guinea," rather often,
    And we always say "I farncy" for "I guess."

We esteem the Revolution as illegal;
    If you mention Bunker Hill to us, we sigh;
We particularly execrate an eagle,
    And we languish on the fourth day of July.

We are not prepared in any foolish manner
    The vulgarities of Uncle Sam to screen;
We dislike to hear that dull "Star-Spangled Banner,"
    But we thoroughly respect "God save the Queen."

We revere the Prince of Wales, though he should prick us
    With a sneer at the republic we obey!

We would rather let his Royal Highness kick us
Than have been the bosom friend of Henry Clay!
Edgar Fawcett.
From "The Buntling Ball."

THE NET OF LAW

THE net of law is spread so wide,
   No sinner from its sweep may hide.

Its meshes are so fine and strong,
They take in every child of wrong.

O wondrous web of mystery!
Big fish alone escape from thee!
James Jeffrey Roche.

A BOSTON LULLABY

BABY'S brain is tired of thinking
   On the Wherefore and the Whence;
  Baby's precious eyes are blinking
With incipient somnolence.

Little hands are weary turning
  Heavy leaves of lexicon;
Little nose is fretted learning
  How to keep its glasses on.

Baby knows the laws of nature
  Are beneficent and wise;
His medulla oblongata
  Bids my darling close his eyes

And his pneumogastrics tell him
    Quietude is always best
When his little cerebellum
    Needs recuperative rest.

Baby must have relaxation,
    Let the world go wrong or right.
Sleep, my darling—leave Creation
    To its chances for the night.
                James Jeffrey Roche.

THE V-A-S-E

FROM the madding crowd they stand apart,
    The maidens four and the Work of Art;

And none might tell from sight alone
In which had culture ripest grown—

The Gotham Millions fair to see,
The Philadelphia Pedigree,

The Boston Mind of azure hue,
Or the Soulful Soul from Kalamazoo;

For all loved Art in a seemly way.
With an earnest soul and a capital A.

  .   .   .   .   .   .

Long they worshipped; but no one broke
The sacred stillness, until up spoke

The Western one from the nameless place,
Who, blushing, said, "What a lovely vace!"

Over three faces a sad smile flew,
And they edged away from Kalamazoo.

But Gotham's haughty soul was stirred
To crush the stranger with one small word;

Deftly hiding reproof in praise,
She cries, "'Tis, indeed, a lovely vaze!"

But brief her unworthy triumph, when
The lofty one from the home of Penn,

With the consciousness of two grandpapas,
Exclaims, "It is quite a lovely vahs!"

And glances round with an anxious thrill,
Awaiting the word of Beacon Hill.

But the Boston maid smiles courteouslee,
And gently murmurs, "Oh, pardon me!

"I did not catch your remark, because
I was so entranced with that charming vaws!"

*Dies erit prægelida
Sinistra quum Bostonia.*
                    James Jeffrey Roche.

THURSDAY

THE sun was setting, and vespers done;
    From chapel the monks came one by one,
    And down they went thro' the garden trim,
In cassock and cowl, to the river's brim.
Ev'ry brother his rod he took;
Ev'ry rod had a line and a hook;
Ev'ry hook had a bait so fine,
And thus they sang in the even shine:
"Oh, to-morrow will be Friday, so we'll fish the
    stream to-day!
Oh, to-morrow will be Friday, so we'll fish the
    stream to-day!
        Benedicite!"

So down they sate by the river's brim,
And fish'd till the light was growing dim;
They fish'd the stream till the moon was high,
But never a fish came wand'ring by.
They fish'd the stream in the bright moonshine,
But not one fish would he come to dine.
And the Abbot said, "It seems to me
These rascally fish are all gone to sea.
And to-morrow will be Friday, but we've caught no
    fish to-day;
Oh, to-morrow will be Friday, but we've caught no
    fish to-day!
        Maledicite!"

So back they went to the convent gate,
Abbot and monks disconsolate;

For they thought of the morrow with faces white,
Saying, "Oh, we must curb our appetite!
But down in the depths of the vault below
There's Malvoisie for a world of woe!"
So they quaff their wine, and all declare
That fish, after all, is but gruesome fare.
"Oh, to-morrow will be Friday, so we'll warm our
    souls to-day!
Oh, to-morrow will be Friday, so we'll warm our
    souls to-day!
           Benedicite!"
              Frederick Edward Weatherly.

A BIRD IN THE HAND

THERE were three young maids of Lee;
    They were fair as fair can be,
    And they had lovers three times three,
For they were fair as fair can be,
These three young maids of Lee.
But these young maids they cannot find
A lover each to suit her mind;
The plain-spoke lad is far too rough,
The rich young lord is not rich enough,
The one is too poor, and one is too tall,
And one just an inch too short for them all.
"Others pick and choose, and why not we?
We can very well wait," said the maids of Lee.
    There were three young maids of Lee;
    They were fair as fair can be,
    And they had lovers three times three

    For they were fair as fair can be,
    These three young maids of Lee.

    There are three old maids of Lee,
    And they are old as old can be,
    And one is deaf, and one cannot see,
    And they are all as cross as a gallows-tree,
    These three old maids of Lee.
Now, if any one chanced—'tis a chance remote—
One single charm in these maids to note,
He need not a poet nor handsome be,
For one is deaf and one cannot see;
He need not woo on his bended knee,
For they all are willing as willing can be.
He may take the one, or the two, or the three,
If he'll only take them away from Lee.
    There are three old maids at Lee;
    They are cross as cross can be;
    And there they are, and there they'll be
    To the end of the chapter, one, two, three,
    These three old maids of Lee.
              Frederick Edward Weatherly.

AN ADVANCED THINKER.

THIS modern scientist—a word uncouth—
    Who calls himself a seeker after truth,
    And traces man through monkey back to
        frog,
Seeing a Plato in each pollywog,
Ascribes all things unto the power of Matter.
The woman's anguish, and the baby's chatter—

The soldier's glory, and his country's need—
Self-sacrificing love—self-seeking greed—
The false religion some vain bigots prize,
Which seeks to win a soul by telling lies—
And even pseudo-scientific clatter—
All these, he says, are but the work of Matter.
Thus, self-made science, like a self-made man,
Deems naught uncomprehended in its plan;
Sees naught he can't explain by his own laws.
The time has come, at length, to bid him pause,
Before he strive to leap the unknown chasm
Reft wide 'twixt awful God and protoplasm.
Brander Matthews.

A THOUGHT

IF all the harm that women have done
  Were put in a bundle and rolled into one,
    Earth would not hold it,
    The sky could not enfold it,
It could not be lighted nor warmed by the sun;
    Such masses of evil
    Would puzzle the devil,
And keep him in fuel while Time's wheels run.

But if all the harm that's been done by men
Were doubled, and doubled, and doubled again,
And melted and fused into vapour, and then
Were squared and raised to the power of ten,
There wouldn't be nearly enough, not near,
To keep a small girl for the tenth of a year.
J. K. Stephen.

A SONNET

TWO voices are there: one is of the deep;
    It learns the storm-cloud's thunderous melody,
Now roars, now murmurs with the changing sea,
Now bird-like pipes, now closes soft in sleep:
And one is of an old, half-witted sheep,
    Which bleats articulate monotony,
    And indicates that two and one are three,
That grass is green, lakes damp, and mountains steep;
And, Wordsworth, both are thine. At certain times
Forth from the heart of thy melodious rhymes,
The form and pressure of high thoughts will burst;
    At other times—good Lord! I'd rather be
    Quite unacquainted with the A B C,
Than write such hopeless rubbish as thy worst.

J. K. Stephen.

THEY SAID

BECAUSE thy prayer hath never fed
    Dark Atë with the food she craves;
    Because thou dost not hate, they said,
  Nor joy to step on foemen's graves;
Because thou canst not hate, as we,
How poor a creature thou must be!
Thy veins as pale as ours are red!
Go to! Love loves thee not, they said.

A Satire Anthology

Because by thee no snare was spread
   To baffle Love—if Love should stray;
Because thou dost not watch, they said,
   To strictly compass Love each way;
Because thou dost not watch, as we,
Nor jealous Care hath lodged with thee,
To strew with thorns a restless bed—
Go to! Love loves thee not, they said.

Because thy feet were not misled
   To jocund ground, yet all infirm;
Because thou art not fond, they said,
   Nor dost exact thine heyday term;
Because thou art not fond, as we,
How dull a creature thou must be!
Thy pulse how slow, yet shrewd thy head!
Go to! Love loves thee not, they said.

Because thou hast not roved to wed
   With those to Love averse or strange;
Because thou hast not roved, they said,
   Nor ever studied artful change;
Because thou hast not roved, as we,
Love paid no ransom rich for thee,
Nor, seeking thee, unwearied sped.
Go to! Love loves thee not, they said.

Aye, so! because thou thought'st to tread
   Love's ways, and all his bidding do;
Because thou hast not tired, they said,
   Nor ever wert to Love untrue;
Because thou hast not tired, as we,
How tedious must thy service be;

Love with thy zeal is surfeited!
Go to! Love loves thee not, they said.

Because thou hast not wanton shed
  On every hand thy heritage;
Because thou art not flush, they said,
  But hast regard to meagre age;
Because thou art not flush, as we,
How strait thy cautious soul must be!
How well thy thrift stands thee in stead!
Go to! Love loves thee not, they said.

And therefore look thou not for bread—
  For wine and bread from Love's deep store,
Because thou hast no need, they said;
  But us he'll feast forevermore!
Because thou hast no need, as we,
Sit in his purlieus, thou, and see
How with Love's bounty we are fed.
Go to! Love loves thee not, they said.
                              Edith M. Thomas.

TO R. K.

> As long I dwell on some stupendous
> And tremendous (Heaven defend us!)
> Monstr'inform' ingens-horrendous
> Demoniaco-seraphic
> Penman's latest piece of graphic.—*Browning.*

WILL there never come a season
    Which shall rid us from the curse
    Of a prose which knows no reason,
And an unmelodious verse?—

When the world shall cease to wonder
  At the genius of an Ass,
And a boy's eccentric blunder
  Shall not bring success to pass?—

When mankind shall be delivered
  From the clash of magazines,
And the inkstand shall be shivered
  Into countless smithereens?—
When there stands a muzzled stripling,
  Mute, beside a muzzled bore?—
When the Rudyards cease from Kipling,
  And the Haggards Ride no more?
                                J. K. Stephen.

TO MIGUEL DE CERVANTES SAAVEDRA

A BLUEBIRD lives in yonder tree,
    Likewise a little chickadee,
    In two woodpeckers' nests, rent free.

There, where the weeping willow weeps,
A dainty house-wren sweetly cheeps;
From an old oriole's nest she peeps.

I see the English sparrow tilt
Upon a limb with sun begilt;
Her nest an ancient swallow built.

So it was one of your old jests,
Eh, Mig. Cervantes, that attests
"There are no birds in last year's nests?"
        Richard Kendall Munkittrick.

WHAT'S IN A NAME?

IN letters large upon the frame,
    That visitors might see,
  The painter placed his humble name:
O'Callaghan McGee.

And from Beersheba unto Dan,
    The critics, with a nod,
Exclaimed: "This painting Irishman
    Adores his native sod.

"His stout heart's patriotic flame
    There's naught on earth can quell;
He takes no wild romantic name
    To make his pictures sell."

Then poets praise, in sonnets neat,
    His stroke so bold and free;
No parlor wall was thought complete
    That hadn't a McGee.

All patriots before McGee
    Threw lavishly their gold;
His works in the Academy
    Were very quickly sold.

His "Digging Clams at Barnegat,"
    His "When the Morning Smiled,"
His "Seven Miles from Ararat,"
    His "Portrait of a Child,"

Were purchased in a single day,
   And lauded as divine.

  .   .   .   .   .

That night as in his *atelier*
   The artist sipped his wine,

And looked upon his gilded frames,
   He grinned from ear to ear:
"They little think my real name's
   V. Stuyvesant De Vere!"
        Richard Kendall Munkittrick.

WED.

FOR these white arms about my neck—
   For the dainty room, with its ordered grace—
For my snowy linen without a fleck—
For the tender charm of this uplift face—

For the softened light and the homelike air—
   The low, luxurious cannel fire—
The padded ease of my chosen chair—
   The devoted love that discounts desire—

I sometimes think, when twelve is struck
   By the clock on the mantel, tinkling clear,
I would take—and thank the gods for the luck—
   One single hour with the boys and the beer,

Where the sawdust-scent of a cheap saloon
   Is mingled with malt; where each man smokes;

Where they sing the street-songs out of tune,
   Talk Art, and bandy ephemeral jokes.

By Jove, I do! And all the time
   I know not a man that is there to-night,
But would barter his brains to be where I'm—
   And I'm well aware that the beggars are right.
H. C. Bunner.

ATLANTIC CITY

O CITY that is not a city, unworthy the prefix Atlantic,
   Forlornest of watering-places, and thoroughly Philadelphian!
In thy despite I sing, with a bitter and deep detestation—
A detestation born of a direful and dinnerless evening,
Spent in thy precincts unhallowed—an evening, I trust, may recur not.
Never till then did I know what was meant by the word God-forsaken:
Thou its betokening hast taught me, being the chiefest example.
Thou art the scorned of the gods; thy sand from their sandals is shaken;
Thee have they left in their wrath to thy uninteresting extensiveness,
Barren, and bleak, and big; a wild aggregation of barracks,

A Satire Anthology

Miscalled hotels, and of dovecotes denominate cottages;
A confusion of ugly girls, of sand, and of health-bearing breezes,
With one unending plank-walk for a true Philadelphia "attraction."
City ambitiously named, why, with inducements delusive,
Is the un-Philadelphian stranger lured to thy desert pretentious?
'Tis not alone that thy avenues, broad and unpaved and unending,
Reecho yet with the obsolete music of "Pinafore,"
Whistled in various keys by the rather too numerous negro;
'Tis not alone that Propriety—Propriety too Philadelphian—
Over thee stretches an ægis of wholly superfluous virtue;
That thou art utterly good; hast no single vice to redeem thee;
'Tis not alone that thou art provincial in all things, and petty;
And that the dulness of death is gay, compared to thy dulness—
'Tis not alone for these things that my curse is to rest upon thee,
But for a sin that crowns thee with perfect and eminent badness,
Sets thee alone in thy shame, the unworthiest town on the sea-coast;
This: That thou dinest at noon, and then in a manner barbarian,

Soupless, and wineless, and coffeeless, untimely and wholly indecent,
As is the custom, I learn, in Philadelphia proper.
I rose, and I fled from thy supper. I said, "I will get me a dinner!"
Vainly I wandered thy streets. Thy eating-places ungodly
Knew not the holiness of dinner. In all that evening I dined not;
But in a strange, low lair, infested of native mechanics,
Bolted a fried beefsteak for the physical need of my stomach.
And for them that have fried that steak, in Aïdes' lowest back-kitchen,
May they eternally broil, by way of a warning to others.
During my wanderings, I met and hailed with delight one Italian,
A man with a name from "Pasquale"—the chap sung by Tagliapietra;
He knew what it was to dine; he comprehended my yearnings;
But the spell was also on him, the somnolent spell Philadelphian,
And his hostelry would not be open till Saturday next; and I cursed him.
Now this is not too much to ask—God knows!—that a mortal should want a
Pint of Bordeaux to his dinner, and a small cigarette for a climax;

A Satire Anthology

But these things being denied him, where, then, is your civilization?
O Coney Island! of old I have reviled and blasphemed thee,
For that thou dousest thy glim at an hour that is unmetropolitan;
That thy frequenters' feet turn townwards ere striketh eleven,
When the returning cars are filled with young men and maidens,
Most of the maidens asleep on the young men's cindery shoulders—
Yea, but I spake as a fool, insensate, disgruntled, ungrateful:
Thee will I worship henceforth in appreciative humility;
Luxurious and splendid and urban, glorious and gaslit and gracious,
Gathering from every land thy gay and ephemeral tenantry,
From the Greek who hails thee "Thalatta!" to the rustic who murmurs "My golly!"
From the Bowery youth who requests his sweetheart to "Look at them billers!"
To the Gaul whom thy laughing waves almost persuade to immersion.
O Coney Island, thou art the weary citizen's heaven—
A heaven to dine, not die in, joyful and restful and clamful.
Better one hour of thee than an age of Atlantic City!
H. C. Bunner.

A Satire Anthology

THE FONT IN THE FOREST

THERE'S a prim little pond
    At the back of Beyond,
    And its waters are over your ears;
It's a sort of a tarn
    Behind Robin Hood's barn,
Where the fish live a million years.

    And the mortals who drink
    At its pebbly brink
Are immediately changed into mullets,
    Whose heads grow immense
    At their bodies' expense,
And whose eyes become bulbous as bullets.

    But they willingly stay
    Who have once found the way,
And they crave neither credit nor blame;
    For to wiggle their tails,
    And to practise their scales,
Is enough in the Fountain of Fame.
              Herman Knickerbocker Vielé.

THE ORIGIN OF SIN

HE talked about the origin
    Of sin;
        But present sin, I must confess,
He never tried to render less;

But used to add, so people talk,
His share unto the general stock—
   But grieved about the origin
     Of sin.

He mourned about the origin
     Of sin;
But never struggled very long
To rout contemporaneous wrong,
And never lost his sleep, they say,
About the evils of to-day—
   But wept about the origin
     Of sin.

He sighed about the origin
     Of sin;
But showed no fear you could detect
About its ultimate effect;
He deemed it best to use no force,
But let it run its natural course—
   But moaned about the origin
     Of sin.

Samuel Walter Foss.

A PHILOSOPHER

ZACK BUMSTEAD useter flosserfize
   About the ocean an' the skies;
   An' gab an' gas f'um morn till noon
About the other side the moon;
An' 'bout the natur of the place
Ten miles beyend the end of space.

An' if his wife she'd ask the crank
Ef he wouldn't kinder try to yank
Hisself out-doors an' git some wood
To make her kitchen fire good,
So she c'd bake her beans an' pies,
He'd say, " I've gotter flosserfize."

An' then he'd set an' flosserfize
About the natur an' the size
Of angels' wings, an' think, and gawp,
An' wonder how they make 'em flop.
He'd calkerlate how long a skid
'Twould take to move the sun, he did;
An' if the skid was strong an' prime,
It couldn't be moved to supper-time.
An' w'en his wife 'd ask the lout
Ef he wouldn't kinder waltz about
An' take a rag an' shoo the flies,
He'd say, " I've gotter flosserfize."

An' then he'd set an' flosserfize
'Bout schemes for fencing in the skies,
Then lettin' out the lots to rent,
So's he could make an honest cent.
An' if he'd find it pooty tough
To borry cash fer fencin'-stuff?
An' if 'twere best to take his wealth
An' go to Europe for his health,
Or save his cash till he'd enough
To buy some more of fencin'-stuff;
Then, ef his wife she'd ask the gump
Ef he wouldn't kinder try to hump

Hisself to t'other side the door,
So she c'd come an' sweep the floor,
He'd look at her with mournful eyes,
An' say, " I've gotter flosserfize."

An' so he'd set an' flosserfize
'Bout what it wuz held up the skies,
An' how God made this earthly ball
Jest simply out er nawthin' 'tall,
An' 'bout the natur, shape, an' form
Of nawthin' that he made it from.
Then, ef his wife sh'd ask the freak
Ef he wouldn't kinder try to sneak
Out to the barn an' find some aigs,
He'd never move, nor lift his laigs;
He'd never stir, nor try to rise,
But say, " I've gotter flosserfize."

An' so he'd set an' flosserfize
About the earth, an' sea, an' skies,
An' scratch his head, an' ask the cause
Of w'at there wuz before time wuz,
An' w'at the universe 'd do
Bimeby w'en time hed all got through;
An' jest how fur we'd have to climb
Ef we sh'd travel out er time;
An' ef we'd need, w'en we got there,
To keep our watches in repair.
Then, ef his wife she'd ask the gawk
Ef he wouldn't kinder try to walk
To where she had the table spread,
An' kinder git his stomach fed,

A Satire Anthology

He'd leap for that ar kitchen door,
An' say, "W'y didn't you speak afore?"
An' when he'd got his supper et,
He'd set, an' set, an' set, an' set,
An' fold his arms, an' shet his eyes,
An' set, an' set, an' flosserfize.
     Samuel Walter Foss.

THE FATE OF PIOUS DAN

"RUN down and get the doctor—quick!"
 Cried Jack Bean with a whoop;
"Run, Dan; for mercy's sake, be quick!
 Our baby's got the croup."
But Daniel shook his solemn head,
 His sanctimonious brow,
And said: "I cannot go, for I
 Must read my Bible now;
For I have regular hours to read
The Scripture for my spirit's need."

Said Silas Gove to Pious Dan,
 "Our neighbour, 'Rastus Wright,
Is very sick; will you come down
 And watch with him to-night?"
"He has my sympathy," says Dan,
 "And I would sure be there,
Did I not feel an inward call
 To spend the night in prayer.
Some other man with Wright must stay;
Excuse me, while I go and pray."

A Satire Anthology

"Old Briggs has fallen in the pond!"
  Cried little 'Bijah Brown;
"Run, Pious Dan, and help him out,
  Or else he sure will drown!"
"I trust he'll swim ashore," said Dan,
  "But now my soul is awed,
And I must meditate upon
  The goodness of the Lord;
And nothing merely temporal ought
To interrupt my holy thought."

So Daniel lived a pious life,
  As Daniel understood,
But all his neighbours thought he was
  Too pious to be good;
And Daniel died, and then his soul,
  On wings of hope elate,
In glad expectancy flew up
  To Peter's golden gate.
"Now let your gate wide open fly;
Come, hasten, Peter! Here am I."

"I'm sorry, Pious Dan," said he,
  "That time will not allow;
But you must wait a space, for I
  Must read my Bible now."
So Daniel waited long and long,
  And Peter read all day.
"Now, Peter, let me in," he cried.
  Said Peter, "I must pray;
And no mean temporal affairs
Must ever interrupt my prayers."

A Satire Anthology

Then Satan, who was passing by,
  Saw Dan's poor shivering form,
And said, "My man, it's cold out here;
  Come down where it is warm."
The angel baby of Jack Bean,
  The angel 'Rastus Wright,
And old Briggs, a white angel, too,
  All chuckled with delight;
And Satan said, "Come, Pious Dan,
For you are just my style of man."
              Samuel Walter Foss.

THE MEETING OF THE CLABBERHUSES

I

HE was the Chairman of the Guild
    Of Early Pleiocene Patriarchs;
  He was chief Mentor of the Lodge
Of the Oracular Oligarchs;
He was the Lord High Autocrat
  And Vizier of the Sons of Light,
And Sultan and Grand Mandarin
  Of the Millennial Men of Might.

He was Grand Totem and High Priest
  Of the Independent Potentates;
Grand Mogul of the Galaxy
  Of the Illustrious Stay-out-lates;
The President of the Dandydudes,
  The Treasurer of the Sons of Glee;

The Leader of the Clubtown Band
  And Architects of Melody.

II

She was Grand Worthy Prophetess
  Of the Illustrious Maids of Mark;
Of Vestals of the Third Degree
  She was Most Potent Matriarch;
She was High Priestess of the Shrine
  Of Clubtown's Culture Coterie,
And First Vice-President of the League
  Of the Illustrious G. A. B.

She was the First Dame of the Club
  For teaching Patagonians Greek;
She was Chief Clerk and Auditor
  Of Clubtown's Anti-Bachelor Clique;
She was High Treasurer of the Fund
  For Borrioboolaghalians,
And the Fund for Sending Browning's Poems
  To Native-born Australians.

III

Once to a crowded social *fête*
  Both these much-titled people came,
And each perceived, when introduced,
  They had the self-same name.
Their hostess said, when first they met:
  "Permit me now to introduce
My good friend Mr. Clabberhuse
  To Mrs. Clabberhuse."

"'Tis very strange," said she to him,
 "Such an unusual name!—
A name so very seldom heard,
 That we should bear the same."
"Indeed, 'tis wonderful," said he,
 "And I'm surprised the more,
Because I never heard the name
 Outside my home before.

"But now I come to look at you,"
 Said he, "upon my life,
If I am not indeed deceived,
 You are—you are—my wife."
She gazed into his searching face,
 And seemed to look him through;
"Indeed," said she, "it seems to me
 You are my husband, too.

"I've been so busy with my clubs,
 And in my various spheres,
I have not seen you now," she said,
 "For over fourteen years."
"That's just the way it's been with me;
 These clubs demand a sight"—
And then they both politely bowed,
 And sweetly said "Good-night."
          Sam Walter Foss.

WEDDED BLISS

"O COME and be my mate!" said the Eagle to the Hen;
"I love to soar, but then
I want my mate to rest
Forever in the nest!"
Said the Hen, "I cannot fly,
I have no wish to try,
But I joy to see my mate careering through the sky!"
They wed, and cried, "Ah, this is Love, my own!"
And the Hen sat, the Eagle soared, alone.

"O come and be my mate!" said the Lion to the Sheep;
"My love for you is deep!
I slay—a Lion should,
But you are mild and good!"
Said the Sheep, "I do no ill—
Could not, had I the will;
But I joy to see my mate pursue, devour, and kill."
They wed, and cried, "Ah, this is Love, my own!"
And the Sheep browsed, the Lion prowled, alone.

"O come and be my mate!" said the Salmon to the Clam;
"You are not wise, but I am.
I know sea and stream as well;
You know nothing but your shell."

A Satire Anthology

Said the Clam, "I'm slow of motion,
 But my love is all devotion,
And I joy to have my mate traverse lake and
  stream and ocean!"
They wed, and cried, "Ah, this is Love, my own!"
And the Clam sucked, the Salmon swam, alone.
        Charlotte Perkins (Stetson) Gilman.

A CONSERVATIVE

THE garden beds I wandered by,
  One bright and cheerful morn,
  When I found a new-fledged butterfly
A-sitting on a thorn—
A black and crimson butterfly,
  All doleful and forlorn.

I thought that life could have no sting
  To infant butterflies,
So I gazed on this unhappy thing
  With wonder and surprise,
While sadly with his waving wing
  He wiped his weeping eyes.

Said I: "What can the matter be?
  Why weepest thou so sore,
With garden fair and sunlight free,
  And flowers in goodly store?"
But he only turned away from me,
  And burst into a roar.

Cried he: "My legs are thin and few,
  Where once I had a swarm;
Soft, fuzzy fur—a joy to view—
  Once kept my body warm,
Before these flapping wing-things grew,
  To hamper and deform."

At that outrageous bug I shot
  The fury of mine eye;
Said I, in scorn all burning hot,
  In rage and anger high,
"You ignominious idiot!
  Those wings are made to fly."

"I do not want to fly," said he;
  "I only want to squirm."
And he dropped his wings dejectedly,
  But still his voice was firm:
"I do not want to be a fly;
  I want to be a worm."

O yesterday of unknown lack!
  To-day of unknown bliss!
I left my fool in red and black,
  The last I saw was this—
The creature madly climbing back
  Into his chrysalis.
        Charlotte Perkins Stetson Gilman.

SAME OLD STORY

HISTORY, and nature, too, repeat themselves, they say;
Men are only habit's slaves; we see it every day.
Life has done its best for me—I find it tiresome still;
For nothing's everything at all, and everything is nil.
  Same old get-up, dress, and tub;
  Same old breakfast; same old club;
  Same old feeling; same old blue;
  Same old story—nothing new!

Life consists of paying bills as long as you have health;
Woman? She'll be true to you—as long as you have wealth;
Think sometimes of marriage, if the right girl I could strike;
But the more I see of girls, the more they are alike.
  Same old giggles, smiles, and eyes;
  Same old kisses; same old sighs;
  Same old chaff you; same adieu;
  Same old story—nothing new!

Go to theatres sometimes to see the latest plays;
Same old plots I played with in my happy childhood's days;

Hero, same; same villain; and same heroine in tears,
Starving, homeless, in the snow—with diamonds in her ears.
    Same stern father making "bluffs";
    Leading man all teeth and cuffs;
    Same soubrettes, still twenty-two;
    Same old story—nothing new!

Friend of mine got married; in a year or so, a boy!
Father really foolish in his fond paternal joy;
Talked about that "kiddy," and became a dreadful bore—
Just as if a baby never had been born before.
    Same old crying, only more;
    Same old business, walking floor;
    Same old "kitchy—coochy—coo!"
    Same old baby—nothing new!
              Harry B. Smith.

HEM AND HAW

HEM and Haw were the sons of sin,
    Created to shally and shirk;
    Hem lay 'round, and Haw looked on,
While God did all the work.

Hem was a fogy, and Haw was a prig,
    For both had the dull, dull mind;
And whenever they found a thing to do,
    They yammered and went it blind.

Hem was the father of bigots and bores;
    As the sands of the sea were they;
And Haw was the father of all the tribe
    Who criticise to-day.

But God was an artist from the first,
    And knew what he was about;
While over his shoulder sneered these two,
    And advised him to rub it out.

They prophesied ruin ere man was made:
    "Such folly must surely fail!"
And when he was done, "Do you think, my Lord,
    He's better without a tail?"

And still in the honest working world,
    With posture and hint and smirk,
These sons of the devil are standing by
    While man does all the work.

They balk endeavour and baffle reform,
    In the sacred name of law;
And over the quavering voice of Hem
    Is the droning voice of Haw.
                    Bliss Carman.

THE SCEPTICS

IT was the little leaves beside the road.

    Said Grass: "What is that sound
So dismally profound,

That detonates and desolates the air?"
    "That is St. Peter's bell,"
    Said rain-wise Pimpernel;
    "He is music to the godly,
    Though to us he sounds so oddly,
And he terrifies the faithful unto prayer."

    Then something very like a groan
    Escaped the naughty little leaves.

    Said Grass: "And whither track
    These creatures all in black,
So woebegone and penitent and meek?"
    "They're mortals bound for church,"
    Said the little Silver Birch;
    "They hope to get to heaven,
    And have their sins forgiven,
If they talk to God about it once a week."

    And something very like a smile
    Ran through the naughty little leaves.

    Said Grass: "What is that noise
    That startles and destroys
Our blessed summer brooding when we're tired?"
    "That's folk a-praising God,"
    Said the tough old cynic Clod;
    "They do it every Sunday,
    They'll be all right on Monday;
It's just a little habit they've acquired."

And laughter spread among the little leaves.
                      Bliss Carman.

THE EVOLUTION OF A "NAME"

WHEN Hill, the poet, first essayed
   To push the goose's quill,
Scarce any name at all he made:
   ('Twas simply "A. H. Hill.")

But as success his efforts crowned,
   Rewarding greater skill,
His name expanded at a bound:
   (It was "A. Hiller Hill.")

Now that his work, be what it may,
   Is sure to "fill the bill,"
He has a name as wide as day:
   ("Aquilla Hiller Hill.")
         Charles Battell Loomis.

"THE HURT THAT HONOUR FEELS"

SUGGESTED BY THE ATTITUDE OF THE FRENCH
PRESS ON THE FASHODA QUESTION

THAT man is surely in the wrong,
   And lets his angry passions blind him,
Who, when a person comes along
   Behind him,

And hits him hard upon the cheek
   (One whom he took to be his brother),
Declines to turn and let him tweak
   The other.

It should be his immediate care,
  By delicate and tactful dealings,
To ease the striker's pain, and spare
      His feelings;

Nor should he, for his private ends,
  Make any personal allusion
Tending to aggravate his friend's
      Confusion.

For there are people built this way:
  They may have scratched your face, or bent it,
Yet, if you reason with them, they
      Resent it!

Their honour, quickly rendered sore,
  Demands that you should suffer mutely,
Lest they should feel it even more
      Acutely.

I knew a man of perfect tact;
  He caught a burglar once, my man did;
He took him in the very act,
      Red-handed;

What kind of language then occurred?
  How did he comment on the jemmy?
Did he employ some brutal word
      Like "demme"?

Or kick the stranger then and there,
  Or challenge him to formal battle?
Or spring upon the midnight air
      His rattle?

Certainly not! He knew too much;
  He knew that, as a bud is blighted,
Your burglar's honour, at a touch,
    Feels slighted.

He saw, as men of taste would see,
  That others' pride should be respected;
Some people cannot bear to be
    Detected.

Therefore his rising wrath he curbed,
  Gave him a smile as warm as may be,
Thanked him because he'd not disturbed
    The baby;

Apologized for fear his guest
  Might deem him casual or surly
For having rudely gone to bed
    So early.

The night was still not very old,
  And, short as was the invitation,
Would he not stay and share a cold
    Collation?

So was his tact not found at fault;
  So was he spared, by tasteful flattery,
What might have ended in assault
    Or battery.

Soft language is the best—how true!
  This doctrine, which I here rehearse, 'll
Apply to nations: it is u-
      -niversal!

Thus England should not take offence
  When from behind they jump upon her;
She must not hurt their lively sense
    Of honour.

For plain opinions, put in speech,
  Might lead to blows, which might be bloody,
A lesson which the press should teach
    And study!
                    Owen Seaman.

JOHN JENKINS

JOHN JENKINS, in an evil day, felt suddenly inclined
  To perpetrate a novel of an unobtrusive kind;
It held no "Strange Adventures" or "Mysterious Events,"
To terrify its readers with exciting accidents.
"I have never," said John Jenkins, "in my uneventful life,
Taken part in revolutions or in sanguinary strife;
My knowledge of historic days is lamentably scant,
But the present will afford me the material I want."
In fact, the rash resolve with which this foolish man set out,
Was just to deal with matters that he really knew about.
He studied all his characters with sympathy sincere;
He wrote, rewrote, and laboured at his chapters for a year;

He found a trusting publisher—one wonders much
    at that—
For this, his first production, fell quite absolutely
    flat.

The critics were benign indeed: "A harmless little
    tale,"
Was what they mostly called it. "While the reader
    cannot fail,"
Another wrote, "to credit it with fluency and grace,
Its fault is that it's really so extremely common-
    place."
A third condemned it roundly as "A simple, shame-
    less sham"
(Finding that alliteration often does for epigram).
And as John Jenkins wearily perused each fresh
    review,
He shook his head, and cried, "Oh, this will never,
    never do!"

Undaunted by catastrophe, John Jenkins tried
    again,
And wrote his second novel in a very different
    strain;
In one short month he finished what the critic at a
    glance
Pronounced a fine example of the latter-day Ro-
    mance.
His characters now figured in that period sub-
    lime
Which, with convenient vagueness, writers call
    "The Olden Time."

They said "Oddsbobs," "Grammercy," and other phrases sweet,
Extracted from old English as supplied in Wardour Street.
Exciting was their wooing, constant battles did they wage,
And some one murdered some one else on every other page;
Whereat the critics flung their caps, and one and all agreed,
"Hail to the great John Jenkins! This is True Romance indeed!"

And so John Jenkins flourishes, and scribbles wondrous fast
A string of such "romances," each exactly like the last;
A score of anxious publishers for his assistance seek;
His "Illustrated Interview" you meet with every week.
Nay, more; when any question, difficult and intricate,
Perplexes the intelligence of ministers of State,
The country disregards them all, and where they fear to tread,
Adventurous John Jenkins rushes boldly in instead,
And kindly (in the intervals of literary cares)
Instructs a grateful nation how to manage its affairs!
So, for all youthful authors who are anxious to succeed,
The moral of John Jenkins is—well, he who runs may read.

Anthony C. Deane.

A CERTAIN CURE

WHEN I look at my diligent neighbours,
    Each wholly convinced in his mind
    That the fruit of his personal labours
  Will be the reform of mankind,
When I notice the bland satisfaction
    That brightens the features of each—
Commendably prudent in action,
    Though mighty in speech—

Observing by dint of persistence
  What wide reputation they gain,
The clew to a happy existence
  Is rendered increasingly plain,
Because the self-satisfied feeling
  I covet may quickly be had
By any one owning (or stealing)
    A suitable fad.

Shall I hotly oppose Vivisection?
  Grow warm on the Drainage of Flats?
Or strive for the Better Protection
  Of Commons, Cathedrals, or Cats?
Perhaps in orations that thrill, I
  For freedom (and fever) will fight—
A portion of small-pox bacilli
    Is simply our right!

However, the choice is a detail;
  Whatever the fad be about,
To trade in it, wholesale and retail,
  To preach it, in season and out,

And so to be reckoned a leader
  (Although there be little to lead),
Yes, that's, O incredulous reader,
    The way to succeed!

You find that existence is hollow,
  The fight for position is hard.
A remedy? Yes, if you'll follow
  This way, to the fad-monger's yard:
Come, here is a hobby—astride it
  You settle; I tighten the girth—
So-off, and good-luck to you! Ride it
    For all it is worth!
Anthony C. Deane.

THE BEAUTIES OF NATURE

A FRAGMENT FROM AN UNPUBLISHED EPIC

HERE, my Amanda, let us seat ourselves;
  Here let us banish sorrow from our minds,
  By contemplating the delightful view
Which stretches all around us. And what joy
To be reminded thus, though far from town,
Of that which glorifies our native land,
Our British Trade! Gaze first at yonder wood:
On every tree is tastefully inscribed
In scarlet letters, "Use Niagara Soap!"
Turn to those meadows (at no distant date
But one uninteresting plain of grass),
Each bears a dozen hoardings, striking, bright,
Decked in resplendent variegated hues,

Telling the reader that Excelsior Pills
Cure influenza; that Brown's Tea is best,
And costs no more than one-and-six the pound;
And that the purchaser, who fain would quaff
Smith's special brand of Sherry, must beware
Of spurious imitations. On that hill
A grand gigantic sky-sign testifies
To Johnson's Hair Renewer; and beyond
You catch a glimpse of ocean, where the boats
Proclaim the message, painted on their sails:
"Robbinson's Boots are Warranted to Wear!"
Oh, does not such a view delight the heart?
Yea, soon the time will come when every inch
Of England shall display advertisements;
When newly taught, the birds shall add their notes
To the glad chorus, "Buy Pomponia Paste!"
The nightingale shall sing, and all the glade
Echo her music—"Buy Pomponia Paste!"
How great a debt of thankfulness we owe
To these the benefactors of our time,
Who both contribute to the human race
Productions to our ancestors unknown,
And also glorify each rural scene
By the announcements of their excellence!
And how we pity those of olden time
Who praised the country, but so little knew
What beauty could be added to the scene
By the artistic advertiser's aid,
To whom the hills, the meadows, and the woods
Brought no glad message, such as we receive,
Of Soaps and Sugars, Pens, Pianos, Pills!
Anthony C. Deane.

PARADISE

A HINDOO LEGEND

A HINDOO died—a happy thing to do
When twenty years united to a shrew.
Released, he hopefully for entrance cries
Before the gates of Brahma's Paradise.
"Hast been through Purgatory?" Brahma said.
"I have been married," and he hung his head.
"Come in, come in, and welcome, too, my son!
Marriage and Purgatory are as one."
In bliss extreme he entered heaven's door,
And knew the peace he ne'er had known before.

He scarce had entered in the Garden fair,
Another Hindoo asked admission there.
The self-same question Brahma asked again:
"Hast been through Purgatory?" "No; what then?"
"Thou canst not enter!" did the god reply.
"He that went in was no more there than I."
"Yes, that is true, but he has married been,
And so on earth has suffered for all sin."
"Married? 'Tis well; for I've been married twice!"
"Begone! We'll have no fools in Paradise!"
George Birdseye.

HOCH! DER KAISER

DER Kaiser of dis Vaterland
   Und Gott on high all dings command—
   Ve two. Ach! don't you understand?
  Myself—und Gott.

Vile some men sing der power divine,
Mein soldiers sing "Der Wacht am Rhine,"
Und drink deir health in Rhenish wine
   Of Me—und Gott.

Dere's France, she swaggers all aroundt;
She's ausgespielt, of no account;
To much ve tink she don't amount;
   Myself—und Gott.

She vill not dare to fight again;
But if she shouldt, I'll show her blain
Dot Elsass und (in French) Lorraine
   Are mein—by Gott!

Dere's grandma dinks she's nicht small beer;
Mit Boers und such she interfere;
She'll learn none owns dis hemisphere
   But me—und Gott!

She dinks, good Frau, fine ships she's got,
Und soldiers mit der scarlet goat.
Ach! Ve could knock dem! Pouf! like dot,
   Myself—mit Gott!

In dimes of peace brebare for wars;
I bear de spear und helm of Mars,
Und care not for a tousand Czars,
    Myself—mit Gott!

In fact, I humour efery vhim,
Mit aspect dark und visage grim;
Gott pulls mit me, und I mit Him,
    Myself—und Gott!
Rodney Blake.

ON A MAGAZINE SONNET

"SCORN not the sonnet," though its strength be sapped,
  Nor say malignant its inventor blundered;
The corpse that here in fourteen lines is wrapped
  Had otherwise been covered with a hundred.
Russell Hilliard Loines.

EARTH

IF this little world to-night
    Suddenly should fall through space
  In a hissing, headlong flight,
Shrivelling from off its face,
As it falls into the sun,
  In an instant every trace
Of the little crawling things—
  Ants, philosophers, and lice,
Cattle, cockroaches, and kings,
  Beggars, millionaires, and mice,

Men and maggots—all as one,
  As it falls into the sun—
Who can say but at the same
  Instant, from some planet far
A child may watch us, and exclaim:
  "See the pretty shooting star!"
Oliver Herford.

A BUTTERFLY OF FASHION

A REAL Butterfly, I mean,
  With Orange-Pointed saffron wings,
And coat of inky Velveteen—
None of your Fashion-Plated Things

That dangle from the Apron-strings
  Of Mrs. Grundy, or you see
Loll by the Stage-Door or the Wings,
  Or sadly flit from Tea to Tea;

Not such a Butterfly was he;
  He lived for Sunshine and the Hour;
He did not flit from Tea to Tea,
  But gayly flew from Flower to Flower.

One Day there came a Thunder-Shower;
  An Open Window he espied;
He fluttered in; behold, a Flower!
  An Azure Rose with petals wide.

He did not linger to decide
  Which Flower; there was no other there.

He calmly settled down inside
  That Rose, and no one said "Beware!"

There was no Friend to say "Take care!"
  How ever, then, could he suppose
This Blossom, of such Colour Rare,
  Was just an Artificial Rose?

All might have ended well—who knows?—
  But just then some one chanced to say:
"The very Latest Thing! That Rose
  In Paris is the Rage To-day."

No Rose of such a Tint *outré*
  Was ever seen in Garden Bed;
The Butterfly had such a Gay
  Chromatic Sense, it turned his head.

"The Very Latest Thing?" he said;
  "Long have I sighed for something New!
O Roses Yellow, White, and Red,
  Let others sip; mine shall be Blue!"

The Flavour was not Nice, 't is true
  (He felt a Pain inside his Waist).
"It is not well to overdo,"
  Said he, "a just-acquired taste."

The Shower passed; he joined in haste
  His friends. With condescension great,
Said he, "I fear your time you waste;
  Real Roses are quite out of date."

He argued early, argued late,
   Till what was erst a HARMLESS POSE
Grew to a Fierce, Inordinate
   Craving for Artificial Rose.

He haunted Garden Parties, Shows,
   Wherever Ladies Congregate,
And in their Bonnets thrust his nose
   His Craving Fierce to Satiate.

At last he chanced—sad to relate!—
   Into a Caterer's with his Pose,
And there Pneumonia was his Fate,
   From sitting on an Ice-Cream Rose.

O Reader, shun the Harmless Pose!
   They buried him, with scant lament,
Beneath a Common Brier-Rose,
   And wrote:
      HERE LIES A DECADENT.
                 Oliver Herford.

GENERAL SUMMARY

WE are very slightly changed
   From the semi-apes who ranged
      India's prehistoric clay;
Whoso drew the longest bow,
Ran his brother down, you know,
   As we run men down to-day.
"Dowb," the first of all his race,
Met the Mammoth face to face

On the lake or in the cave,
Stole the steadiest canoe,
Ate the quarry others slew,
    Died—and took the finest grave.

When they scratched the reindeer-bone,
Someone made the sketch his own,
    Filched it from the artist—then,
Even in those early days,
Won a simple Viceroy's praise
    Through the toil of other men.

Ere they hewed the Sphinx's visage,
Favouritism governed kissage,
Even as it does in this age.

Who shall doubt the secret hid
Under Cheops' pyramid
Was that the contractor did
    Cheops out of several millions?
Or that Joseph's sudden rise
To Comptroller of Supplies
Was a fraud of monstrous size
    On King Pharaoh's swart Civilians?

Thus, the artless songs I sing
Do not deal with anything
    New or never said before.
As it was in the beginning,
Is to-day official sinning,
    And shall be for evermore.
                  Rudyard Kipling.

THE CONUNDRUM OF THE WORKSHOPS

WHEN the flush of a new-born sun fell first on Eden's green and gold,
Our father Adam sat under the Tree and scratched with a stick in the mould;
And the first rude sketch that the world had seen was joy to his mighty heart,
Till the Devil whispered behind the leaves, "It's pretty, but is it Art?"

Wherefore he called to his wife, and fled to fashion his work anew—
The first of his race who cared a fig for the first, most dread review;
And he left his lore to the use of his sons, and that was a glorious gain
When the Devil chuckled, "Is it Art?" in the ear of the branded Cain.

They fought and they talked in the North and the South, they talked and they fought in the West,
Till the waters rose on the pitiful land, and the poor Red Clay had rest—
Had rest till that dank blank-canvas dawn when the dove was preened to start,
And the Devil bubbled below the keel, "It's human, but is it Art?"

They builded a tower to shiver the sky and wrench the stars apart,
Till the Devil grunted behind the bricks, "It's striking, but is it Art?"

The stone was dropped at the quarry-side, and the idle derrick swung,
While each man talked of the aims of Art, and each in an alien tongue.

The tale is as old as the Eden Tree, and new as the new-cut tooth,
For each man knows, ere his lip-thatch grows, he is master of Art and Truth;
And each man hears, as the twilight nears to the beat of his dying heart,
The Devil drum on the darkened pane, "You did it, but was it Art?"

We have learned to whittle the Eden Tree to the shape of a surplice-peg;
We have learned to bottle our parents twain in the yolk of an addled egg;
We know that the tail must wag the dog, for the horse is drawn by the cart;
But the Devil whoops, as he whooped of old, "It's clever, but is it Art?"

When the flicker of London Sun falls faint on the Club-room's green and gold,
The sons of Adam sit them down and scratch with their pens in the mould;
They scratch with their pens in the mould of their graves, and the ink and the anguish start,
For the Devil mutters behind the leaves, "It's pretty, but is it Art?"

Now, if we could win to the Eden Tree where the
    Four Great Rivers flow,
And the Wreath of Eve is red on the turf as she
    left it long ago,
And if we could come when the sentry slept and
    softly scurry through,
By the favour of God we might know as much—as
    our father Adam knew!
Rudyard Kipling.

EXTRACTS FROM THE RUBAIYAT OF OMAR CAYENNE

WAKE! for the Hack can scatter into flight
    Shakespeare and Dante in a single Night!
        The Penny-a-Liner is Abroad, and
    strikes
Our Modern Literature with blithering Blight.

Before Historical Romances died,
Methought a Voice from Art's Olympus cried,
    "When all Dumas and Scott is still for Sale,
Why nod o'er drowsy Tales, by Tyros tried?"

A Book of Limericks—Nonsense, anyhow—
Alice in Wonderland, the Purple Cow
    Beside me singing on Fifth Avenue—
Ah, this were Modern Literature enow!

Ah, my Beloved, write the Book that clears
To-Day of dreary Debt and sad Arrears;

To-morrow!—Why, To-Morrow I may see
My Nonsense popular as Edward Lear's.

And we, that now within the Editor's Room
Make merry while we have our little Boom,
   Ourselves must we give way to next month's
      Set—
Girls with Three Names, who know not Who from
      Whom!

As then the Poet for his morning Sup
Fills with a Metaphor his mental Cup,
   Do you devoutly read your Manuscripts
That Someone may, before you burn them up!

And if the Bosh you write, the Trash you read,
End in the Garbage-Barrel—take no Heed;
   Think that you are no worse than other Scribes,
Who scribble Stuff to meet the Public Need.

So, when WHO's-WHO records your silly Name,
You'll think that you have found the Road to Fame;
   And though ten thousand other Names are there,
You'll fancy you're a Genius, just the Same!

Why, if an Author can fling Art aside,
And in a Book of Balderdash take pride,
   Were't not a Shame—were't not a Shame for
      him
A Conscientious Novel to have tried?

And fear not, if the Editor refuse
Your work, he has no more from which to choose;

A Satire Anthology

The Literary Microbe shall bring forth
Millions of Manuscripts too bad to use.

The Woman's Touch runs through our Magazines;
For her the Home, and Mother-Tale, and Scenes
   Of Love-and-Action, Happy at the End—
The same old Plots, the same old Ways and Means.

But if, in spite of this, you build a Plot
Which these immortal Elements has not,
   You gaze To-Day upon a Slip, which reads,
"The Editor Regrets"—and such-like Rot.

Waste not your Ink, and don't attempt to use
That subtle Touch which Editors refuse;
   Better be jocund at two cents a word,
Than, starving, court an ill-requited Muse!

Strange—is it not?—that of the Authors who
Publish in England, such a mighty Few
   Make a Success, though here they score a Hit?
The British Public knows a Thing or Two!

The Scribe no question makes of Verse or Prose,
But what the Editor demands, he shows;
   And he who buys three thousand words of Drool,
He knows what People want—you Bet He knows!

Would but some wingéd Angel bring the News
Of Critic who reads Books that he Reviews,
   And make the stern Reviewer do as well
Himself, before he Meed of Praise refuse!

Ah, Love, could you and I perchance succeed
In boiling down the Million Books we read
  Into One Book, and edit that a Bit—
There'd be a WORLD'S BEST LITERATURE indeed!
                              Gelett Burgess.

BALLADE OF EXPANSION

1899

TIME was he sang the British Brute,
    The ruthless lion's grasping greed,
    The European Law of Loot,
  The despot's devastating deed;
  But now he sings the heavenly creed
Of saintly sword and friendly fist,
  He loves you, though he makes you bleed—
The Ethical Expansionist!

He loves you, Heathen! Though his foot
  May kick you like a worthless weed
From that wild field where you have root,
  And scatter to the winds your seed;
  He's just the government you need;
If you object, why, he'll insist,
  And, on your protest, "draw a bead"—
The Ethical Expansionist!

He'll take you to him *coute que coute!*
  He'll win you, though you fight and plead.
His guns shall urge his ardent suit,
  Relentless fire his cause shall speed.

A Satire Anthology

In time you'll learn to write and read,
(That is, if you should then exist!)
You won't, if you his course impede—
The Ethical Expansionist!

ENVIO

Heathen, you must, you shall be freed!
It's really useless to resist;
To save your life, you'd better heed
The Ethical Expansionist!
Hilda Johnson.

FRIDAY AFTERNOON AT THE BOSTON SYMPHONY HALL

SINCE Bach so well his clavier tuned, since
Palestrina wrote his Masses,
Since Modes Ecclesiastical began to puzzle music-classes,
All Anglo-Saxondom has tried, by teaching of its lads and lasses,
The gift of Orpheus to acquire,
Whilst substituting for his lyre
The concert-room's imposing choir—string-orchestra, wood, wind, and brasses.

Hallé in Free Trade Hall I heard when first I took the music craze on;
Later, in Sydney, New South Wales, I listened to Roberto Hazon;

Berlin's "Philharmonie," which plays the winter through alternate days on,
    Took my spare cash from time to time,
    And I may add, for sake of rhyme,
Richter at Bradford, quite sublime! Pauer and Colonne in the *Saison*.

Lest I should make the list too short, and show a lack of erudition,
I'd better mention Cowan, who ruled at the Melbourne Exhibition,
Villiers Stanford, Auguste Mannés, and Thomas, whose keen intuition
    Carried him westward from New York
    To the Metropolis of Pork,
Where, thanks to his devoted work, Beethoven found superb rendition.

All these I've heard, and others, too—poor Seidl, who has talked with Charon;
Nikisch, whose eager gestures make it difficult to keep your hair on;
Then there's a chap whose name I've lost (I think he wrote "The Rose of Sharon");
    Wood, of Queen's Hall, in London Town;
    Strauss, for his programme-music known;
Dozens whose brains the genius own that's common to the seed of Aaron.

But if good music is the thing your inmost soul would fain get fat on,
Avoid, I pray, good Boston town, where, though no male may keep his hat on,

The ladies talk the whole show through, and you
    will certainly be sat on
        If you protest, for they will say
        "We have the right to, if we pay
Each for a seat, and chat away in time with the
    conductor's baton."

Oft that October day I see—delightful month,
    June's elder sister;
The splendid Hall was opened, and a poem read
    by Owen Wister
(So kind the Muse, 'twas plain to see in Philadel-
    phia he had kissed her).
        Missa Solennis, then, in B,
        Proud to be in such company
Of fair-clad girls, and panoply of bright new paint
    without a blister.

Nowhere on this broad earth, I grant, is music
    played to such perfection;
Even strict Apthorp will admit that false notes are
    a rare exception;
But what avail such wond'rous play, when to the
    Hall for friend's inspection
        Each lady takes some little thing—
        New-purchased pocket-book, or ring—
Or in loud voice the matrons sing the dangers of
    small-pox infection.

To Mendelssohn's Scotch Symphony I've heard of
    Johnny's scarlet fever;
Bizet's Arlesienne Suites I link with Kate's sore
    throat that wouldn't leave her;

A Satire Anthology

Oft to Wagnerian strains I've heard eager dispute
of seal and beaver,
 To clasp fair Mabel's dainty throat,
 Or make for Madge a winter coat,
As seen on transatlantic boat, from Messrs. Robinson and Cleaver.

Pray do not think that Boston girls all talk such
feeble stuff as this is;
To Glazounoff's inspiring notes they'll quote from
Phillips's "Ulysses";
To Massenet's caressing phrase admire Burne-Jones's long-necked misses;
 Ask what of Ibsen you may think,
 Of Nietzsche or of Maeterlinck,
And tell, to score of Humperdink, Buddha's most
esoteric blisses.

A concert it is hard to turn into a *conversazione*,
Except with consequences which would make the
softest heart quite stony,
Unless 'tis done in restaurant where foreigners eat
macaroni,
 And greasy dago tips a stave,
 Or where the blue Atlantic wave,
While pallid shop-girls misbehave, doth cool the
verdant Isle of Coney.

Forgive me if I criticise; I love you none the less,
Priscilla,
And when the concert's o'er, we'll go where Huyler
serves his best vanilla;

A Satire Anthology

Talk as you will, I love you still; I'd live with you
    in flat or villa,
        For never, never you'd commit
        A split infinitive, and it
Is certain you would not omit in proper place the
    French cedilla.
Faulkner Armytage.

WAR IS KIND

DO not weep, maiden, for war is kind.
    Because your lover threw wild hands towards the sky,
And the affrighted steed ran on alone,
        Do not weep.
        War is kind.

Hoarse, booming drums of the regiment,
Little souls who thirst for fight,
    These men were born to drill and die.
The unexplained glory flies above them,
Great is the battle-god, great, and his kingdom—
    A field where a thousand corpses lie.

Do not weep, babe, for war is kind.
Because your father tumbled in the yellow trenches,
Raged at his breast, gulped and died,
        Do not weep.
        War is kind.

Swift-blazing flag of the regiment,
Eagle with crest of red and gold,

These men were born to drill and die.
Point for them the virtue of slaughter;
Make plain to them the excellence of killing,
    And a field where a thousand corpses lie.

Mother, whose heart hung humble as a button
On the bright splendid shroud of your son,
        Do not weep.
        War is kind.

Stephen Crane.

LINES

A LITTLE ink more or less!
    It surely can't matter?
    Even the sky and the opulent sea,
The plains and the hills, aloof,
Hear the uproar of all these books.
But it is only a little ink more or less.

A MAN said to the universe,
    "Sir, I exist!"
    "However," replied the universe,
"The fact has not created in me
A sense of obligation."

THE Wayfarer,
    Perceiving the pathway to truth,
    Was struck with astonishment.
It was thickly grown with weeds.
"Ha," he said,

"I see that none has passed here
In a long time."
Later he saw that each weed
Was a singular knife.
"Well," he mumbled at last,
"Doubtless there are other roads."

"HAVE you ever made a just man?"
"Oh, I have made three," answered God,
"But two of them are dead,
And the third—
Listen! listen,
And you will hear the thud of his defeat."

THREE little birds in a row
Sat musing.
A man passed near that place.
Then did the little birds nudge each other.
They said, "He thinks he can sing."
They threw back their heads to laugh.
With quaint countenances
They regarded him.
They were very curious,
Those three little birds in a row.

A YOUTH, in apparel that glittered,
Went to walk in a grim forest.
There he met an assassin
Attired all in garb of old days;

He, scowling through the thickets,
And dagger poised quivering,
Rushed upon the youth.
"Sir," said the latter,
"I am enchanted, believe me,
To die thus
In this mediæval fashion,
According to the best legends;
Ah, what joy!"
Then took he the wound, smiling,
And died, content.

A MAN saw a ball of gold in the sky;
    He climbed for it,
    And eventually he achieved it;
It was clay.
Now this is the strange part:
When the man went to the earth
And looked again,
Lo, there was the ball of gold.
Now this is the strange part:
It was a ball of gold.
Aye, by the heavens, it was a ball of gold.

"THINK as I think," said a man,
    "Or you are abominably wicked;
    You are a toad."
And after I had thought of it,
I said, "I will, then, be a toad."

A Satire Anthology

UPON the road of my life,
    Passed me many fair creatures,
    Clothed all in white, and radiant;
To one, finally, I made speech:
"Who art thou?"
But she, like the others,
Kept cowled her face,
And answered in haste, anxiously,
"I am Good Deed, forsooth;
You have often seen me."
"Not uncowled," I made reply.
And with rash and strong hand,
Though she resisted,
I drew away the veil,
And gazed at the features of Vanity.
She, shamefaced, went on;
And after I had mused a time,
I said of myself, "Fool!"
                    Stephen Crane.

FROM THE HOUSE OF A HUNDRED LIGHTS

WHAT! doubt the Master Workman's hand
    Because my fleshly ills increase?
No; for there still remains one chance
    That I am not His masterpiece.

Out of all Epicurus' train
    I wonder which class is sincerest,

The drones, or workers, who believe
   This doctrine of "Believe-the-Nearest."

You invalids who cannot drink
   Much wine or love, I say to you,
"Content yourselves with laughing at
   The antics of the fools who do."

Bad-liver says each morning's sun
   Is but to him a juggling bawd,
That opens up for man's deceit
   Only another chest of fraud.

Old Ash-in-Blood still deals advice
   To Rose-of-Youth, and as he deals it,
Rolls piously his eyes; but ah,
   He knows the pain whose body feels it.

In youth my head was hollow, like
   A gourd, not knowing good from ill;
Now, though 'tis long since then, I'm like
   A reed—wind-shaken, hollow still.

Said one young foolish mouth with words
   As many as the desert sands,
"My grandfather took daily baths
   In rose-water; just smell my hands!"

And now young poets will arise
   And burst earth's fetters link by link,
And mount the skies of poesy,
   And daub Time's helpless wings with ink!

A Satire Anthology

In youth I wrote a song so great,
    I thought that, like a flaring taper,
'Twould shine abroad; and so it did,
    To the four corners of the—paper.

And, poet, should you think your songs
    Must, or even will, be read,
Bethink thee, friend, what fine springs rise
    Impotently from the sea's bed.

I marvelled at the speaker's tongue,
    And marvelled more as he unrolled it.
How strange a thing it was, and yet
    How much more strange if he could hold it!

A little judge once said to me,
    "Behold, my friend, I caused these laws!"
But I knew One who, strange to say,
    Had been the Causer of this Cause.

See fathoms deep, midst gold and gems,
    Life sits and weeps on ocean's floor;
But though on land no treasure is,
    Life laughs and stands. I'll stay on shore.

This mess of cracked ice, stones and bread,
    Of sweetness savours not a bit,
And yet, my friends, I'm satisfied,
    For lo! I—I—invented it!
              Frederic Ridgely Torrence.

THE BRITISH VISITOR

ARRIV'D, at last, Niagara to scan,
   He walks erect and feels himself a man;
   Surveys the cataract with a "critic's eye,"
Resolv'd to pass no "imperfections by"—
Niag'ra, wonder of the Deity,
Where God's own spirit reigns in majesty.
With sullen roar the foaming billows sweep;
A world of waters thunders o'er the steep;
The unmingled colours laugh upon the spray,
And one eternal rainbow gilds the day.
Oh, glorious God! Oh, scene surpassing all!
"True, true," quoth he, "'tis something of a fall."
Now, shall unpunish'd such a vagrant band,
Pour like the plagues of Egypt on the land,
Eyeing each fault, to all perfection blind,
Shedding the taint of a malignant mind?
               From the Trollopiad.

A MATCH

IF I were Anglo-Saxon,
    And you were Japanese,
   We'd study storks together,
Pluck out the peacock's feather,
And lean our languid backs on
   The stiffest of settees—
If I were Anglo-Saxon,
   And you were Japanese.

A Satire Anthology

If you were Della-Cruscan,
   And I were A.-Mooresque,
We'd make our limbs look less in
Artistic folds, and dress in
What once were tunics Tuscan
   In Dante's days grotesque—
If you were Della-Cruscan,
   And I were A.-Mooresque.

If I were mock Pompeian,
   And you Belgravian Greek,
We'd glide 'mid gaping Vandals
In shapeless sheets and sandals,
Like shades in Tartarean
   Dim ways remote and bleak—
If I were mock Pompeian,
   And you Belgravian Greek.

If you were Culture's scarecrow,
   And I the guy of Art,
I'd learn in latest phrases
Of either's quaintest crazes
To lisp, and let my hair grow,
   While yours you'd cease to part—
If you were Culture's scarecrow,
   And I the guy of Art.

If I'd a Botticelli,
   And you'd a new Burne-Jones,
We'd dote for days and days on
Their mystic hues, and gaze on

With lowering looks that felly
    We'd fix upon their tones—
If I'd a Botticelli,
    And you'd a new Burne-Jones.

If you were skilled at crewels,
    And I a dab at rhymes,
I'd write delirious "ballads,"
While you your bilious salads
Were stitching upon two ells
    Of coarsest crash, at times—
If you were skilled at crewels,
    And I a dab at rhymes.

If I were what's "consummate,"
    And you were quite "too, too,"
'Twould be our Eldorado
To have a yellow dado,
Our happiness to hum at
    A teapot tinted blue—
If I were what's "consummate,"
    And you were quite "too, too."

If you were what "intense" is,
    And I were like "decay,"
We'd mutely muse, or mutter
In terms distinctly utter,
And find out what the sense is
    Of this æsthetic lay—
If you were what "intense" is,
    And I were like "decay."

If you were wan, my lady,
  And I your lover weird,
We'd sit and wink for hours
At languid lily-flowers,
Till, fain of all things fady,
  We faintly—disappeared—
If you were wan, my lady,
  And I your lover weird.

Punch.

WANTED—A GOVERNESS

A GOVERNESS wanted—well fitted to fill
    The post of tuition with competent skill—
    In a gentleman's family highly genteel;
Superior attainments are quite indispensable,
With everything, too, that's correct and ostensible;
Morals of pure unexceptionability;
Manners well formed, and of strictest gentility.
The pupils are five—ages, six to sixteen,
All as promising girls as ever were seen;
And besides (though 'tis scarcely worth while to put that in),
There is one little boy, but he only learns Latin.
The lady must teach all the several branches
Whereinto polite education now launches.
She's expected to speak the French tongue like a native,
And be to her pupils of all its points dative.
Italian she must know *à fond*, nor need banish
Whatever acquaintance she may have with Spanish;

Nor would there be harm in a trifle of German,
In the absence, that is, of the master, Von Hermann.
The harp and piano—*cela va sans dire*—
With thorough-bass, too, on the plan of Logier.
In drawing in pencil, and chalks, and the tinting
That's called Oriental, she must not be stint in;
She must paint upon paper, and satin, and velvet;
And if she knows gilding, she's no need to shelve it.
Dancing, of course, with the newest gambades,
The Polish mazurka, and best gallopades;
Arithmetic, history joined with chronology,
Heraldry, botany, writing, conchology,
Grammar, and satin stitch, netting, geography,
Astronomy, use of the globes, and cosmography.
'Twere also as well she should be calisthenical,
That her charges' young limbs may be pliant to any call.
Their health, play, and studies, and moral condition
Must be superintended without intermission.
At home she must all habits check that disparage,
And when they go out must attend to their carriage.
Her faith must be orthodox, temper most pliable,
Health good, and reference quite undeniable.
These are the principal matters—*Au reste*,
Address, Bury Street, Mrs. General Peste.
As the *salary's moderate*, none need apply
Who more on that point than on *comfort* rely.

Anonymous.

LINES BY AN OLD FOGY

I'M thankful that the sun and moon
  Are both hung up so high,
  That no presumptuous hand can stretch
And pull them from the sky.
If they were not, I have no doubt
  But some reforming ass
Would recommend to take them down
  And light the world with gas.

Anonymous.

INDEX OF TITLES

INDEX OF TITLES

		PAGE
ADDRESS TO THE UNCO GUID, OR THE RIGIDLY RIGHTEOUS	Robert Burns	86
Advanced Thinker, An	Brander Matthews	282
Aesthete, The	W. S. Gilbert	260
All-Saints	Edmund Yates	237
Anglicised Utopia	W. S. Gilbert	252
Annuity, The	George Outram	156
Ape and the Lady, The	W. S. Gilbert	250
Ass's Legacy, The	Rutebœuf	7
Atlantic City	H. C. Bunner	290
BALLADE OF EXPANSION	Hilda Johnson	331
Ballade of Literary Fame	Andrew Lang	274
Ballade of Old-Time Ladies, A (Translated by John Payne)	François Villon	11
Battle of Blenheim, The	Robert Southey	97
Beauties of Nature, The	Anthony C. Deane	317
Bird in the Hand, A	Frederick E. Weatherly	281
Boston Lullaby, A	James Jeffrey Roche	277
British Visitor, The	From the Trollopiad	343
Butterfly of Fashion, A	Oliver Herford	322
CACOËTHES SCRIBENDI	Oliver Wendell Holmes	166
Carman's Account of a Lawsuit, A	Sir David Lyndsay	12
Certain Cure, A	Anthony C. Deane	316
Character of Holland, The	Andrew Marvell	35
Chorus of Anglomaniacs (From "The Buntling Ball")	Edgar Fawcett	275
Chorus of Women	Aristophanes	3
Christmas Out of Town	James Smith	103
Cockle v. Cackle	Thomas Hood	140
Cologne	Samuel T. Coleridge	96

A Satire Anthology

		PAGE
Conservative, A	Charlotte Perkins (Stetson) Gilman	304
Constant Lover, The	Sir John Suckling	27
Contentment	Oliver Wendell Holmes	171
Conundrum of the Workshops, The	Rudyard Kipling	326
Country House Party, A	Lord Byron	127
Country Squire, The	Tomas Yriarte	80
Critics	Elizabeth Barrett Browning	164
Cui Bono?	Thomas Carlyle	135
Cynical Ode to an Ultra-Cynical Public	Charles Mackay	192
Damages, Two Hundred Pounds	William Makepeace Thackeray	182
Description of Holland	Samuel Butler	30
Devil at Home, The	Thomas Kibble Hervey	149
Diamond Wedding, The	Edmund Clarence Stedman	240
Distiches	John Hay	264
Dr. Delany's Villa	Thomas Sheridan	52
Duke of Buckingham, The	John Dryden	37
Earth	Oliver Herford	321
Eggs, The	Tomas Yriarte	83
Elegy on the Death of a Mad Dog, An	Oliver Goldsmith	72
Epistle to Sir Robert Walpole, An	Henry Fielding	65
Epitaph, An	George John Cayley	64
Epitaph, An	Matthew Prior	43
Eternal London	Thomas Moore	105
Etiquette	W. S. Gilbert	254
Evolution of a "Name," The	Charles Battell Loomis	310
Extracts from the Rubaiyat of Omar Cayenne	Gelett Burgess	328
Faithful Picture of Ordinary Society, A	William Cowper	74
Fame	James Herbert Morse	269

Index of Titles

		PAGE
Fame's Penny Trumpet	Lewis Carroll	238
Familiar Letter to Several Correspondents, A	Oliver Wendell Holmes	167
Fate of Pious Dan, The	Samuel Walter Foss	298
Father-Land and Mother-Tongue	Samuel Lover	135
Father Molloy	Samuel Lover	136
Five Lives	Edward Rowland Sill	270
Font in the Forest, The	Herman Knickerbocker Vielé	294
Fragment, A	Grace Greenwood	212
Friar of Orders Gray, The	John O'Keefe	79
Friday Afternoon at the Boston Symphony Hall	Faulkner Armytage	332
Friend of Humanity and the Knife-Grinder, The	George Canning	92
From "A Fable for Critics"	James Russell Lowell	201
From "As You Like It"	Shakespeare	22
From "English Bards and Scotch Reviewers"	Lord Byron	125
From "King Henry IV."	Shakespeare	20
From "Love's Labour's Lost"	Shakespeare	21
From "The Devil's Drive"	Lord Byron	123
From "The Epistle to Dr. Arbuthnot"	Alexander Pope	60
From "The Feast of the Poets"	James Henry Leigh Hunt	116
From "The House of a Hundred Lights"	Frederic Ridgely Torrence	340
From "The Love of Fame"	Edward Young	50
Furniture of a Woman's Mind, The	Jonathan Swift	48
GAFFER GRAY (FROM "HUGH TREVOR")	Thomas Holcroft	139
General Summary	Rudyard Kipling	324
Giles' Hope	Samuel T. Coleridge	96
Give Me a Theme	Richard Watson Gilder	274
Great Critics, The	Charles Mackay	193
Greediness Punished	Friedrich Rückert	130
HE AND SHE	Eugene Fitch Ware	272
Hem and Haw	Bliss Carman	307

A Satire Anthology

		PAGE
Hen, The	Matthew Claudius	77
Hiding the Skeleton	George Meredith	229
Hoch! der Kaiser	Rodney Blake	320
Holy Willie's Prayer	Robert Burns	88
Horace Concocting an Ode	Thomas Dekker	23
How to Make a Man of Consequence	Mark Lemon	173
How To Make a Novel	Lord Charles Neaves	150
"Hurt that Honour Feels, The"	Owen Seaman	310
Introduction to the True-Born Englishman	Daniel Defoe	41
Job	Samuel T. Coleridge	95
John Jenkins	Anthony C. Deane	313
King of Yvetot, The (Version of W. M. Thackeray)	Pierre Jean De Béranger	109
Kitty of Coleraine	Edward Lysaght	91
Latest Decalogue, The	Arthur Hugh Clough	200
Laureate, The	William E. Aytoun	194
Let Us All Be Unhappy Together	Charles Dibdin	78
Life in Laconics	Mary Mapes Dodge	263
Lines	Stephen Crane	337
Lines by an Old Fogy	Anonymous	348
Literary Lady, The	Richard Brinsley Sheridan	84
Lost Leader, The	Robert Browning	186
Love-Letter, The	Austin Dobson	267
Lying	Thomas Moore	108
Malbrouck	Translated by Father Prout	161
Manly Heart, The	George Wither	26
Man's Requirements, A	Elizabeth Barrett Browning	163
Match, A	Punch	343
Meeting of the Clabberhuses, The	Samuel Walter Foss	300

Index of Titles

		PAGE
Midges	*Robert Bulwer Lytton*	230
Miser, The	*Edward Fitzgerald*	166
Modern Puffing System, The	*Thomas Moore*	106
Modest Wit, A	*Selleck Osborn*	112
Mourner à la Mode, The	*John Godfrey Saxe*	197
Mr. Barney Maguire's Account of the Coronation	*Richard Harris Barham*	119
Mr. Molony's Account of the Ball Given to the Nepaulese Ambassador by the Peninsular and Oriental Company	*William Makepeace Thackeray*	179
My Lord Tomnoddy	*Robert Barnabas Brough*	227
NET OF LAW, THE	*James Jeffrey Roche*	277
Nora's Vow	*Sir Walter Scott*	94
Nothing to Wear	*William Allen Butler*	213
OF A CERTAIN MAN	*Sir John Harrington*	16
Of Propriety	*Charles Stuart Calverley*	235
On a Magazine Sonnet	*Russell Hilliard Loines*	321
On Don Surly	*Ben Jonson*	24
On Johnson	*John Wolcott (Peter Pindar)*	75
On Lytton	*Alfred Tennyson*	177
On Shadwell	*John Dryden*	38
On Smollett	*Charles Churchill*	73
Origin of Sin, The	*Samuel Walter Foss*	294
Our Village	*Thomas Hood*	145
Ozymandias	*Percy Bysshe Shelley*	134
PARADISE. A HINDOO LEGEND	*George Birdseye*	319
Pauper's Drive, The	*Thomas Noel*	175
Peace: A Study	*Charles Stuart Calverley*	236
Pelters of Pyramids	*Richard Hengist Horne*	155
Philosopher, A	*Samuel Walter Foss*	295
Philosopher's Scales, The	*Jane Taylor*	114
Pious Editor's Creed, The	*James Russell Lowell*	206
Poem to the Critic, The	*Richard Watson Gilder*	274
Poet and the Critics, The	*Austin Dobson*	265
Poet of Fashion, The	*James Smith*	101
Pope and the Net, The	*Robert Browning*	188
Positivists, The	*Mortimer Collins*	225

A Satire Anthology

		PAGE
Precise Tailor, A	*Sir John Harrington*	16
Public Breakfast, The	*Christopher Anstey*	67
QUIDNUNCKIS, THE	*John Gay*	54
RELIGION OF HUDIBRAS, THE	*Samuel Butler*	31
Remedy Worse Than the Disease, The	*Matthew Prior*	45
Remonstrance, The	*Sir John Suckling*	28
Reporters	*George Crabbe*	85
Revelry in India	*Bartholomew Dowling*	210
Review, A	*Bayard Taylor*	221
Rich and Poor; or, Saint and Sinner	*Thomas L. Peacock*	117
Rich and the Poor Man, The (From the Russian of Kremnitzer)	*Sir John Bowring*	132
SAILOR'S CONSOLATION, THE	*William Pitt*	152
Saintship versus Conscience	*Samuel Butler*	29
Same Old Story	*Harry B. Smith*	306
Sandys' Ghost	*Alexander Pope*	57
Satire on Edward Howard	*Charles Sackville, Earl of Dorset*	39
Satire on the Scots	*John Cleiveland*	32
Sceptics, The	*Bliss Carman*	308
Scholar and His Dog, The	*John Marston*	25
Schoolmaster Abroad with His Son, The	*Charles Stuart Calverley*	233
Sick Man and the Angel, The	*John Gay*	55
Sky-Making	*Mortimer Collins*	226
Sleep On	*W. S. Gilbert*	249
Sly Lawyers	*George Crabbe*	85
Soliloquy of the Spanish Cloister	*Robert Browning*	190
Song	*Richard Lovelace*	34
Sonnet, A	*J. K. Stephen*	284
Sorrows of Werther	*William Makepeace Thackeray*	178
Soul's Errand, The	*Sir Walter Raleigh*	13
St. Anthony's Sermon to the Fishes	*Abraham á Sancta-Clara*	39
Sympathy	*Reginald Heber*	111

Index of Titles

		PAGE
THERE IS NO GOD	Arthur Hugh Clough	199
They Said	Edith M. Thomas	284
Thought, A	J. K. Stephen	283
Three Black Crows	John Byrom	63
Thursday	Frederick Edward Weatherly	280
To Boswell	John Wolcott (Peter Pindar)	76
To Miguel de Cervantes Saavedra	Richard Kendall Munkittrick	287
To R. K.	J. K. Stephen	286
To the Terrestrial Globe	W. S. Gilbert	240
To Woman	Lord Byron	126
Too Late	Fitz-Hugh Ludlow	261
Tool, The	Richard Watson Gilder	273
True to Poll	Frank C. Burnand	247
Twelve Articles	Jonathan Swift	46
Two Characters	Henry Taylor	151
UNCERTAIN MAN, THE	William Cowper	74
V-A-S-E, THE	James Jeffrey Roche	278
Verses on Seeing the Speaker Asleep in His Chair During One of the Debates of the First Reformed Parliament	Winthrop M. Praed	154
WANTED—A GOVERNESS	Anonymous	346
War Is Kind	Stephen Crane	336
Wed	H. C. Bunner	289
Wedded Bliss	Charlotte Perkins (Stetson) Gilman	303
Well of St. Keyne, The	Robert Southey	99
What Will We Do?	Robert J. Burdette	272
What's In a Name?	Richard Kendall Munkittrick	288
Widow Malone, The	Charles Lever	173
Will, The	John Donne	18
Wish for Length of Life, The	Juvenal	6
Woman	Fitz-Greene Halleck	132
Woman's Will	John Godfrey Saxe	196
Would-be Literary Bore, A	Horace	4

INDEX OF AUTHORS

INDEX OF AUTHORS

ANONYMOUS   PAGE
   Lines by an Old Fogy 348
   Wanted—A Governess 346
ANSTEY, CHRISTOPHER
   The Public Breakfast 67
ARISTOPHANES
   Chorus of Women 3
ARMYTAGE, FAULKNER
   Friday Afternoon at the Boston Symphony Hall . . 332
AYTOUN, WILLIAM E.
   The Laureate 194

BARHAM, RICHARD HARRIS
   Mr. Barney Maguire's Account of the Coronation . . 119
BIRDSEYE, GEORGE
   Paradise. A Hindoo Legend 319
BLAKE, RODNEY
   .Hoch! der Kaiser 320
BOWRING, SIR JOHN
   The Rich and the Poor Man (From the Russian of
      Kremnitzer) 132
BROUGH, ROBERT BARNABAS
   My Lord Tomnoddy 227
BROWNING, ELIZABETH BARRETT
   Critics 164
   A Man's Requirements 163
BROWNING, ROBERT
   The Lost Leader 186
   The Pope and the Net 188
   Soliloquy of the Spanish Cloister 190
BUNNER, H. C.
   Atlantic City 290
   Wed 289

A Satire Anthology

	PAGE
BURDETTE, ROBERT J.	
What Will We Do?	272
BURGESS, GELETT	
Extracts from the Rubaiyat of Omar Cayenne	328
BURNAND, FRANK C.	
True to Poll	247
BURNS, ROBERT	
Address to the Unco Guid, or the Rigidly Righteous	86
Holy Willie's Prayer	88
BUTLER, WILLIAM ALLEN	
Nothing to Wear	213
BUTLER, SAMUEL	
Description of Holland	30
The Religion of Hudibras	31
Saintship versus Conscience	29
BYROM, JOHN	
The Three Black Crows	63
BYRON, LORD	
A Country House Party	127
From "English Bards and Scotch Reviewers"	125
From "The Devil's Drive"	123
To Woman	126
CALVERLEY, CHARLES STUART	
Of Propriety	235
Peace: A Study	236
The Schoolmaster Abroad with His Son	233
CANNING, GEORGE	
The Friend of Humanity and the Knife-Grinder	92
CARLYLE, THOMAS	
Cui Bono?	135
CARMAN, BLISS	
Hem and Haw	307
The Sceptics	308
CARROLL, LEWIS	
Fame's Penny Trumpet	238
CAYLEY, GEORGE JOHN	
An Epitaph	64
CHURCHILL, CHARLES	
On Smollett	73
CLAUDIUS, MATTHEW	
The Hen	77
CLEIVELAND, JOHN	
Satire on the Scots	32

Index of Authors

CLOUGH, ARTHUR HUGH
    The Latest Decalogue 200
    There Is No God 199
COLERIDGE, SAMUEL TAYLOR
    Cologne 96
    Giles' Hope 96
    Job 95
COLLINS, MORTIMER
    The Positivists 225
    Sky-Making 226
COWPER, WILLIAM
    A Faithful Picture of Ordinary Society 74
    The Uncertain Man 74
CRABBE, GEORGE
    Reporters 85
    Sly Lawyers 85
CRANE, STEPHEN
    Lines 337
    War Is Kind 336

DEANE, ANTHONY C.
    The Beauties of Nature 317
    A Certain Cure 316
    John Jenkins 313
DE BÉRANGER, PIERRE JEAN
    The King of Yvetot (Version of W. M. Thackeray). 109
DEFOE, DANIEL
    Introduction to the True-Born Englishman . . . 41
DIBDIN, CHARLES
    Let Us All be Unhappy Together 78
DEKKER, THOMAS
    Horace Concocting an Ode 23
DOBSON, AUSTIN
    The Love-Letter 267
    The Poet and the Critics 265
DODGE, MARY MAPES
    Life in Laconics 263
DONNE, JOHN
    The Will 18
DOWLING, BARTHOLOMEW
    Revelry in India 210
DRYDEN, JOHN
    The Duke of Buckingham 37
    On Shadwell 38

A Satire Anthology

	PAGE
FAWCETT, EDGAR	
Chorus of Anglomaniacs (From "The Buntling Ball")	275
FIELDING, HENRY	
An Epistle to Sir Robert Walpole	65
FITZGERALD, EDWARD	
The Miser	166
FOSS, SAMUEL WALTER	
The Fate of Pious Dan	298
The Meeting of the Clabberhuses	300
The Origin of Sin	294
A Philosopher	295
GAY, JOHN	
The Quidnunckis	54
The Sick Man and the Angel	55
GILBERT, W. S.	
The Aesthete	260
Anglicised Utopia	252
The Ape and the Lady	250
Etiquette	254
Sleep On	249
To the Terrestrial Globe	240
GILDER, RICHARD WATSON	
Give Me a Theme	274
The Poem, to the Critic	274
The Tool	273
GILMAN, CHARLOTTE PERKINS (Stetson)	
A Conservative	304
Wedded Bliss	303
GOLDSMITH, OLIVER	
An Elegy on the Death of a Mad Dog	72
GREENWOOD, GRACE	
A Fragment	212
HALLECK, FITZ-GREENE	
Woman	132
HARRINGTON, SIR JOHN	
Of a Certain Man	16
A Precise Tailor	16
HAY, JOHN	
Distiches	264
HEBER, REGINALD	
Sympathy	111

Index of Authors

	PAGE
HERFORD, OLIVER	
A Butterfly of Fashion	322
Earth	321
HERVEY, THOMAS KIBBLE	
The Devil at Home	149
HOLCROFT, THOMAS	
Gaffer Gray (From "Hugh Trevor")	139
HOLMES, OLIVER WENDELL	
Cacoëthes Scribendi	166
Contentment	171
A Familiar Letter to Several Correspondents	167
HOOD, THOMAS	
Cockle v. Cackle	140
Our Village	145
HORACE, QUINTUS HORATIUS FLACCUS	
A Would-Be Literary Bore	4
HORNE, RICHARD HENGIST	
Pelters of Pyramids	155
HUNT, JAMES HENRY LEIGH	
From "The Feast of the Poets"	116
JOHNSON, HILDA	
Ballade of Expansion	331
JONSON, BEN	
On Don Surly	24
JUVENAL	
The Wish for Length of Life	6
KIPLING, RUDYARD	
The Conundrum of the Workshops	326
General Summary	324
LANG, ANDREW	
Ballade of Literary Fame	274
LEMON, MARK	
How to Make a Man of Consequence	173
LEVER, CHARLES	
The Widow Malone	173
LOINES, RUSSELL HILLIARD	
On a Magazine Sonnet	321
LOOMIS, CHARLES BATTELL	
The Evolution of a "Name"	310

A Satire Anthology

LOVER, SAMUEL	PAGE
Father-Land and Mother-Tongue	135
Father Molloy	136
LOVELACE, RICHARD	
Song	34
LOWELL, JAMES RUSSELL	
From "A Fable for Critics"	201
The Pious Editor's Creed	206
LUDLOW, FITZ-HUGH	
Too Late	261
LYNDSAY, SIR DAVID	
A Carman's Account of a Lawsuit	12
LYSAGHT, EDWARD	
Kitty of Coleraine	91
LYTTON, ROBERT BULWER	
Midges	230
MACKAY, CHARLES	
Cynical Ode to an Ultra-Cynical Public	192
The Great Critics	193
MARSTON, JOHN	
The Scholar and His Dog	25
MARVELL, ANDREW	
The Character of Holland	35
MATTHEWS, BRANDER	
An Advanced Thinker	282
MEREDITH, GEORGE	
Hiding the Skeleton	229
MOORE, THOMAS	
Eternal London	105
Lying	108
The Modern Puffing System	106
MORSE, JAMES HERBERT	
Fame	269
MUNKITTRICK, RICHARD KENDALL	
To Miguel de Cervantes Saavedra	287
What's in a Name?	288
NEAVES, LORD CHARLES	
How to Make a Novel	150
NOEL, THOMAS	
The Pauper's Drive	175

Index of Authors

O'KEEFE, JOHN   PAGE
    The Friar of Orders Gray 79
OSBORN, SELLECK
    A Modest Wit 112
OUTRAM, GEORGE
    The Annuity 156

PEACOCK, THOMAS L.
    Rich and Poor; or, Saint and Sinner 117
PITT, WILLIAM
    The Sailor's Consolation 152
POPE, ALEXANDER
    From "The Epistle to Dr. Arbuthnot" 60
    Sandys' Ghost 57
PRAED, WINTHROP M.
    Verses on Seeing the Speaker Asleep in His Chair During one of the Debates of the First Reformed Parliament 154
PRIOR, MATTHEW
    An Epitaph 43
    The Remedy Worse Than the Disease 45
PROUT, FATHER
    Malbrouck 161
PUNCH
    A Match 343

RALEIGH, SIR WALTER
    The Soul's Errand 13
ROCHE, JAMES JEFFREY
    A Boston Lullaby 277
    The V-A-S-E 278
    The Net of Law 277
RÜCKERT, FRIEDRICH
    Greediness Punished 130
RUTEBŒUF
    The Ass's Legacy 7

SACKVILLE, CHARLES, EARL OF DORSET
    Satire on Edward Howard 39
SANCTA-CLARA, ABRAHAM Á
    St. Anthony's Sermon to the Fishes 39

	PAGE
SAXE, JOHN GODFREY	
The Mourner à la Mode	197
Woman's Will	196
SCOTT, SIR WALTER	
Nora's Vow	94
SEAMAN, OWEN	
"The Hurt that Honour Feels"	310
SHAKESPEARE, WILLIAM	
From "As You Like It"	22
From "Love's Labour's Lost"	21
From "King Henry IV."	20
SHELLEY, PERCY BYSSHE	
Ozymandias	134
SHERIDAN, RICHARD BRINSLEY	
The Literary Lady	84
SHERIDAN, THOMAS	
Dr. Delany's Villa	52
SILL, EDWARD ROWLAND	
Five Lives	270
SMITH, HARRY B.	
Same Old Story	306
SMITH, JAMES	
Christmas Out of Town	103
The Poet of Fashion	101
SOUTHEY, ROBERT	
The Battle of Blenheim	97
The Well of St. Keyne	99
STEDMAN, EDMUND CLARENCE	
The Diamond Wedding	240
STEPHEN, J. K.	
To R. K.	286
A Sonnet	284
A Thought	283
SUCKLING, SIR JOHN	
The Constant Lover	27
The Remonstrance	28
SWIFT, JONATHAN	
The Furniture of a Woman's Mind	48
Twelve Articles	46
TAYLOR, BAYARD	
A Review	221
TAYLOR, HENRY	
Two Characters	151

Index of Authors

	PAGE
TAYLOR, JANE	
The Philosopher's Scales	114
TENNYSON, ALFRED	
On Lytton	177
THACKERAY, WILLIAM MAKEPEACE	
Damages, Two Hundred Pounds	182
Mr. Molony's Account of the Ball Given to the Nepaulese Ambassador by the Peninsular and Oriental Company	179
Sorrows of Werther	178
THOMAS, EDITH M.	
They Said	284
TORRENCE, FREDERIC RIDGELY	
From "The House of a Hundred Lights"	340
TROLLOPIAD, FROM THE	
The British Visitor	343
VIELÉ, HERMAN KNICKERBOCKER	
The Font in the Forest	294
VILLON, FRANÇOIS	
A Ballade of Old-Time Ladies (Translated by John Payne)	11
WARE, EUGENE FITCH	
He and She	272
WEATHERLY, FREDERICK EDWARD	
A Bird in the Hand	281
Thursday	280
WITHER, GEORGE	
The Manly Heart	26
WOLCOTT, JOHN (PETER PINDAR)	
On Johnson	75
To Boswell	76
YATES, EDMUND	
All-Saints	237
YOUNG, EDWARD	
From "The Love of Fame"	50
YRIARTE, TOMAS	
The Country Squire	80
The Eggs	83

053157

ST. MARY'S COLLEGE OF MARYLAND
ST. MARY'S CITY, MARYLAND